WE LEARNED TO SKI

WE LEARNED TO SKI

Harold Evans, Brian Jackman and Mark Ottaway

of

THE SUNDAY TIMES

St. Martin's Press   New York

While the authors have taken every care to ensure that the
advice given in this book is in accordance with the
best ski-ing practice, no liability can be accepted for the
consequences of accidents to skiers which may occur as
a result of their attempts to follow the advice.

Library of Congress Cataloging in Publication Data

Evans, Harold.
  We learned to ski.

  Includes index.
  1. Skis and skiing. I. Jackman, Brian, joint
author. II. Ottaway, Mark, joint author.
III. Title.
GV854.E9 1975   796.9'3   74-33905

PREFACE TO THE THIRD EDITION

The authors are gratified that in eight years this book has been immensely popular; even more exciting is the knowledge that people have been known to learn to ski with no more than our words, our illustrations, and a sense of fun, a quality that remains more important than acquiring the quadraceps of a weight-lifter. If you are a beginner, you can do it; if you are a frightened intermediate you can become a confident adventurer. We know that is what has happened to hundreds of skiers who have written to us. We have added new material throughout this edition, but we want to emphasise Chapters 1 (on equipment), 9 (what the ski will do for you), 12 (the basic swing) and 19 (carving the turn). This book teaches both skidded (flat ski) turns and carved (edged ski) turns. Most people are taught to skid first but the sooner you try carving the better. These terms will mean more to you when you've dipped into the book and had a ski holiday or two. But you will discover that we are obsessed with *knees* as the key to exhilarating and relaxed ski-ing in which the skis are made to work efficiently. There is, admittedly, a little more to it than that —hence the succeeding pages—but we like to feel, and have some very good days on snow to encourage us, that we have simplified our work from the first edition. In this we have been greatly assisted by Alasdair Ross, senior trainer for the British Association of Ski Instructors and teacher at the Swiss Ski School, Wengen.

This book is a team effort. It began with an enthusiasm for ski-ing and a conviction about its teaching shared between *The Sunday Times* and Collins Publishers. The words have been written by Harold Evans, Brian Jackman and Mark Ottaway of *The Sunday Times*; Edwin Taylor, *Sunday Times*, director of design, was put on skis for the first time in his life so that later he could more sensibly direct the presentation by his group, led by Victor Shreeve. Photographers Frank Herrmann and Bryan Wharton skied scores of mountain slopes with pack and cameras and took many vital reference photographs.

Our first thanks to others must go to the ski instructors who uncomplainingly skied the same movement superbly a hundred times for us. We must thank also Warren Witherell, Director of Burke Mountain Alpine Training Centre, Vermont, for advice on carving turns; Horst Abraham of Vail, Colorado, chairman of the technical committee of the US Professional Ski Instructors' Association; Douglas Godlington, who runs his own ski school in Scotland, and is also technical adviser to the Ski Club of Great Britain; and John Sheddon, chairman of the coaching committee of the National Ski Federation of Great Britain.

We have a special debt to the French ski resort of Les Arcs, where we went to study the ski-évolutif method. The Ski Club of Great Britain, in particular Ruth Elcome, helped us on resorts, and Major Peter Forbes and Peter Henry with advice on equipment. Major General Ian Graeme of the National Ski Federation was also guide and critic.

And, not least, we thank and salute those fellow skiers who have over the years skied with us in groups, written to us by the thousand and in the resorts rambled on over tea and cream cakes about the mysteries and wonders of ski-ing. We hope the book increases their ranks.

Section

1 Before you begin

2 Lessons for beginners

3 The first turns

The snowplough

Chapter	page

Section

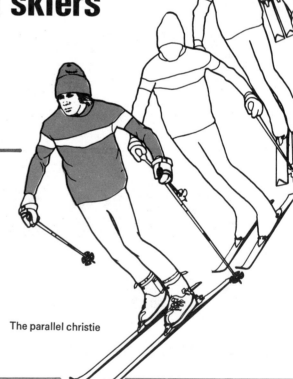

The parallel christie

Chapter	page

Skiing the back bowls at Vail, Colorado

The dreams that lure us to the mountains . . .

INTRODUCTION

The ski bug bites people in different ways. Some become obsessed by the thrill of speed, ecstatic birdmen winging through sunlit mountain passes. Some ski for solitude, meditative loners in the spectacular theatre of the peaks. Some ski for the companionship of the slopes and the jolliness of the resorts. And some people never get bitten at all. For a start, the boots hurt. The skis don't work properly; they keep slipping. Then, every time you fall there is this incomprehensible foreigner telling you to do impossible things. Well, he knows what he can do with his knees—and you there with your stuff about romance and adventure in the Alps.

The authors of this book, of whom more later, have all been bitten. But one of us nearly missed the intoxication because of a bad beginning, and all of us have been impressed, not to say dismayed, by the number of people who give up learning to ski. It is not, mostly, their fault. Anybody who is normally active can get fun out of ski-ing. There is no sex or age barrier. Girls pick it up as quickly as boys, and muscular young men are frequently upstaged by delicate girls. Every day on the slopes young men, inert with an attack of nerves, are passed by middle-aged matrons doing neat, safe turns. Many of us who take it up later naturally feel enraged, if not humiliated, by the sight of five-year-old Austrians buzzing down the mountainside at absurd speeds. But you will soon get over this, and learn to enjoy your own achievements. After all, kids go too fast to appreciate the view, and they're in bed by the time the *après-ski* starts. One of us took up ski-ing after the age of 40 and can now come down any slope. Families can hope to ski together. We would not advise taking children under eight, as it often means that, in practice, mothers fall behind from looking after a grumpy child. But beyond that ski-ing offers a unique family holiday. Parents and children who move at the same speed in their lessons can stay together, or they can split up into different groups and swap experiences in the evenings.

The trouble is, too many people are taught badly. Too many are sold the wrong holidays in the wrong places at the wrong time. Too many are allowed to hire unsuitable skis, boots and poles. This book is an attempt to correct all these unhappy antidotes to catching the ski-ing bug. It is addressed mainly

High adventure begins by overcoming fear

to the unbitten, but we hope it will be of value to all recreational skiers and especially those with less than, say, three years' experience. It advises generally on resorts and equipment and clothing, but our main impetus is a conviction about the teaching of ski movements.

This is best illustrated by a chance remark by the famous French racer Jean-Claude Killy. Discussing the 'fall line' in an article in the British magazine *Ski World* (in February 1973), Killy said this: 'When you are learning—and it is so long ago for me that I have almost forgotten it—you may suffer a moment of anxiety as your skis slide faster and faster.' Many people who teach ski-ing have, like Killy, forgotten what it is like learning to ski. And it is because Killy has forgotten what it is like to learn that he can say, in all honesty, that the learner 'may suffer a *moment* of anxiety' as his skis slide faster and faster. *May* indeed! In the normal ski school, he will and does suffer prolonged periods of fright. No wonder the ski learner—and even the intermediate to advanced skier —poised on some precipice, has bitter moments reflecting whether he inhabits the same universe as the teacher. No wonder ski teachers are bewildered by the failure of their students.

The best teachers have retained enough sympathetic imagination to remember what it was like learning, to recognize the fears and to cope with the fact that they are often asking their pupils to do something that goes against their deepest instincts. But, generally:

There are far too many experts teaching and far too few expert teachers. There are too many who do not ski the way they tell the class to ski, who have forgotten how they ski themselves.

There is not enough analysis. This is different from description. You get such complicated descriptions of what you should do with every part of your body that you might be training for bull-fighting or ballet. The lessons have gone too far away from the basic concept of what is happening to the ski and why. It is extraordinary that hardly anywhere is the skier told what are the qualities in the ski which he can exploit. How many are told of the differences between skidded and carved turns? The skis might as well be two bits of board instead of ingeniously engineered tools.

There is far too little interest in the suitability and efficiency of the skier's equipment. This is our collective view based on personal experiences, and talks with other learners, in Europe and North America, but before we decided to produce this book we checked our impressions by formal interviews with a group of 40 university students ski-ing in the Dolomites.

Some were beginners, some had up to ten years' experience, and some had taught ski-ing. They told us about a lot of things they thought should be in a book like this, but the overwhelming message was that they felt their teachers had failed to identify their problems because it was so long since they themselves had experienced them.

This book is different from other ski books for this reason. It is by a group of people who have learned to ski recently enough to know what it is like learning. We came together at our newspaper, *The Sunday Times*, London, because of our enthusiasm for ski-ing and our exasperation with traditional teaching and books. We are of a wide range of experience and athletic abilities, and differ in our ski-ing standards, which run from intermediate to advanced. But we all remember vividly what it was like when the skis slid faster, or the 'moguls', those small hills of hardened snow, appeared as sinister blisters, or the ski equipment worried us, or when every turn ended in a spreadeagle of skis and sticks; and we all remember what helped us to overcome all this and get real enjoyment from our expeditions. When we decided to set down these conclusions, we were able to enlist three kinds of valuable assistance. First, the graphic skills of *The Sunday Times*, secondly the interest of the travel department (*Compass*) and thirdly the ski-ing skills of some excellent individual instructors in Europe and America (we think particularly of Alasdair Ross, Jean Pierre Gasset, Pierre Filiatrault, Romano Bossi and Freddy Reilly, senior instructor at London's Crystal Palace training centre. They and the Ski Club of Great Britain, joined in with enthusiasm when we explained what we were about. We are grateful to them, especially Ross, though we accept full responsibility for the actual contents of this book. We also remember with affection and sadness our talks and ski-ing with Robert Blanc, the pioneer of the short-ski method at Les Arcs who died trying to rescue some skiers in an avalanche in 1980. We have tried both revolutionary and orthodox methods. We went as a party— writers, photographers, and designers — to Les Arcs in the French Alps to try out Blanc's short-ski method of beginning parallel ski-ing on mini-skis and graduating to longer ones. It is called ski-évolutif in Europe, GLM (graduated length method) in the USA. One of our more practised skiers, who had learned the traditional way, tried it, and so did two of the party who were beginners. We describe the lessons of the mini-ski or progressive ski teaching in Chapter 18. We believe progress is faster by graduating the length of the ski. We do not agree, however, that the mini-ski method, with its more direct approach to the admired parallel turn, makes the stem and stem christie turns obsolete. Far from it. Inevitably there will always be some people who will get more enjoyment out of ski-ing if they can rely on these so-called defensive turns. Irwin Shaw, the American writer, assessed their need correctly when he said that parallel ski-ing was something he indulged in only when stopping in front of a restaurant.

We have attempted, in setting out our lessons, to make the analytical drawings, photographs, and words work together. The book does not require consecutive reading or that you should search for the graphics for explanation. Each lesson has been tested by a group of skiers. Of course, some are more difficult to do than others, and some will have to be read more than once for the point to sink home. All of them are given, however, in the context of ski-ing in an effort to keep reminding you that they are not a set of bedroom exercises but actions to help you on a mountain in all kinds of conditions. There is, naturally, no substitute for getting out on the mountain and we would not want the criticisms we have made of general teaching attitudes to put you off joining a ski school. You must do that. You can learn a lot trying to follow a good skier on movements in your range; you will be encouraged to venture further than you would alone; you will enjoy trying exercises in a group; and you will pick up a great deal of value about where to ski. The best way of learning, we believe, is to combine three things:

1. The discipline of regular lessons.

2. An hour or so a day of concentrated practice on your own or with a friend perfecting some movement on an easy slope for confidence, and then gradually pushing yourself to trying it on something tough.

3. Some theoretical knowledge so that you can fill in the gaps of the formal lessons, seize on the essentials, and avoid bad habits in your own practice. It is this third role which this book fills.

We suggest you browse in the chapters which concern you before you go. At the resort, put the book aside for the first lessons, but when you are ruminating, having a hot soak or a drink at night, scan it again and try to identify points where you have succeeded and points where you have failed. Our own experience is that you learn more easily if you concentrate on *one* key point at a time. Some of the ski instructors shout so much about 'bend-the-knees-keep-the-uphill-ski-in-front-watch-that-shoulder-back-with-those-poles' that you end up not being able to tell your knee from your nose. Resolve to concentrate on one essential at a time – knees forward, say, or knees-into-the-hill. When that becomes second nature, you can concentrate on hip-into-the-hill, or pole-planting. And so on. You will not be able to memorize a whole chapter. What we have done is to add at the end of most teaching sections a few simple slogans that you can easily memorize. Say them to yourself on the slope. This may sound eccentric, but it helps—the ski slopes are full of people talking themselves into a better performance. Even the expert, as he comes down, is feeding inspiring little messages to himself. We hope that with the help of this book you will not be confused by various rival schools or distracted by the latest fad. It is as sure as sun melting snow that between the writing and publication of this book some esoteric new turn will have been invented and urged on the credulous as the only 'natural' way or the way this or that racer skis. Well, let him. You are out to enjoy yourself. And if there are moments when the short-swing parallel or the jet turn seems to be a bit beyond you, never mind. Reflect on the fact that usually the most bored (and boring) men and women in the resort are the skiers so expert that all challenge has vanished.

Ski-ing for fun : one of the authors at Les Menuires, France.

1 Before you begin

1 WHERE TO GO: Snow conditions. The right resort. Ski schools. Nordic ski-ing.
2 WHAT TO WEAR: All you need to know about boots and ski clothes.
3 SKIS AND BINDINGS: Choosing the right equipment.

1 WHERE TO GO

Go West, young man : instructors of the Aspen ski-school

HOW TO PICK A SKI HOLIDAY

There are a lot of reasons for postponing a ski holiday, perhaps for ever. Snow is cold, grey, mushy stuff. Ski resorts are full of 'beautiful people'. It costs money. You break your legs. The children are too young. It is all very confusing about where to go. You really were never the star athlete at school. Perhaps next year. . .

For several years reasons like these kept us from trying ski-ing. We look back on them with resentment. For the youngest of us there is now probably only 25 years of ski-ing left, and it is too little. There is so much to try, so many places to explore, such excitement in prospect each winter. This does not mean there is nothing in the inhibitions. In particular, selecting a resort and a time are crucial, and not easy. You must have the right clothes and equipment, and this can be expensive. But some of the routine excuses for staying at home can be discounted fairly quickly. Cold it can be, especially at

14

high altitudes in December and January, or in the eastern United States, but the right clothing can keep you snug. But when the sun is shining, the mountains are usually the warmest place to be. And it is more likely to be shining high above the clouds than it is down in the valleys. If someone threw the word 'ski-ing' at us, we would be more likely to come back with 'sunburn' than with 'cold feet'.

The high risk of injury was another fear that proved to be an exaggeration. Again we would neither wish to minimize the fact that ski-ing *is* dangerous, nor suggest that you throw all caution to the winds. But just how dangerous do you calculate two weeks by the seaside abroad to be? Well, insurance companies, who are hard-headed parties, reckon it to be about as dangerous as a week's ski-ing. The test of their sincerity is that they will charge you about the same premium for both. (Although you would be wise to take out a heftier cover for ski-ing, since a ski-ing injury can be more expensive than a seaside one. The cost of an air-ambulance, for instance, is obviously greater than that of an ordinary one.) The statisticians, as always, seem unable to agree. It seems we risk having an accident needing medical attention between once in every 200 days ski-ing (US figure), and once in every 400 days (worldwide figure). Few of us are likely to ski that much in a lifetime.

Children may be a problem. There is too much facile talk about putting five-year-olds on skis and away they go. It only seems to work with other people's children. Ski-ing with your own can result in hours doing up laces and rushing back down to the resort when classes are due to end. Some resorts have a kindergarten where children can play, and this is a more realistic proposition for younger children. We know the Austrians ski in their cradles, but you will probably only have two weeks; so finding a resort with a playgroup is better than not going at all. Only when children reach the age of seven or eight, depending on their daring, can you safely plan a family ski-ing holiday.

There are, it is true, a few 'beautiful people', but they are not intimidating. Most of them seem to do their ski-ing with their bottoms on the bar stools in the village, and the majority of our fellow-skiers turned out to be without a yacht to their name. True, too, ski-ing is expensive, and always will be. Yet we are not at all sure we really care about that any more. It is worth saving for the perfect winter tonic: sun, fresh clean air and, above all, total absorption. You can take your preoccupations onto a golf course, but not on to a ski-slope.

No, the real things to worry about before you go are the facilities of the resort. These are a complex matter. The check

list of the things you need to know about winter sport is far more detailed than a check-list for a summer one, and the information you need is a lot harder to come by. It is this shortage of detailed, accurate, impartial and up-to-date information which makes the choice difficult.

The information famine is to an extent a fact of life. Snow, for instance, is completely unpredictable. Even the Swiss Meteorological Office cannot guarantee 24 hours in advance that it will snow in any given resort. Yet 'Will there be snow?' is clearly at the top of any check-list for a ski-ing holiday.

With snow, therefore, you are reduced to working on probabilities. They are strong probabilities, however, and we shall be dealing with them.

We are not quite so philosophical about some of the other information you must know about resorts and which the brochures rarely tell us.

Would you buy a television set merely on the dealer's description of the wonderful programmes that are broadcast? Well, we would not. Yet travel agents often expect you to spend much the same sort of money on winter holidays on little more than an assurance as to what fun they are. Much of the vital technical data you need is missing from their brochures.

We do not believe that the travel companies are guilty of deliberate obscurity: the fault is more that of uncritical customers. If enough people asked the right questions, more of the answers would be printed in the brochures. If you are prepared to be persistent enough to ask them you may well be doing a favour to your fellow-skiers as well as to yourself.

Brochures are promotional literature. They should therefore be perused with scepticism. For this reason alone it is worth joining a ski club, or your national ski federation. They will not know everything, but they will certainly be the most impartial and up-to-date source of information available to you.

Despite our criticism of travel agency brochures the fact remains that packaged holidays by air with a company that has a large ski programme offer significant economies in time, trouble and money. You might not dream of taking a package holiday in summer, but in winter we advise it, and the sales talk about the wisdom of booking early is usually true. The sacrifice in personal freedom on a winter ski package is virtually nil. You will travel on the same plane as others in the group, but once in your accommodation you are free as you care to be, and the bigger agencies usually have someone on the spot who can advise you on slopes, lifts, eating places and tours, and help if there are any unexpected difficulties about returning.

SNOW

The knowledge you must have before you choose a holiday begins with snow.

To the man in the slush snow is simply cold, white and wet. To us it is something far more subtle, a substance capable of almost infinite variations. To list some of the factors that can change snow, and hence the ski-ing surface: sun and shade, wind and shelter, temperature, altitude, time of day, time of year, depth of snow, the angle and shape of the slope and the direction it faces.

So, ski-ing from the top to the bottom even of a single mountain you are likely to encounter different kinds of snow. With experience you will learn to 'read' snow. You will know the signs that warn you that your ski-ing surface is about to change, and you will adjust your technique accordingly. But that is for the future; for the moment all you need to know are the different types of snow the skier encounters, when and where he is likely to find them, and what he thinks of them.

Powder snow is the stuff of dreams. It is our favourite snow. It is fresh snow when temperatures are below freezing. Hold it in your hands. It is dry. It runs through the fingers like white sand. You cannot make snowballs with it. It creaks when you walk on it. It hisses when you ski on it, every turn of the skis throwing up a billowing spray of drifting crystals in your wake. No other snow condition is more flattering to your style. It slides smoothly under your skis. Turning on four to six inches of powder snow on a firm base is easy. Friction between skis and snow is minimal.

Deep powder snow, say a foot or more, is something else, however. When we were beginners it was a very long way indeed down our list of favourite snow conditions. Ski-ing in it requires a more advanced technique, not to mention a good deal more courage and confidence. The expert, on the other hand, who is perfectly capable of ski-ing with his skis and calves out of sight under the powder, may love deep powder snow best of all.

Cold hard-packed snow is what happens to powder snow when lots of people have skied over it, or it has been packed by a machine. (These snow-cats, as they are known, are crosses between caterpillar tractors, rollers and lawn mowers. They trundle up and down the slopes, breaking up ice and bumps, packing the snow tightly and smoothly into the ground.) Some of us liked this just as much as the powder snow.

Spring or corn snow is thought by many to be at least as good as powder snow. However you look at it, spring snow is nothing to grumble about, and it is what we pray for towards the end of the season. Spring snow is powder snow that has started to melt, but which has frozen again during the cold night hours. The result is a texture like granulated sugar—lots of little particles of dry, icy snow.

Spring snow can be hard work first thing in the morning. The little granules have stuck together, and are lumpy and icy. As the sun loosens them the ski-ing improves, but then around 11 a.m.—on south facing slopes—the snow becomes too mushy. It is then time to go over the mountain, or across the valley, to the Northern slopes which catch less sun and where the spring snow is still at its best.

Hard, wet or heavy snow makes for mediocre ski-ing conditions, but is no reason to pack up and go home. This can result from fresh snow that has fallen when it is relatively warm (around freezing point only), or from powder snow that has been rained upon, or from powder snow that is thawing, and not re-freezing at night.

It is wet: good for snowballs, but not so good for ski-ing. It is difficult: we had to work twice as hard to turn our skis. It is a nuisance: it stuck on the soles of our boots in thick wedges when we walked. It is also the most dangerous snow of all in which to fall. The ski can plunge into the snow, exerting leverage on your leg if the binding does not open. We often had to take off our skis when we fell in deep heavy snow. It gripped them mercilessly. This is why it is dangerous.

Crust is a layer of ice on top of the spring or powder snow. It can be caused by wind, or by the sun. Like snow itself, crust produces a variety of ski-ing conditions, some pleasurable, others plain murderous.

We did not mind when the crust was very thin, so that it would break under the slightest pressure. This gave us conditions very similar to spring snow.

Then there was the sort of crust formed by wind on exposed slopes with powder snow. It usually broke into large slabs as we skied across it. This we tried to avoid.

There were two kinds of crust, however, we did *not* like. We were not at all sure which was worse. One was the kind of crust which was just thick enough to support us most of the time, but which always seemed to break just when we didn't want it to, usually when turning.

The other was crust so thick that, while it would take our weight at all times, it was in practice the equivalent of ski-ing on ice. The Americans call this 'boiler-plate'.

As beginners we were inclined to rate ski-ing on ice as the most frightening snow condition of all. Our skis could not 'bite' the ice. We slid all over the place at first, although later we learned to cope with it better. There is one consolation about crust, however: it is usually spring snow in the making.

Once it has been broken up by the passage of skiers or the snow-cats, the result is spring snow.

That leaves us with the snow conditions which, if they are at all widespread, make us want to go home. The only thing we can hope for these is a fresh fall of snow.

Heavy, rotten 'porridge' or 'mashed potato' explains itself. The snow is in an advanced state of decomposition. It is wet, slushy, difficult, dangerous and sometimes almost impossible to ski. This is a particular problem for beginners, for not only do they find it hard-going but if these conditions exist anywhere in the resort it will be on the lower slopes where the beginners are taught.

Icy Ruts: if there is a sharp frost at night the porridge can freeze solid. You then have all the difficulties of ski-ing on an icy piste plus a highly irregular surface.

As skiers pass over porridge they create ruts in the snow, usually with a little pool of water at the bottom. In a freeze ruts result that are solid and icy. We found it almost impos-

sible to control our skis in these conditions. The worst thing was when one ski stuck in one rut and the other stuck in a rut going in a different direction. This is fine in Charlie Chaplin films; in reality it produces either a nasty case of the splits, or crossed skis. These are not leg breaking conditions so much as muscle-pulling ones. A fall can be particularly painful and can even result in your cutting yourself if you are not well padded.

Thin snow cover: the rockier and bumpier the terrain, the more snow needed to smooth it out. It is therefore difficult to specify a minimum snow cover for ski-ing, but anything less than five inches (12 cm) could create difficulties.

Not only might there be rocks, mud or roots showing through the snow, but these absorb heat from the sun better than the snow and will cause rapid melting of the snow around them. In conditions like this you have to pick your way slowly down the slope, seeking out the good patches, avoiding the bad ones. This is tedious, and takes much of the fun out of ski-ing.

The factors affecting snow conditions

The non-skier always assumes that the mountains are full of snow. It takes but one holiday where you are ski-ing on porridge and iced mud and grass to persuade the most lackadaisical of us to devote our lives to a study of snow.

Although weather can change daily, three factors affect the probability of your finding snow on any given bit of mountain: the time of year, its altitude, and the direction in which it faces.

As a general and not altogether surprising rule, when ski-ing weather is at its best prices are at their highest. Christmas and Easter are exceptions. The ski-ing is often mediocre, high-season prices are charged, and resorts are crowded.

Winter in the Alps

Late November   The foundations for the ski-ing season are, literally, being laid. Hard frosts freeze the ground. When the air is humid and temperatures drop to around the freezing mark the first snow falls on the higher slopes. The flakes are big, often the size of a man's wristwatch. This is not a windy time of year, and usually the snow will fall evenly across the mountainside. The skier is hoping that it will provide an even cover of around a metre in depth. It may well turn into rain. This is not always the skier's enemy, however. Rain packs the snow down to a depth of about 20 cm and, after a good night's freeze, the result is a firm base of lower snow, wet and heavy. Unless you happen to be in the mountains anyway it is too early to think about ski-ing. The quantity and staying power of the snow is still too uncertain.

December   Conditions are still unreliable, especially at lower altitudes. It can be very cold. The skier is waiting for powder snow, hoping that, when it comes, it will adhere to the November base. If it is too cold for snow to adhere to the base or if there is no base the slopes may be 'blown'—that is, the winds will just sweep the powder away.

Until the powder comes the snow-cat machines will be beating down the heavy snow on the 'piste' (the name given to the carefully marked out runs you will use). The result can be eminently skiable, even if it tends to be a rather grey and chilly time. Skis will slide easily over the snow which is soft enough for them to 'bite' and to make turning fairly easy. This is what we meant by a 'cold, well-packed surface'. At lower altitudes, however, the snow can still be wet.

Towards Christmas the air becomes drier. Temperatures are lower, fluctuating between −5° and −15° centigrade. Powder snow is on its way. With luck it might even begin to fall now.

January to mid-February   This is perhaps the ideal time for the beginner. During what the French call *le trou* (approximately 5 January to 5 February) the resorts are comparatively empty and are back on low season prices. If it does not snow now it maybe never will. This is the ideal time for powder snow. A two day fall could give 60 cm (2 ft) or more of powder snow cover, but it is still cold, and remember—if it is snowing then the sun cannot be shining. You may well come home with a tan, but it is not what you go for in *le trou*. You go for low prices and the best snow.

Late February and March   This is the high season in the Alps. It is just as expensive as Christmas and Easter, but often less crowded, especially in the smaller resorts.

The snow monsoon is over, and the sun is rising higher in the sky. You can ski in the warmth of the sun before it has had time to melt too much of the snow. Then, as the sun gets to work, spring snow will spread, first to the southern facing slopes, then to the northern ones. During the transition period the northern slopes will still have plenty of powder.

Towards the end of March few southern slopes are skiable after midday. If you go in March you must, therefore, go to a resort with northern as well as southern slopes. Many resorts are charging only mid or even low season prices at this time (especially if they do not have good northern slopes).

April   This when prices go up again. The snow is in rapid retreat up the mountain, and the ski instructors are bored and wondering how to pass the summer. Yet Easter is probably the most crowded time of all. Why? The answer is the tyranny of the fixed holiday. Many of us can only ski at Christmas or Easter, and most of us would rather have dubious snow and sunshine than dubious snow and no sunshine. Northern facing slopes and a good altitude (at least 5,000 feet, or 1,500 metres) are prerequisites of any ski resort in April. (We shall be dealing with the effects of altitude on snow.) Southern facing slopes where there is still snow are often wet and unskiable for most of the day. But April can bring unexpected and often violent snow storms, especially at high altitudes.

May   This can often afford glorious ski-ing at high altitudes, for April and May can bring the heaviest snowfalls of the year. This is so utterly unpredictable, however, that we do not advise holidaying in May. It is the month for impulse holidays to places with good snow reports, and it is too much of a gamble to book more than a week or two in advance. You should also check that the ski schools are still functioning.

Winter in the American West

You have few worries about snow if you ski the West, especially if you ski the Rockies. Moisture-laden air currents sweep in from the Pacific and there are heavy falls as early as Thanksgiving in the Pacific Northwest and California–Nevada. Some Washington and Oregon resorts have an average yearly snowfall of up to 25 feet. The snow lasts too, often into May, but having come straight from the ocean it can be heavy and wet. This is where the Rockies score. The season is not as long as in the Sierras, but the snow is every skier's dream. The air currents, having lost much of their moisture in the West, cross the dry temperate plateau and then have to climb suddenly 14,000 feet to cross the Rockies. They lose more of their moisture as light, dry snow; even if it is moist when it hits the ground, the humidity is so low the snow changes quickly from crystalline to gaseous form—in short to the most superb ski-ing powder. Some of the Rocky Mountain resorts help it to settle by making an artificial snow base in the heavy traffic areas of the slopes— or *pistes* as we prefer to say. That's a French word meaning slope or trail; it is used round the world and since this book is international we will use piste throughout when referring to slopes or trails. The Rockies have another appeal. Since the resorts are basically in a temperate zone, the snow often falls at night, when it is colder, and you ski powder in sunshine the next day.

Winter in the East and Midwest

If you learn to ski in the East and Midwest, they say, you can ski anywhere. It's partly a way of conceding that the snow conditions are tougher. Amounts may vary widely, depending on the frequency and intensity of individual storms, and what falls often becomes hard-packed by the skiers, mogulled and icy. Yet the best resorts make up for this by manufacturing snow with zeal and profusion, and man-made snow can be excellent in texture. We skiied Killington one sunny Thanksgiving with Warren Witherell, on an inch of light man-made snow on a firm base, and the skis turned beautifully. Among resorts with good snow-making systems are Hunter Mountain and Catamount in New York; Jiminy Peak and Brodie Mountain in Massachusetts; and Bromley and Killington in Vermont. We would not chance anywhere East for a holiday that did not have a good snow-making system.

Stretching the season

Artificial snow is virtually unknown in Europe. But resorts with early snow records include: St Anton, Zürs (Austria); Davos, Klosters, Flims (Switzerland); Tignes, Val d'Isère (France); Courmayeur (Italy). Best late bets: St Moritz, Zermatt, Verbier (all have early snow also) Saas Fee (Switzerland).

Altitude in the Alps

The higher you go, the greater the probability of snow (and cold and wind). It is a probability that is strong enough to form the basis of every skier's calculations. It is particularly important for the beginner. Every skier needs snow, but if it is to be found anywhere at a resort it is on the highest runs. And the highest runs are usually the most difficult. This is all very well for the expert, but frustrating for the beginner who may be confined to the lower slopes. You should not, therefore, be dazzled by the highest altitude given for a resort unless you can check whether there are accessible nursery slopes of that height. It is the height of the beginners' slopes that counts. Broadly speaking, on any mountain the skier is interested in the area from 2,000 feet (600 m) or so below the treeline upwards. The treeline is the level at which the coniferous forests end. Only scattered trees are to be found above it in the Alps. It is entirely different in the Rockies where even at 10–11,000 feet you ski through spruce and pine. Most people prefer the uncluttered terrain above it for ski-ing. Narrow, icy woodland paths, on the other hand, are a nightmare. Yet trees are also the skiers' friend—in a 'white-out' the visi-

The skier's mountain: no two mountains are quite the same, but the potential ski-ing areas are fairly predictable

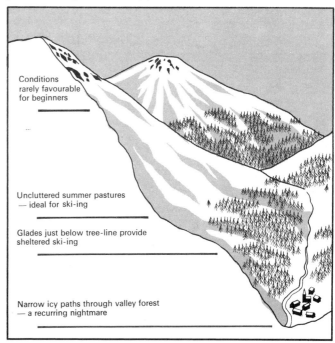

Conditions rarely favourable for beginners

Uncluttered summer pastures — ideal for ski-ing

Glades just below tree-line provide sheltered ski-ing

Narrow icy paths through valley forest — a recurring nightmare

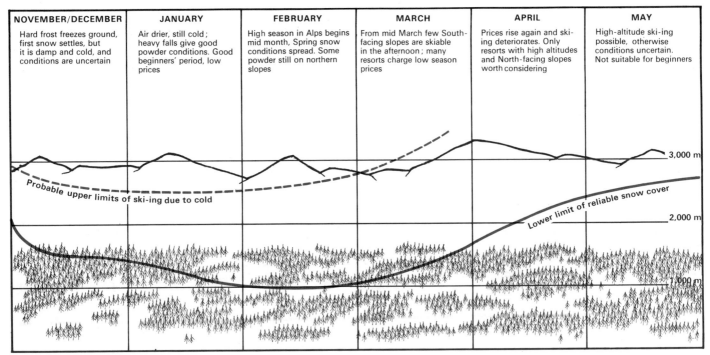

NOVEMBER/DECEMBER	JANUARY	FEBRUARY	MARCH	APRIL	MAY
Hard frost freezes ground, first snow settles, but it is damp and cold, and conditions are uncertain	Air drier, still cold; heavy falls give good powder conditions. Good beginners' period, low prices	High season in Alps begins mid month, Spring snow conditions spread. Some powder still on northern slopes	From mid March few South-facing slopes are skiable in the afternoon; many resorts charge low season prices	Prices rise again and ski-ing deteriorates. Only resorts with high altitudes and North-facing slopes worth considering	High-altitude ski-ing possible, otherwise conditions uncertain. Not suitable for beginners

The skier's Alpine calendar

bility is better near or among trees. If the damp snow which falls early in the winter is blown from the slopes, then the later powder snow may never settle properly. Trees prevent this—and they also shelter *you* from icy winds. Many resorts suited to beginners have little or no ski-ing above the treeline.

In springtime it is the sun that is the enemy. The 'freeze and thaw' process produced by cold mountain nights and hot sunny days results in slopes that can be crusty and icy in the morning and mushy for the rest of the day—hardly ever just right. This is particularly true of south facing slopes. Once again, trees can help prevent this.

As a result the ski-ing can sometimes be better below the tree-line than above it. The skier naturally prefers his trees to be in well-ordered glades rather than crowding around the piste. Such glades account largely for the reputation of the splendid north-facing runs into the Klosters valley. So, with height, what you must look for is this: a resort which enables you to ski below the treeline and from at least 2,000 feet (600 m) higher up. The higher the better. This, as a general rule of thumb, rules out most Alpine resorts where the ski-ing is below 4,000 feet (1,200 metres), except in New England. Furthermore, at the beginning and end of the season (December and mid-March on), when snow is uncertain, seek out slopes *suitable to your own abilities* that end at not less than

5,000 feet (1,500 m). There is also an upper limit to your ski-ing that is likely to be imposed by the cold. This is around 8,500 feet (2,600 m) in December and early January. And 9,000 feet (2,750 m) until the end of February. So at Christmas and the New Year at least, the parameters are tight: 5,000 to 8,500 feet (1,500–2,600 m). Like all rules, the '4,000 feet (1,200 m) minimum' has exceptions. These are the 'snow pockets', which get more snow than a glance at their altitude would lead you to believe. Kitzbühel is a notable example. At 2,600 feet (790 m) it has the sort of snow record you would expect to find at 5,000 feet (1,500 m). Fieberbrunn, St Johann, Westendorf, Niederau, Oberau, and Auffach, also in Austria, are snow pockets, as is the St Cergue region of the Swiss Jura. Norway is a case apart. The Norwegians claim that 2,000 feet (600 m) should be added to their heights for a fair comparison with Alpine resorts (their distance north compensating for their lack of height). We have found no reason to take issue with them on this. But height is altogether a less important factor in Norway (which is totally covered with snow for much of the winter) than it is in the Alps. Otherwise, with the added proviso that going further north in Norway has the same effect, what is true of the Alps is true of Norway: the higher you go the more sure you can be of snow in April—and of being cold in January and February.

The way the slopes face

Finally, the direction in which the ski slopes face has a direct bearing on the snow—an important point to remember when choosing a resort. The main points to consider are as follows:

NORTH FACING SLOPES

Advantages: These receive little sunshine—mostly only weak slanting rays—or no sun at all if shaded by woods. The cold and the low ground temperatures keep the snow good and powdery for much longer periods. North-facing slopes also retain their snow later into the season.

Disadvantages: Following a period of thaw ice may persist until there is a fresh snowfall.

Uphill transport by open lift (eg by chairlift) can be bitterly cold, especially early in the season.

SOUTH FACING SLOPES

Advantages: Hot sun by day and cold night temperatures combine to create the much-vaunted spring snow conditions in mid-season.

Disadvantages: Being exposed to the direct rays of the sun for most of the day, powder snow is short-lived unless the weather is overcast. Off-piste, south-facing slopes are liable to form crust between December and the end of February. In late season, unless there have been substantially heavy pre-season falls to form a good base, the piste begins to wear thin, and in any case the snow tends to become slow and heavy after mid-day.

EAST AND WEST FACING SLOPES

These share the features of both south- and north-facing slopes, although they are less pronounced. Thus they are warmer than northern slopes, and snow lasts longer than on the southern slopes. The only difference between eastern and western slopes, of course, is that the sun shines on the eastern slopes in the morning and on the western in the afternoon. You would therefore tend to ski on the eastern slopes before lunch, and on the western ones after lunch.

Intermediate points: Mountainsides do not point obligingly due north, south, east or west. A north-western slope would have most of the characteristics of a northern one. Not least, expect it to have more skiable pistes towards the end of the season than a south-westerly one.

The snow reports

Season, altitude and aspect, then, all have some bearing on snow conditions, but they only tell you what are the *probabilities*. For more precise information the skier turns to snow reports, although even these have snags for those who live far from the ski-ing areas. The reports are printed in newspapers and, in resort areas, broadcast by radio stations. In the United States summaries of these reports appear in many major newspapers in cities that are close to ski resorts. Often these reports appear only on Thursdays and Fridays, although some major ski cities (Denver, Salt Lake City) publish daily reports. Generally the resorts themselves originate these reports. They supply the information to services such as Ellis Ski Information Center.

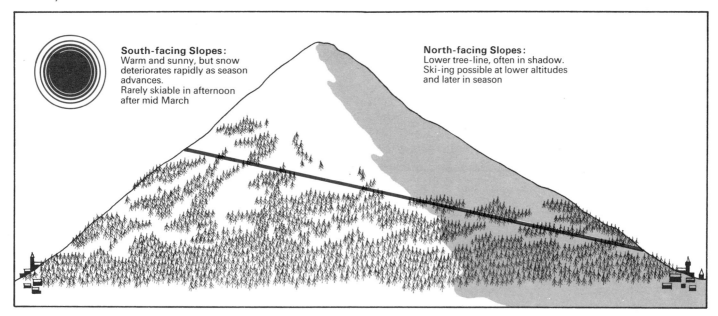

South-facing Slopes:
Warm and sunny, but snow deteriorates rapidly as season advances.
Rarely skiable in afternoon after mid March

North-facing Slopes:
Lower tree-line, often in shadow.
Ski-ing possible at lower altitudes and later in season

Obviously the resort could have a vested interest in writing glowing reports. Newspapers assured us that no resort would do this because each is only too aware that consistent misreporting would backfire. Yet commercial urges cannot be ignored. It is not unknown for ski resorts to be badgered about adverse reports by the local hotel managements, or for tourist offices to fail to file a report at all rather than confess there is no snow. Wilful misreporting is not the main problem, however. This is the practical difficulty of reporting snow conditions over a large area in a way that means something to the skier who has not yet arrived there. First, between the filing of a good snow report and your own contemplation of mushy slopes several days later there could have been a sudden thaw or warm winds. Alternatively, to look on the bright side, if your January or February holiday is preceded by poor snow reports you may arrive to find snow has fallen and you have powder.

Secondly, snow conditions can vary considerably in one resort. How do you fairly average snow depth or conditions when there is little on the peaks because of winds, plenty in the more protected middle ranges, little in the village, but a tolerable amount on one north-facing nursery slope? Something like that is a frequent pattern.

Many newspapers and some radio stations try to overcome this problem by adding their own commentary, sometimes by a columnist who has visited resorts during the week.

Even if the snow reports have problems, they remain a vital part of your check list and are worth examining. Illustrated at right is a report on ski conditions that appeared in *The New York Times* one day in February. Only resorts in New England are mentioned. Generally newspapers only report on their own region. For more distant resorts you can call airlines serving that part of the country, state tourist boards or travel agencies. Many resorts also have toll-free 800 or WATS telephone lines where you can dial straight through for the facts.

Let us now examine the report (but please remember that this is for a day in 1975 and is not to be taken as any kind of guide to your current holiday).

The base: Two figures follow the resort name. These give the depth of the snow base in inches. The first (and smaller) of these numbers is more important because it gives the depth of the base at its lowest point. A minimum base for ski-ing varies between 8 to 12 inches; anything less means you may hit rocks or bare spots. On this report for this time the Catskill resort, with only a 2-inch base, was not really a good bet. The higher of the base numbers is less meaningful. It is usually measured in a snow drift and is useful only as a general guide to the average snow depth.

Reports on Skiing Conditions

(Reports are supplied by resort owners.)

NEW YORK

Belleayre—18-to-38 inch base; 5 inches new packed powder; skiing excellent.
Big Birch—12-24; packed powder; excellent.
Big Tupper—6-34; 1 new powder; excellent.
Big Vannila (Davos)—12-36; 5 new powder; excellent.
Catamount—20-62; 4 new powder; excellent.
Catskill—2-14; 5 new windblown packed powder; good.
Cortina Valley—28-40; 8 new packed powder; excellent.
Dutchess—20-40; 8 new packed powder; excellent.
Fahnestock—18-36; 10 new powder; excellent.
Gore Mt.—9; 1 new packed powder; good-excellent.
Holiday Mt.—36; 6 new powder; excellent.
Hunter Mt.—24-70; 4 new artificial powder; excellent.
Mt. Peter—25-40; 8 new artificial powder; excellent.
Plattekill—6-15; 3 new packed powder; excellent.
Scotch Valley—10-35; 3 new packed powder; good-excellent.
Silvermine—23-36; packed powder; excellent.
Snow Ridge—26; 2 new packed powder; excellent.
Sterling Forest—12-46; 12 new packed powder; excellent.
West Mt.—36-68; 3 new packed artificial powder; excellent.
Whiteface Mt.—10-40; packed artificial powder; good-excellent.

NEW HAMPSHIRE

Bretton Woods—34-42; packed powder; excellent.
Cannon Mt.—12-22; packed powder; excellent.
Mittersill—12-22; 5 powder; excellent.
Waterville Valley—15-38; packed powder; good-excellent.
Wildcat—15-25; packed powder; good excellent.

VERMONT

Bromley—16-50; 4 powder; excellent.
Glen Ellen—40-55; 1 powder; excellent.
Haystack—23-30; 4 powder; excellent.
Jay Peak—30-40; 2 powder; excellent.
Killington—26-65; 1 powder; excellent
Mad River—12-36; 1 powder; excellent.
Magic Mt.—40; 3 powder; excellent.
Mt. Snow—15-39; 4 powder; excellent.
Okemo—20-36; packed powder; excellent.
Pico Peak—25-48; packed powder; excellent.
Round Top—12-16; 1-2 new powder; excellent.
Smugglers Notch—36-51; 3 powder; excellent.
Stowe—28-34; packed powder; excellent.
Stratton—28; packed powder; excellent.
Sugarbush—2-44; packed powder; excellent.
Woodstock Ski Area—22-32; packed powder; excellent.

CONNECTICUT

Mohawk Mt.—8-15; 6 powder; excellent.
Powder Ridge—20-40; 10 powder; excellent.

SKI INFORMATION

Round-the-clock toll free information is available at Ellis Ski Information Center.
From New York—800-243-3430.
From Maine, Vermont, Pennsylvania, Delaware, Virginia and Washington, D. C 800-243-3430.
From Connecticut—800-992-3420.

New snow: After the base figure, the report tells what, if any, new snow has fallen and what type of snow it is. Thus, if the report says '4 new powder', as it does for Catamount, it means that on top of the base is 4 inches of new powder that makes up the current ski-ing surface. Once this new snow is packed down it becomes a part of the figure for the base. If there has been no new snow, the depth of the base will be followed by a description of the ski-ing surface—powder, hard-packed, granular, icy, etc. You will note that new snow has been more plentiful in New York than in Vermont or New Hampshire. However, the northern resorts have a greater base.

Snow condition: Finally, there is an evaluation of the condition of the snow generally. This will range from poor through fair and good to excellent, with frequent combinations (eg fair to good). This last part of the report is the most difficult to assess. Obviously it involves a subjective judgement by the resort owner, who has a vested interest in reporting conditions likely to attract customers. The best advice we can give here is to watch the resort's reporting practises. Do some comparison shopping on adjectives. Be suspicious of a resort, for instance, that reports 'excellent' when everyone else within 100 miles is reporting 'fair'. Some resorts have a reputation for scrupulous honesty in reporting their own snow. Try to learn which they are.

Artificial snow: The report also indicates which resorts make artificial snow (Hunter Mountain, for instance, reports '4 inches new artificial powder'). Artificial snow is often a little heavier and denser in texture than natural snow; but in the East we rate very highly the ability of the resort to provide a skiable area artificially.

The main thing to note about the reports printed by *The New York Times* on this February 1975 day is how great the ski-ing is. Most of the resorts have a good enough base, which has been topped with new powder snow. An overwhelming majority list their conditions as 'excellent'. Reports like these mean it is time to pack your skis and head for the pistes, with the awareness, though, that thousands of other skiers are going to have the same idea.

The Weather Map: This is a neglected source for saving ski holidays. The average skier sets off on the basis of ski conditions in his paper on Thursday, which have been filed by the resorts on Wednesday. By the time he reaches those pistes on Saturday, this report will be more than three days old. A lot can happen to snow in three days. If you learn to read the weather map you can have a good idea of how much the snow conditions in that area are likely to change between the Wednesday report and your Saturday arrival. Take temperature. Read-

ings are taken towards nightfall. If they are above freezing, then the chances of a good frost to preserve melting snow are poor. Winds are also bad news for snow.

What can you do if the snow report is bad? First, remember that it can change quite quickly. Secondly, if your resort is bad check on nearby resorts. A resort further down the valley or just over the mountain might well have ideal snow—and your resort could well share its lift system. At the very least it is worth budgeting a little extra for local transport, rather than cancelling your holiday. Here, of course, is the main disadvantage of having to book long in advance. The odds in the snow gamble can be improved by studying the records of resorts and their altitude-slope complexion; or by booking only the air passage in advance and taking pot luck with accommodation where the snow reports are good (which is an expensive way of ski-ing, as you do not have the economies of a package holiday). That gamble is up to you; we would not care for the responsibility of recommending it. We have done it, but with varying success, sometimes finding room in the resort easily, especially out of season, sometimes having to travel a long way daily for accommodation: good snow reports attract other skiers like flies, especially locals and week-enders.

Choosing a country

Most American skiers stay at home. You can learn to ski, and have great fun for a few days, on some of the modest knobs of hills in the East and Midwest. For those who want to adventure and really experience mountain solitude on a long day's run, the choice is between Europe and the American West. We have skied both. The pull of Europe lies in: longer, more romantic runs, especially between linked ski resorts such as Davos-Klosters, Lech-Zurs, Courchevel-Meribel; *après-ski* life in old towns of aesthetic appeal (Zermatt especially); and good food, notably in France. The pull of the Rockies is first and foremost the snow—even as we write we can feel ourselves drifting down through unbeatable powder, in brilliant sunshine; secondly, the organisation of ski schools and lifts and the maintenance of trails is superior in the U.S. We will describe the best areas we have skied ourselves in the U.S. For those we miss (there are about 1,500 across the country), and as a check on our judgements, we urge on you the paperback *Where to Ski*, by William I. Berry (Signet $1.95, 1974). In the areas we know personally we haven't been able to fault his frank and lively assessments.

You should always write to a fancied resort and check the brochures against the tests we suggest later on in this chapter. An example to all ski states is *Colorado Ski Country USA* (1461

Larimer Square, Denver), a succinct tabulated guide to 29 resorts.

Here are our judgements on areas in the U.S. and Europe, beginning with the U.S.

The American West

We think the hottest thing in the West is Colorado, which has more of the best resorts; the other major states are Utah, Idaho, California, Nevada, Wyoming, New Mexico, Washington, Oregon and, in Canada, Alberta and British Columbia. In Colorado we pick out Vail, Snowmass, Copper, Keystone, Aspen, Aspen Highlands, Aspen Buttermilk, Breckenridge, Steamboat and Winter Park. In Utah it is Park City, Snowbird and Alta. In Idaho, Sun Valley; in California, Heavenly Valley and Alpine Meadows; in Wyoming, Jackson Hole (stay at Teton Village); in New Mexico, Taos. Beginners and worriers should avoid Aspen, Jackson Hole and Snowbird. Vail is a resort for skiers of all grades and, if costly, it is also arguably the finest in the U.S. There are eleven square miles of ski country, a 3,000-foot vertical drop and a 5-mile run. The trails overlooking and flowing down to the twin resorts of Vail Village (mock but appealing Swiss-Austrian) and Lionshead (high-rise hotels with redeeming pedestrian squares) are wide, superbly groomed, varied runs; and over the crest of the mountain are the famous back bowls—huge, open, treeless areas where you turn when you feel like it, or practise really long carved turns. Intermediates can enjoy Game Creek Bowl; experts head for Sun, Sun Down and Forever. Snowmass—not to be confused with Aspen, which is 12 miles away—can be strongly recommended for families. It is a chic but cosy village of lodges and condominiums built right on the slopes. Years ago there was a forest fire that left huge open areas on the mountain called the Big Burn, so that the ski-ing, if a little more limited than Vail, has plenty of interest for a full holiday. Children and handicapped people get special attention here.

Neither of these excellent resorts is as colourful and fascinating a town base as Aspen, Park City (Utah), Breckenridge or Steamboat, each with a honky tonk echo of the Old West. Park City, a 30-minute drive from Salt Lake City, was a bonanza silver mining town, and amid the lodges are old miners' houses, false front stores and original saloons (beer, not hard liquor). Excellent ski-ing for all levels. It was gold at Breckenridge, cattle at Steamboat and silver at Aspen. In Aspen there are red-plush and gold saloons, with stained glass and chandeliers, and you can sit and watch the snow slanting past the street lights and the men (freshly gnarled from New York) with Stetsons supported by moustaches. Expect to carry your

skis as well as your drink; and the mountain is tough.

Finally, we pick Sun Valley (Idaho) and Heavenly Valley (Lake Tahoe, California). Sun Valley is a complete ski resort with one mountain (Dollar) for beginners and another (Baldy) for the rest; bowls with a great variety of steepness (if not length); and, of course, the essential 'ego snow' as they call the powder there, which makes you feel like a hot-dog champion. Lake Tahoe has about six separate ski resorts around its shores. Heavenly Valley we liked best, with its unusual ridge runs from California into Nevada, views over the lake and considerable terrain.

East Coast

The great thing about the East is variety—somewhere in Maine, Vermont, New Hampshire, Connecticut, New York, Massachusetts (or Quebec in Canada), there is the hill/mountain matched with the quiet/roaring resort for every taste. The snow does not compare to the West; the trails, swathed through woodland, are narrower; and you can be so cold you wonder where you lost your fingers (down-filled mitts are vital).

Yet there can be some fine ski-ing in places like Vermont's Jay Peak, Killington, Sugarbush, Stratton, Magic Mountain,

Little more than sheep meadow a dozen years ago, Vail's Alpine-style village in Colorado is the showpiece of a giant ski area with easy boulevard runs, great middle-grade ski-ing and tough stuff in the back bowls. Car free Zermatt (*left*), is a real Swiss Alpine village, one of the world's great ski resorts. You really do take a horse-and-buggy ride to the cable car stations

Mount Snow, and Bromley; New Hampshire's Waterville, Cannon Mountain, Loon, Wildcat, Cranmore and Sunapee; Maine's Sugarloaf; New York's Hunter and Whiteface (less good for intermediates). The teaching is generally good, the nightlife is often exuberant and the New England villages can be as charming as anything in Europe. But always check the snow report and the resort's snow-making capacity before you set off.

Europe

Austria Once a by-word for cheap winter sports, it is losing a lot of its competitive edge. This is particularly true of the smaller resorts. As prices rise there is a tendency for cheese-paring on package holidays. They look relatively cheap in the brochure, but sometimes essentials like three square meals a day are omitted.

However, if you want cuckoo clocks, *glühwein*, Christmas card villages and beery, cheery *après ski* at a reasonable price, then this is still the country. It is winter sports as all except the ultra chic have always imagined it.

The charm of Austria is that its mountain villages have doubled up as ski resorts. The community came first, the skiers second. This makes for atmosphere, but also, on occasions, long journeys to the slopes.

Austrian instruction is thorough, though there is resistance to new ideas like the short-ski methods developed by the French and Americans (see Chapter 18) and too much emphasis on exaggerated upper body positions. Some resorts do claim to have adopted the short-ski method of teaching, but it is often their own variety. Otherwise this is the traditional country for beginners.

Many resorts feature ski-touring. This is a leisurely perambulation on loose bound skis along prepared paths (see page 47).

This is a trifle less adventuresome than the Norwegian cross country ski-ing, where you just head off across the mountain.

Italy Coming up fast. The ski-ing here is much as you would expect: sunny, noisy, fast, colourful and somewhat undisciplined. The food is not bad, and the wine cheap. Pistes have been constructed with the beginner and intermediate skier in mind. The instruction, although no great shakes, is tolerable in the larger resorts. Instructors rarely speak English. A good place to take children, and to avoid if you cannot stand them. If you are anywhere near a big city, stand by to be engulfed at weekends by hordes of Italians with little ski technique and even fewer ski manners.

Spain A surprisingly late starter in the winter sports stakes, with a lot going for it—not least, it has sunshine and wide treeless slopes. It is much the same as Italy, except that there is less here against which the expert skier can pit himself. Here, too, the presence of Austrian or French instructors in a ski school is the best guarantee that your instruction will be adequate. There are two main areas (that around Madrid not being worthy of consideration), the Pyrenees and the Sierra Nevada. Both have a longer season than you would imagine. Although the actual ski-ing (ie lift passes) are expensive, the cost of living is low.

France Should be given serious consideration by any beginner who can afford it (French resorts are not cheap), and for the advanced skier the challenges are second only to Switzerland. French teaching is probably now the best in the world. The snag is that few instructors can speak English. Many schools now teach Ski Evolutif, the French short-ski method (see Chapter 18). Food, of course, is excellent. Night life is studiedly casual: don't expect to find yourself having a ball with the locals.

Norway The antithesis of France, and unlikely to find favour with the sybarite or the expert downhill skier. Food, especially the famous Norwegian 'cold table' breakfast and lunch, is wholesome and plentiful, while drinks are phenomenally expensive. Slopes are often difficult to reach, and not as challenging as Alpine ones.

Switzerland is outrageously expensive, and to some tastes a trifle dour. What does it offer? Higher mountains, surer snow, a touch of glamour in Zermatt, St. Moritz. Pistes and lifts impeccably maintained. The independent traveller will appreciate the superb public transport system and some people believe that a great merit lies in most of the hotels having public lounges. The big expense is extras such as drinks, discos and general apres-ski jollification. The really keen skier who is prepared to do with little or none of these will survive on the euphoria of the long runs and may argue that Switzerland gives the best value for money. But beginners are better off in Spain or Austria.

Ski instruction is competent (though some fashionable resorts have little interest in beginners) and most instructors, particularly in German speaking areas, have good English.

Scotland This is the only place in Britain with proper ski-ing facilities. It does not offer the Alps serious competition and will never appeal to those for whom a major part of a ski holiday is the acquisition of a sun tan and mingling with the jet set. But Scotland is beginning to look good value for money. The official season is December to May, but, though the late ski-ing can be good, snow is always uncertain, and the weather is fickle and often bitterly cold. What brings people here is the excellence of the (obviously) English language tuition and, believe it or not, the informal but lively night life (it helps to like pubs). The major centre is Aviemore in the Cairngorms.

Australasia Has lots of potential and boasts more snow than Switzerland, but there is little development, and the best facilities do not coincide with the best snow. The South Island of New Zealand can be relied on for waist-deep powder snow for much of the season (June to October) but has few lifts. The North Island resort of Ruapehu, a 9,000 foot extinct volcano, is well equipped and lively, but the snow more fickle. Australia has less spectacular mountains and less reliable snow than New Zealand, but facilities and night life tend to be better. Thredbo and Perisher in NSW and Mount Buller in Victoria are the major resorts.

Choosing a resort

The fact that a resort exists at all means that at least some people believe it provides reasonable ski-ing at the price. But it is crucial to check everything in advance, so that you are able to make up your mind. 'Reasonable ski-ing at the price' is a subjective assessment. It requires not merely choosing the resort but being honest with ourselves.

What type are you?

- First, your abilities: if you are a beginner there is not much point in going to St Moritz; a small Austrian village would be much better. There might not be much there, but providing there is a reasonable ski school and a few beginners' slopes, there will be all you need for your ski-ing. It is not merely foolish to pay for the privilege of access to some of the best ski-ing in the world if you cannot ski the slopes. It is also a matter of morale. Nothing can shatter it more quickly than inconsiderate advanced skiers carving you up. The temptation of armchair skiers

is to opt for something beyond their ability and regret it on the snow. It is generally better to risk some boredom than complete demoralization.

Conversely, once you have experience you are going to look for something more challenging than a resort with short easy runs that are cluttered with beginners.

- Second, your preferences: you need to ask yourself: Would I like a resort where there is something other than downhill ski-ing? Skating, ski-bobbing, tobogganing, ice-hockey, curling, sleigh rides, swimming, walking, excursions or even cross country ski-ing? A cinema perhaps? How important is night life? Or do I want a quiet village atmosphere? Davos, for instance, would disappoint someone bred on the tranquility of Saas Fee, where there are sleighs but no cars; on the other hand, it is a good town for shopping, cinemas and eating.

On a personal note, we would add that we found none of those extra mountain sports or activities significant. We had neither the energy nor the inclination for anything other than ski-ing. Nevertheless, a certain amount of risk-spreading can be advisable for the beginner. If you find you do not after all like ski-ing, then there will always be something else to do. This is clearly also a consideration if you are travelling with a non-skier—or a suspected one! —or with children.

- Third, ask yourself: do I prefer small resorts or big ones? Do I want the Christmas card cosiness of a traditional resort, or the convenience of a purpose-built one? And, as a corollary of this: should I go high up in the mountains where there is likely to be more snow—even at the risk of it being colder, and there being precious little to do if the weather is wrong? Do I prefer the 'all mucking in' atmosphere of Austria? Or the clockwork efficiency of Switzerland?

The quest for an ideal resort usually begins with a visit to the local travel agent to collect a pile of brochures. But there are ways to read brochures, for the omissions can be as significant as what is included. Beginners at least have one security as they burrow in them. They may come across modest little resorts masquerading as major ones, but never the reverse. So it is the competent skier who runs the risk of being lured to a resort better suited for beginners rather than the other way around.

Left: East Coast ski terrain: a woodland trail at Cannon Mountain, New Hampshire

The resorts in close-up

These are the things you should hope to learn about a resort from your brochure:

- The type of resort.
- The length and vertical rise of the lifts.
- The type of lifts (cable car, chair lift, tow).
- The altitude of the resort.
- The length and difficulty of runs.
- The existence of any 'bottlenecks' on the lifts or slopes.
- The direction the slopes face.
- The exact position of the treeline.
- The position of the hotel (ie how far to the lifts?).
- The position of the beginners' slopes: are they in such a situation and at such an altitude that there is a reasonable expectation of their being skiable?
- If you are only moderately proficient, are the slopes appropriate to your ability range linked by pistes on which you are capable of ski-ing?

All this is vital information. A map can show it all. *Yet we have never seen a map in a travel agent's brochure which enables the skier to go through this check list.* Often there is no map at all. Of course there will be difficulty in the agency getting good maps for all resorts, but they are infinitely more worth space and colour printing than the usual run of giggling girls on nursery slopes or vague views of mountains. Some brochures, you will notice, are better than others.

A golden rule of choosing a resort is therefore *never book until you have seen a decent map.* You can write to the resort if the agency or ski club is unhelpful. For a few European resorts, there are excellent little booklets by Rob Tillard, published by Ski Europe, 2 West Eaton Place, London SW1. Prices from 50p.

The type of resort

Winter sports resorts, broadly speaking, divide into three types. Brochures usually contain enough information for you to tell which type it is.

The pre-Alpine resorts

These are the lowest and cheapest resorts. They are usually below 1,400 m (4,600 feet) and nestle deep in a valley. These were thriving communities long before ski-ing became an industry. But, since they were not settled with ski-ing in mind, there is unlikely to be much ski-ing near the village or town other than for beginners, especially early or late in the season. Intermediate skiers would expect a long journey by cable car which will take them up into the surrounding mountains.

Many of the Austrian resorts fall into this category. On the face of it, resorts like this can offer the beginner and intermediate skier the best of both worlds: a charming village in the evenings and broad high snowscapes in the daytime. But, as we shall show you, there can be hidden snags.

The traditional Alpine resorts

These are where holiday ski-ing began, in the days before lifts allowed the pre-Alpine resorts to compete. These are in the 1,400 to 1,800 m (4,600–5,900 feet) bracket. There will be adequate ski-ing around the town itself, and a lift system opening up the higher reaches of the mountains. Even here, however, a lift outside your hotel door is not a foregone conclusion. Most of the famous Swiss resorts are like this.

Purpose-built resorts

The purpose-built resort is to be found from 1,600 m (5,250 feet) up. Built where there was nothing before but mountains, you will have lifts and nursery slopes at your doorstep. This takes a lot of work out of a ski holiday. For this reason, beginners should not be deterred from these resorts simply by the vague idea that the higher the resort the more difficult the ski-ing. Beginners have to work more than intermediates, because they spend so long side-stepping up the nursery slopes. Carrying skis a long way is an unnecessary extra burden, particularly for beginners who are not used to it. These resorts are often split into two or more residential complexes: with one at, say, 1,600 m (5,250 feet), another at 2,000 m (6,560 feet) and a third at 2,700 m (8,850 feet).

Even the pistes are purpose-built in resorts like this. Pistes in the older resorts tend to follow a woodland path or a cattle path here, a logging road there. This is especially true of the pre-Alpine resorts. In the purpose-built resort the pistes go down the mountain the way the *skier* would want to go—not a cow, a timber lorry or a hiker. This involves a certain amount of mountain sculpting, the felling of a few trees to broaden the way through the forest, the removal of a boulder and the filling in of a gully. The result is not necessarily the environmental rape it suggests. The designer of one purpose-built resort told us that one of his priorities was maintaining the traditional summer grazing of the pastures by cattle. This was because long ungrazed grass would not hold the snow properly in winter. And the best way to halt the drift of population away from the mountains, he reasoned, was to provide the local

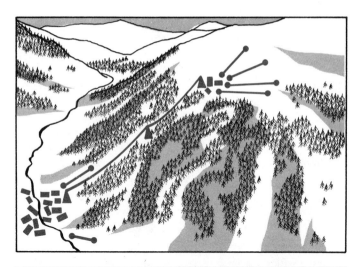

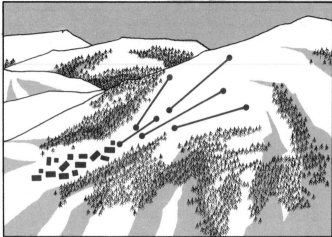

(Top right) Pre-Alpine resort
(middle) Traditional resort
(bottom) Purpose-built resort

people with a handsome winter income from tourism.

Like anything built with efficiency as its foremost criterion, the purpose-built resort tends to lack charm, atmosphere and character. They are as high rise housing to the nostalgic chaos of the old houses that have been bulldozed away. They are efficient and convenient ski-ing machines—and dismal ones when the weather is bad. We do not recommend them for non-skiers.

The length and vertical rise of the lifts

These should be ascertainable from the resort map in the brochure and its key. Most brochures contain at least a minimal map, showing the lift system and usually the pistes of a resort. We shall be taking a more detailed look at these maps and what they can, or should, tell us. All you need to know at this point is that the lifts are the straight lines and the pistes (if they are marked) the squiggly ones. A key to the map will tell you what type of lift it is (we describe the types in the next section), how long it is, and how high up the mountain it will take you (ie its vertical rise or lift). It may also tell you how long it takes and how much it costs.

What you want to know, of course, is what sort of a run any lift will give you. The lift's length is pretty meaningless in this context, although it will be some indication of how long the ride takes, a matter worth consideration on a bitter day. For a beginner, a tow of longer than a kilometre (3,280 feet) could be very unpleasant. The rise of the lift is more relevant to the kind of run it serves, but it is still only a comparative guide. You must hope to find more concise information about the actual pistes to deduce the length and difficulty of runs to which this lift would take you.

Types of lift

Illustrated right are the four basic types of lift. Top is a cable car, the fastest and most expensive way up a mountain. You would hope to use it for those big jumps up the mountain, or across difficult or unskiable terrain. Below it is a chair lift. Next is a 'telecabine' or 'gondola', a cross between the previous two, and more comfortable than either.

And bottom is a ski tow, otherwise known as a tow lift or a T-bar. It is the cheap, slow—and sometimes cold and un-comfortable—way up a mountain, but nevertheless is the sort of lift you are most likely to use. It tows you uphill on your skis, and so is useless when slopes are bare: a point to remember when planning a holiday at the beginning or end of the season. Some of the older resorts also have funicular railways. They may be cheap and fun, but they are also slow.

The altitude of a resort, and what it means

The height of the resort is probably its most vital statistic. Every brochure gives this information, though you need to know how to interpret it and how to calculate the heights of the runs themselves.

Officially a resort's height is that of the local church above sea level, but some resorts, especially the purpose-built ones, do not have a church. In this case, and also where a town has sprawled up the mountainside with the advent of ski-ing, the height will often be the uppermost limit of the town or village. Far from being a false figure, this is often a more valid statistic, for the uppermost limits of the town are usually where the slopes begin.

It is more usual to find two figures quoted (ie '3,436–6,200 ft'). The lower figure is the height of the town; the other is the altitude of the top of its highest lift. Together they tell the skier what he really wants to know: the zones within which he is most likely to ski (assuming he can cope with the highest run, and that the snow extends all the way down to the resort). Resorts *have* been known to quote the height of a neighbouring and totally unskiable peak for the upper figure. This is meaningless, dishonest, and, fortunately, very rare.

For a pre-Alpine resort, these figures will not necessarily tell the whole story. If the ski-ing slopes are reached by a long cable car journey this is because the terrain between the top of the cable car and the town is not always skiable. Take our imaginary resort Anyalp (*top right*). It is low, so if snow is scarce you may only be able to ski from A to B, not A to C. A truer picture of the ski-ing potential of Anyalp is therefore given by subtracting the vertical rise of the cable car (2,106 feet) from the altitude figures.

If the figures quoted are from, say, 4,000 to 10,000 feet (1,216 to 3,047 m), such a calculation would be mere hair-splitting. On the other hand, if they were from, say, 3,000 to 5,000 feet (912–1,523 m) and the initial lift accounted for 1,000 (304 m) of them, then it could be vital.

Similarly, when a brochure lumps together twin resorts sharing a lift system and gives only one set of altitude figures, this can be misleading. For instance, this is often done for Sölden and Hochsölden in Austria, with the figures 4,600–10,000 feet (1,400–3,047 m) quoted. But the higher slopes can be reached only by a cable car from Sölden (see map). From Hochsölden, the higher resort, the lift system extends only up to 8,250 feet (2,513 m). To get higher than 8,250 feet skiers staying at Hochsölden must therefore go down to Sölden and then back up the mountain. The pistes at this height are, in this instance, only suited to expert skiers anyway, and so it is not a problem

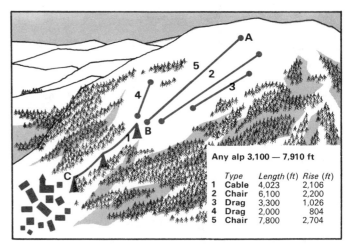

Any alp 3,100 — 7,910 ft

	Type	Length (ft)	Rise (ft)
1	Cable	4,023	2,106
2	Chair	6,100	2,200
3	Drag	3,300	1,026
4	Drag	2,000	804
5	Chair	7,800	2,704

most of us will face at this particular resort. But there are three ways down to Sölden: on skis (the most agreeable way), by chair lift, (A), or by road (B). Now the skier will probably want to get to the upper slopes precisely because there is little or no snow on the lower ones. Ski-ing down is therefore out. He must make the tedious chair lift journey down to Sölden, then a long walk to the cable car (C), and then back up again (unless his hotel provides transport or he can afford a taxi).

The altitude of Hochsölden, incidentally, is 6,857 feet (2,087 m). Its lift system, as we have already noted, extends up to 8,250 feet (2,513 m). But, as a glance at the resort map will instantly tell you, this does not mean that the skier using the Hochsölden lift system has only 1,393 feet (426 m) in which to ski. He can ski below Hochsölden as well as above it. This

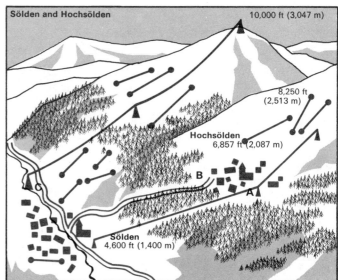

Sölden and Hochsölden

10,000 ft (3,047 m)

8,250 ft (2,513 m)

Hochsölden 6,857 ft (2,087 m)

Sölden 4,600 ft (1,400 m)

is true of a number of the higher resorts.

It is worth noting, in passing, one more hidden snag of the twin resort. The lift passes (of which more later) might be valid for one system but not for the other. If you are counting on using both systems, check this when working out your budget.

The pistes (or ski runs)

Clearly, a map that does not show you the pistes tells you nothing about the ski-ing you will be able to do in a resort. An amazing number do not. They show only the lifts—and, as we have noted, however much information you have about these, you are still little the wiser about the pistes they serve. Fortunately, the majority of operators do at least show you the pistes. This, as we shall see, does enable you to clear up some of the points on your check list, but not all of them. We have never found a travel agent's map which both (a) tells us just how hard these pistes are; and (b) includes every piste in the resort.

First, however the things this kind of 'map' can tell you:

Altitude of pistes To gauge this, add together the vertical rise of the lifts you need to take to get to the top of a piste, and then add this to the base height of the resort. A good resort map will make this easy for you either by giving you the height of each lift station or by actually giving the height of the piste (which by convention is the height of the upper station of the

lift serving it). This information, if it is given at all, is usually contained in the key to the map.

The only reason that most people usually want this information is because they plan their holiday early or late in the season when snow is uncertain, and they want to know what the relative chances are that the pistes they will be using will have a good snow cover. Unfortunately, even after all your calculations, this question will still be unanswered. You will not know which slopes are for beginners and which are for experts, and so you will not know which lifts and pistes *you* are likely to be using.

Bottlenecks There are two kinds of bottlenecks: lift bottlenecks and piste bottlenecks. The typical lift bottleneck is where everyone has to use the same (or a limited number) of lifts to get into the lift system. A piste bottleneck is where there is only one (or a limited number) of pistes back down to the resort. Both are to be avoided, and both are of particular concern to the beginner. Since he tends to ski on the lower slopes, it will probably be his lift and piste everyone is using. Nothing is more demoralizing for a beginner than having all the skiers in the resort bombing past him to the restaurants. Our map of another imaginary resort, Goodalp (*below*), would suggest it has no obvious defects on this score. A reasonable ratio of lifts (four out of nine) provide access to the lift system, at points A, B, C, and D. And, once they have used these lifts, the skiers on the upper slopes have no need to return to them

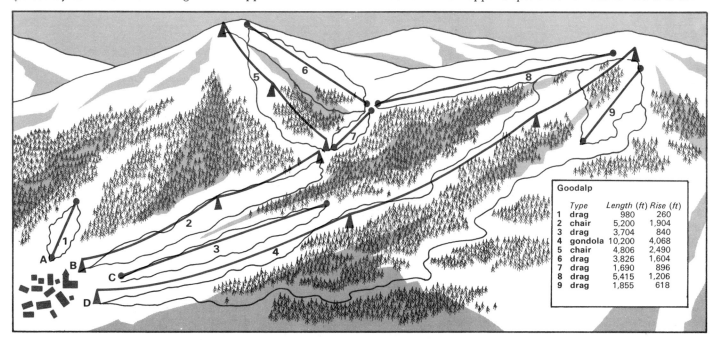

	Goodalp		
	Type	*Length* (ft)	*Rise* (ft)
1	drag	980	260
2	chair	5,200	1,904
3	drag	3,704	840
4	gondola	10,200	4,068
5	chair	4,806	2,490
6	drag	3,826	1,604
7	drag	1,690	896
8	drag	5,415	1,206
9	drag	1,855	618

during their day's ski-ing. Thus the beginners, who will presumably be using the lower slopes (we still do not know), will be left in peace.

Below, on the other hand, is another resort map—also imaginary—which reveals horrendous bottlenecks. All skiers, except those using pistes A and B, will have to return to the bottom of lift 1 at the end of every run. This will create a bottleneck both on this lift—with massive queues—and on the piste leading to it. Even skiers on pistes A and B will have to go through the piste bottleneck when returning to the village for lunch (presuming there are no restaurants on the slopes) and use lift 1 at the beginning of the day. We would rate long waits for lifts high on our list of potential disasters for a holiday. We shall be giving you further guidance on how to spot the likelihood of these. For the moment it is worth noting that the most common type of lift bottleneck, however, is where the resort is below the ski-ing area, and linked to it by a single cable car, as in many pre-Alpine resorts. Monstrous jams are liable to build up here at the beginning and end of each ski-ing day.

This map emphasizes yet again your need to know just how difficult each piste is. If, for instance, piste E is the *only* beginners' slope, then: (*a*) half of it consists of the bottleneck. (*b*) the beginners are going to spend much of their time queueing at the bottom of lift one. (*c*) it is far too long. (*d*) in bad snow, since this is the lowest piste, beginners are either going to have to stop ski-ing or will be forced uphill in their search of snow onto pistes beyond their ski-ing ability.

Also, to continue our argument, what if pistes A, B, and C were the intermediate slopes, and slope D a difficult one? The only way the intermediate slopes can be reached for the first run of the day is up lifts 1 and 2, and then down slope D, the difficult one, which is beyond an intermediate skier's abilities. We would emphasize that we would never expect to find a resort quite as badly designed as this, but we have found some that run it quite close. So check this sort of detail.

This type of map does give you *some* clue about the relative difficulty of the pistes. Clearly a piste which is served by a 2,800 ft lift with a vertical rise of only 670 feet is going to be a lot easier than one served by a 2,200 foot lift with a 830 foot rise—unless, of course, the second piste meanders lazily down the mountain while the first is virtually straight. So you are still without all the information you need, unless you have the length of the piste itself. And we see no reason why you should be expected to do all these sums. What you *will* need is a map which does them for you and marks the grade of each piste. It is at this point therefore that your researches are usually brought to a halt by the inadequacies of the maps in travel agents' brochures. It is a rare brochure indeed that enables you to clear up this or any of the other remaining points. Most skiers accept this resignedly as a fact of life, and so just do not bother with them—or else rely on other people's advice. We used to be the same, but not any longer. We have made mistakes in choosing resorts, and now know they could have been avoided. So, even if you know someone who knows a

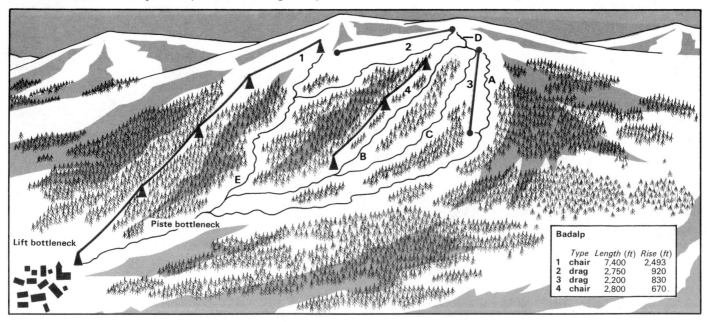

Lift bottleneck

Piste bottleneck

1 2 3 4 A B C D E

Badalp			
	Type	Length *(ft)*	Rise *(ft)*
1	chair	7,400	2,493
2	drag	2,750	920
3	drag	2,200	830
4	chair	2,800	670

resort well—and especially if you do not—always try to get a decent map of a resort before booking a holiday there. Fortunately, these may usually be obtained either from the resort itself or from the tourist board of the country concerned. Even maps from these sources do not always tell you everything, but they are consistently better than those you will find in a winter sports brochure from a package tour company.

This is how to apply the remainder of your check list to a detailed map.

The direction the slopes face

You can deduce the direction the resort's slopes face from the compass rose on the map. In this example (below) they face east (slope A), south (slope B), and west (Slope C). The more ways the slopes face the better: variety will increase the probability of your finding good snow conditions. These are the vital points about the direction the slopes with pistes face when choosing a resort.

1. At all times try to avoid resorts that do not have a west- or a north-facing slope.

2. After February *never* go to a resort that does not have either north-, north-east, or north-west-facing slopes.
 • There may be little snow.
 • What snow there is may have become icy and rutted overnight.
 • Most slopes will be unskiable in the afternoon.

3. We would also advocate a resort where the south facing slopes are higher than the northern ones (if they are on opposite sides of the valley). This would give the northern slopes some protection from the wind.

Grading of pistes

A good resort will mark the grades of any piste on its map. The colour or pattern in which the pistes are printed should relate to a key which tells you its grade. The pistes themselves should also be clearly marked. Appropriately coloured (see below) marker poles guide you down the piste and should be numbered: you should be able, for instance, to report that an injured skier is lying between markers 10 and 11 on piste number four.

Systems of grading can vary, but they are the best guide you will have about what to expect. Sometimes categorization is the responsibility of the resort itself, and in some countries the national ski club determines gradings.

There will be between three and four grades. Confirming that the local system follows on the international pattern should be one of the first items on your checklist when you reach the resort. You cannot always assume that this year's resort has quite the same grading system as last year's, especially if it is in a different country. However, here is what we have found to be the general pattern of designation in Europe. Black: experts only. Red: difficult, for advanced intermediates and above. Blue: easy intermediate runs which you can expect to use at the end of your first holiday. Green: easy, for beginners. The American system is similar: a green circle marks the easiest runs; a blue square is more difficult, and a black triangle the toughest. The American blue runs have sections that would be red in Europe. Pistes are graded according to their average difficulty. Skiers need an occasional challenge to improve, so you can push yourself up the colour scale a bit. But do it judiciously; go up the scale when you are fresh, when the snow is good, and always with a companion, preferably one who is a stronger skier. Do not be deluded by the start of a run. A black run, for instance, may start with an easy descent, but there will be sharp, narrow drops to come, and if you are not up to that kind of ski-ing you may lose your nerve and have to side-step carefully down quite a long way while the experts buzz irritatingly around you.

You may also encounter on an 'easy' run grades that for a short stretch you feel would be better described as intermediate. But the hardest stretch on any given run will never be significantly harder than the run's overall rating. We have never come across a piece of grading with which we would seriously quarrel.

To be of any real use, then, a resort map should show the runs and their grades. This is not just a matter of beginners' caution. The intermediate skier and good skier has even more need of a proper map. The good skier contemplating a new resort must study the runs more, and especially work out these permutations:

1. Can I go up the mountain all day? In other words, when I get to the top are there several local lifts which will enable me to ski a variety of runs at my own grade, or will I just have to ski straight back down again?

2. As a corollary to this, is there a 'circus' of runs somewhere on the mountain with which I can play? In other words, will I be able to go up one lift, ski down to the beginning of another lift, go up that, ski down a new piste to a third lift, go up that, and then, say, ski back to my starting point? Not only will such a 'circus' of lifts lessen the chance of queueing, but ski-ing down the same piste all day is a bore. If lifts and pistes are not linked in this way then the only means of reaching a new slope may well be by walking—which is not only tedious, but also exhausting if you are carrying or wearing skis.

3. Will I be bored on the fourth day doing the same runs or is there sufficient variety, given the time of year and slopes?

4. What are the possibilities of ski-ing my way back home down the mountain at different times? For instance, if the only way home is down a Southern facing slope, this could be a drawback at Easter, when conditions are likely to be wet and slushy in the afternoon, but a bonus in January, because the run home could well be in sunshine.

It is astonishing how many good skiers do not attempt such calculations before they go.

The map that tells it all

This (*right*) is the kind of map the skier needs for picking a resort and planning a day. We have used a system of dots and dashes, instead of colour, to distinguish the grade of piste. In addition you can see which way the slopes face, whether the run is across open snowscapes or down woodland trails, how lifts and pistes connect, what kind of lifts there are, where to find the mountain restaurants, how varied a week you can have. In other words it tells you exactly how you can expect to ski this resort, which is Zürs in Austria.

On the back of a good map you may well find a table giving the length and **vertical rise of each lift,** : so you can gauge **whether a ski tow is likely to prove** boringly long or awkwardly steep. It is more comfortable by cable-car but the map shows that no beginner should go up in the Trittkopf cable-car, unless he merely intends to have a drink, enjoy the view, and come back down in it again. This is because this lift (vertical rise 703m) serves pistes which only brave intermediates and experts can tackle (and the intermediates should stick to the middle one.)

The Zürs lift system connects with Lech, which is just off this map to the north (i.e. below it). There is a tempting circus of lifts for intermediate or expert skiers coming up from Lech. They can, for instance, come up the **Rüfikopf-Bahn. The experts can then ski straight down to Zürs; the inter-**mediates can turn left and ski down to the Trittalm lift. From the top of that there is an easy run to Zürs. The map suggests—accurately—that the skier can return to Lech by going from Zürs up to the Seekopf and Madloch and enjoying the long unbroken run from the Madloch back to Lech. The experts have the option of using the piste which hugs the higher slopes of the valley.

(*Map based on original by Berann, printed by F. Sochor, Zell am See.*)

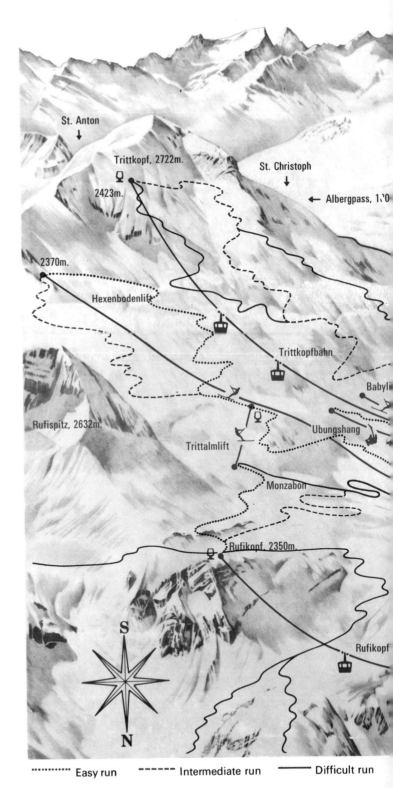

············ Easy run   ------ Intermediate run   —— Difficult run

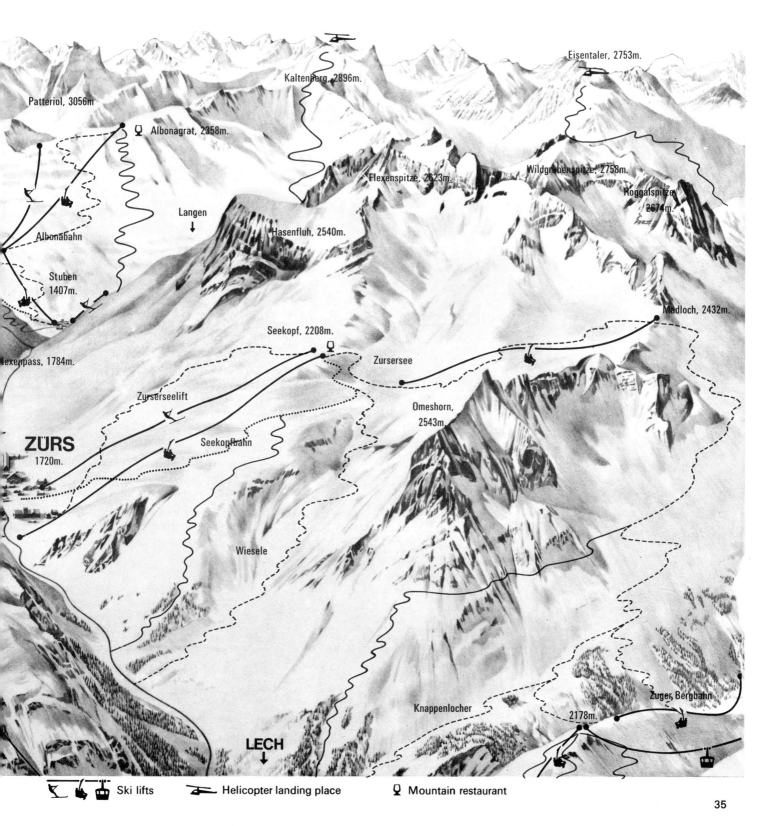

Patteriol, 3056m.

Kaltenberg, 2896m.

Eisentaler, 2753m.

Albonagrat, 2358m.

Wildgrubenspitze, 2758m.

Flexenspitze, 2623m.

Roggalspitze, 2674m.

Langen

Hasenfluh, 2540m.

Albonabahn

Madloch, 2432m.

Stuben
1407m.

Seekopf, 2208m.

Flexenpass, 1784m.

Zursersee

Zurserseelift

Omeshorn,
2543m.

ZÜRS
1720m.

Seekopfbahn

Wiesele

Zuger Bergbahn

Knappenlocher

2178m.

LECH

| ☖ ☖ 🚠 Ski lifts | ✈ Helicopter landing place | ♟ Mountain restaurant |

The beginners' slopes

The beginner has few options. He is limited by his abilities to the beginners' slopes (though the short-ski learners venture further more quickly, and can overcome this liability).

The beginners' nursery slopes are nearly always lower and fewer than the other runs. They are the most vulnerable to thaw and mountain shadow. The beginner runs the risk of finding himself stuck on rocky and patchy pistes down in the valley, shivering in the shadow of the nearby mountain while his more skilful brethren are ski-ing high above in perfect snow and sunshine. It is the worst possible introduction to ski-ing. Never, never believe anybody who says beginners need not worry too much about snow conditions. It is heartbreaking and sometimes even impossible to learn in bad snow. The beginner needs pampering more than anyone else. For this reason we urge beginners not to fall for economy. The cheaper resorts are lower. Beginners try to cut costs—and risk an unpleasant initiation through unfavourable snow. If you are thinking of taking up ski-ing it is crazy to take a risk like this. For the same reason we would urge beginners not to be put off by high altitude resorts straight away: check whether they have adequate beginners' slopes. If they do they are a better bet.

Children from three to six years old in the Kinderheim Playschool, Snowmass, Colorado

Finally, we are sorry to see beginners forced by rigid holiday patterns to risk Easter ski-ing. When this is combined with a low resort, there is a very good chance of a disastrous holiday. You want snow!

Beginners should always take a particularly close look at the map of the resort. You should look for a good variety of beginners' slopes. This is the sort of thing you will want:

- Slopes facing in at least two directions, preferably north-facing and south-facing, to increase your chances of good snow. The beginner is also more prone to cold than other skiers, since a lot of time can be spent hanging around watching the instructor and others in the group. We would therefore hope you will be taught on south- or east-facing slopes in the morning to catch the sun, and north or west ones in the afternoon when temperatures have risen and the morning slopes are more likely to melt and become difficult to ski.
- Wide nursery slopes not hemmed in entirely by rocks, gulleys or trees.
- Two distinct areas of beginners' slopes are an advantage: one below the treeline, the other above it (or in any case one beginners' area well above the other). Once again you are seeking a maximum possible variety of snow conditions. You particularly want to avoid the possibility that all pistes you can ski are either cold or 'blown' (if they are high) or bare (if they are on the lowest slopes).
- Avoid slopes where you will be shivering in the mountain shadow much of the day. This is only a problem with resorts deep in a valley surrounded by high steep mountains.

  It is most likely to affect slopes at the bottom of a steep north- or north-east-facing mountainside, or pistes surrounded by trees. But this is a difficult phenomena to check, since the projection of most resort maps has the effect of flattening the mountains to show the pistes clearly. Sunshine figures for a resort can be a rough guide (make sure they are for the month you are going), but the sunshine man might not take his readings from the spot you are learning to ski. The only sure check on this one is with your ski club. For instance, this is what the SCGB says about Zürs in Austria: 'The village is in shadow from about 2 pm onwards during January. Later on in the season there is sun in clear weather from 7.30 am until 6 pm.'
- Make sure that your pistes will not be the main artery down to the restaurants or the resort. You will not want to be *too* cut off from 'real' skiers (which can result in a leper complex) but nor do you want to be in their way.
- Nor, conversely, do you want your ski lifts to be part of the main arterial *up* the mountain. The top of the beginners' lifts are ideally the end of the line, and not an 'all-change' point for skiers going further up the mountain.
- You will surprise yourself after a day or two by not wanting *all* the beginners' pistes to be short and stunted. After the first few days we found we learned more on longer slopes, and were looking for ones at *least* a kilometre in length. You learn more on one kilometre run than you do on two 500 metre ones. Not only will the two short runs take longer but you will find frequent lift journeys will break your concentration. You start at the top. You will no doubt get something wrong. Try again. Get it a little better. Then, just as you are nearly getting it right, you will run out of piste and have to go back again.
- Be an optimist. Take a look at the intermediate slopes to which you hope to graduate. Are they near the beginners' slopes, so that you could beat a hasty and not-too-wearisome retreat if you find yourself out of your depth? Are there a couple of short ones for your first tentative attempts? And some longer ones for when you have confidence?
- It is a relief if your resort lists a 'baby ski' or practice lift, or has one with virtually no vertical lift. This is an indication that there is a lift beginners can use on their very first day, thus avoiding the exhausting necessity of walking up or side-stepping slopes. Some resorts have them and do not bother to list them.
- Finally, like everyone else, you will want to make sure that you can get from your hotel to the slopes with ease — preferably by just stepping outside. Be particularly wary of resorts where you need to take a long ride by cable car to get to the beginners' slopes.

Resorts can change. An outstanding ski school mesmerised by success can easily become conservative and old-fashioned. A pleasant resort that spends too much money on hotels and too little on lifts and/or piste maintenance can soon become tatty. And, one year, the snow may just not come. But we feel that the following resorts (while quite suitable for experienced skiers) should be considered for beginners — always providing you check them in the way we have described.

Austria: Alpbach, Brand, Lech, Serfaus, Niederau/Oberau.
Italy: Sestriere.
France: Les Arcs, La Plagne, Isola 2000, Courchevel.
Switzerland: Wengen.
USA: Aspen Highlands, Snowmass, Vail, Sun Valley.

Intermediate slopes

People who go ski-ing the second or third year and who have advanced beyond beginners' classes need a range of interesting and more challenging slopes. It is a mistake to assume either that these will be found in good beginners' resorts or that getting to the intermediate stage opens up every resort. Take the SGGB report on Zürs again, for instance. The ski-ing in Zürs is not bad for beginners, because of the extensive practice slopes near the village; there have also been some good instructors and the snow record is good. But away from the practice slopes the ski-ing is steep to moderate, and is only for fairly accomplished skiers. The second or third year intermediate would be trapped between boredom and terror. Once again, a good map helps, but here are some resorts with enjoyable intermediate slopes:

American West: Sun Valley, Copper Mountain, Alpine Meadows, Vail, Steamboat.

American East: Cranmore, Great Gorge, Loon, Stratton.

Austria: Hinterglemm, Saalbach, Kirchberg, Kitzbühel.

France: Les Gets, Morzine, Courchevel.

Switzerland: Wengen, Verbier, Flims.

Piste maintenance

The most ideal pistes are nothing without good maintenance —especially at the beginning and end of the season. You can expect the 'Ratrac' machines to be out after a heavy snowfall beating down the pistes. Later in the season you can hope that the tops would be shaved off the bigger moguls and spread over their often bare sides or in the hollows between them. Up until the point that the maintenance men conclude they are fighting a losing battle against thaw you should also expect them to cover any rocks, roots, grass or mud showing through on the pistes and ski tow tracks.

Towards the end of the season the 'Ratracs' should be shredding up ice and crust on slopes that are too treacherous otherwise.

Markers should be in correct colour and sequence, and they should clearly indicate any pistes that are closed. The sign for this will usually be two crossed sticks (rather like those gardeners use for runner beans) with flags on them. *Gesperrt*

Preparing to ski one of the scenic trails of Heavenly Valley above South Lake Tahoe, California

is German for 'closed', *Fermé* (French), *Chiuso* (Italian), and *Cerrado* (Spanish). Hazards should be clearly marked and isolated trees and lift pylons near pistes should be padded.

Piste maintenance is expensive, and the better it is the more expensive a resort is likely to be. None of the more glamorous resorts would ever have achieved their fame—or got away with their prices—without it.

There is no sure guide to a resort's standard of piste maintenance other than its reputation. The only way to learn this is to talk to your ski club or those who have skied there.

The treeline

A good map should also show the trees. It should let you know what number and type of run there is below the treeline, and give some idea of whether the pistes go through spacious glades or narrow paths. A feature to avoid if you are at all nervous, for instance, is a woodland gulley, especially near a waterfall, where several pistes converge. It will be icy, crowded, narrow and dangerous (trees are harder than snow when you hit them).

The hotel

The nearer your hotel is to the slopes the better. The ideal hotel has a lift outside the door. In a village or small resort this lift is only likely to serve a beginners' slope, but it is the beginners who most need to be spared the fatigue of a long trek to the lifts each day.

If your brochure has no town map (as is more than likely) then look out for the phrase 'free bus service to the lifts'. It may sound like a bonus, but it is this that tells you that the hotel is nowhere near the main ski-ing area, and also lets you know you are liable to run up a big taxi bill. For if the 'free bus service' is to the valley station of a cable car that is merely the beginning of a long journey up to the main ski-ing area, then the likelihood is that the 'bus service' will only be twice a day —out in the morning, back in the evening.

In a resort like this (which is likely to be a pre-Alpine one) you will take lunch at a restaurant by the upper cable car station from which the lift system proper radiates.

If, on the other hand, the bus service takes you to the ski-ing area proper, then there will probably be a lunchtime service as well. (After all, the hotel is anxious to sell you as many meals as possible.) But you can still face long walks or expensive taxi journeys if you get hungry or tired before or after the bus driver thinks you should.

A detailed map will tell you exactly where you stand. The map of the slopes may show the resort itself as merely a homogeneous huddle of buildings ___ you should attempt either to obtain ___ from the tourist office of the co___ badger your travel agent to tell you ___ is. *Be particularly persistent if you are sta___* Such research will also unmask th___ rare—practice of describing a hotel or chalet ___ being 'in' a resort, when in fact it is some distance outside it. In which case you will also have to take taxis to go into town in the evening.

Lunch

Whatever the maps show, the question of where to have lunch is important and should feature in your checklist. Hotels prefer you to return for lunch, but there is nothing more frustrating than paying for full board and then finding you are wasting a lot of valuable time each day returning to the hotel at midday. Take a good look at your maps, and try to assess how much of a problem this may be. Having gone beyond intermediate none of us now takes full board: we prefer the freedom to eat in the mountain restaurants and to try different places at night. But for a family this might be awkward and expensive.

Where it is manifestly impracticable to return to your hotel for lunch, a travel agent may offer you full board with luncheon vouchers. These can be used in the restaurants up on the slopes. But be warned: these will not always purchase what all of us would regard as a square meal. If you have luncheon vouchers then budget a little extra to be safe. Ski-ing is hungry work.

Hotels where you depend on road transport to get to the lifts are best avoided. They are, however, often cheaper than more conveniently situated hotels. But reflect that this *can* be a false economy, as we have shown.

Roads

Busy main roads are another hidden snag—noisy, dangerous, and not at all what you want on a ski-ing holiday. They also bring hoards of trippers, particularly at week-ends. To establish just how busy any road is, a quick look at a road map for the area may be necessary. In general, roads that end at the resort are best. No roads at all are even better, but a rare luxury. Zermatt, Saas Fee, and Wengen are car-free resorts reached by railways.

Railways

You may well feel similarly ill-disposed about these, especially if you have to cross the tracks to get to the slopes.

many ski-ing holidays are ruined by the misery of long queues for lifts. These can be the result of haphazard development, lack of liaison between the people who are building the hotels and the people who are building the lifts—or simple avarice. We have already mentioned bottlenecks, but unfortunately there is no foolproof way to avoid crowds. A resort that has plenty of spare lift capacity one year can have it all taken up the next, once the word has got around.

Certain general probabilities can, however, be used as a guideline. This is the kind of resort which is least likely to have a crowded lift system:

- It is purpose built.
- There are no large centres of population nearby.
- There is no through road.
- There is no main line railway.
- It has not recently been the site of a major ski-ing event, nor have you seen it featured in the gossip columns.
- There are plenty of other resorts nearby.
- A new lift system has just been installed.
- The lift system has a number of access points (ie everybody does not have to start out on the same lift first thing in the morning).
- There is a high proportion of intermediate pistes (these always tend to be the most crowded), and they do not use the beginners' lifts.

Now some qualifications: There are plenty of traditional ski-ing resorts which are not full of people. But we repeat: what you must beware of here is any large valley resort from which the ski-ing terrain is reached only by a single cable car. Once you are through this initial bottleneck on the way up, however, the lifts on the slopes themselves may have no queues at all. Some such resorts stamp your ski with a number or give you a disc so you can have a drink while you wait. Others have even been driven to introducing an overnight reservation system (ie the night before you book a place on the 9.20 am cable car back up the mountain the next morning).

Resorts, aware that there is a limit to their customers' patience, are doing their best to eradicate such bottlenecks. We were, for instance, going to single out Mayrhofen as a resort with a particularly serious problem in this respect, but the recent installation of another lift has eased the situation.

The nearby big cities will only be a real problem at weekends. If it is a city you would like to see anyway then this is not necessarily a fault: you visit the city at weekends, while all its inhabitants are out ski-ing. It could be a welcome break. You tend to ski better for a short break in a long holiday.

If you are at all inclined towards mathematics, you can go one stage further than probabilities. We asked a number of top designers of ski resorts how *they* tried to design away queues. We were not altogether surprised to discover that this is still an infant science. No two designers are altogether of the same mind. On three points, however, they all concur. What they must take into account are:

1. The capacity of the lifts which start at the resort—ie the 'base lifts' which grant access to the system.
2. The capacity of all the lifts in the resort.
3. The bed capacity of the resort.

All agree these figures are vital. What they do not altogether agree on is how to interpret them. This was partly because they were designing different types of resort. Statistic Three, the bed capacity of a resort, is of importance because it is an indication of the number of people who will be using the lifts. But it is only an indication. A resort near a big town will obviously have many more skiers than its bed capacity. In the same way, a remote resort with many alternative activities to ski-ing can expect fewer skiers than its total bed capacity.

All the designers agreed that a simple ratio between bed capacity and hourly lift capacity was useless without Statistic One—the capacity of the base lifts. There is no point in having a resort with a phenomenal lift capacity in relation to its number of beds if there is only one base lift with a low capacity. That spells bottleneck: everyone will be queuing at the base lift waiting to get up to the empty lifts high above the resort.

There is, however, one relatively unconfusing rule. A resort should have base lifts with two-thirds of its bed capacity, and a total lift capacity of between its number of beds and double that amount. The nearer it is to double the better.

In other words, a resort with 6,000 beds should have base lifts capable of carrying 4,000 people an hour. Its total lift capacity should then be not less than 6,000 per hour. If it is 12,000 we can be confident that normally there will be no queues.

If you are that mathematical maniac we mentioned, then perhaps you would like to pit yourself against a refinement of this rule. Some designers are now arguing that it is the *power* of a lift that counts, and there is no point in adding together two lifts with an hourly capacity of 600 each and getting 1,200 if one lift has a much greater vertical rise than the other. The figure that should really be used, they say, is the capacity of the lift times its *vertical rise* (ie a lift taking 600 people an hour up 1,000 *metres* [*not* feet] is rated as 600,000). This is regarded as its power. Do this sum for every lift in the resort, add them all together, and then you have the resort's total lift power. If this is then divided by the number of beds in the resort, yet another figure is obtained. A designer doing his sums would want this final figure to work out at not less than 700. A figure of 1,400, which some of the French resorts, such as Flaine, are claiming, can be regarded as very good indeed.

Apart from the fact that we are not all math wizards, the statistics we need for these sums are almost impossible to obtain. The day may come when the resorts and the tourist agencies are prepared to do our sums for us. Until then the safest way of finding out about crowds is still to check with your ski club, or with people who have recently been ski-ing at the same resort. (They should, incidentally, be of the same ski-ing standard as yourself. The slopes may well have been empty where *they* skied. If they are experts and you are a beginner, then this is no guarantee that they will be empty down where you will be ski-ing. Nor, if they found a resort empty in February, will it necessarily be the same at Easter.)

Money

The package holiday has taken most, but not all, of the surprises out of ski-ing budgets. Travel, hotels, meals, ski rental, lift passes, insurance and lessons can all be paid for in advance. The prices quoted in the brochures are also a safe enough guide to the relative costs of different resorts. The first general rule you will notice is that the higher you go the more it costs.

The price of the package is not quite the end of the story, however. *All* ski resorts are expensive. This is partly due to the cost of transporting materials up the mountain, partly due to their limited season, and partly, too, it should be said, because they have what is very much a captive clientele. All these items can affect your budget:

- If your hotel room has no bathroom, check that baths and showers are free.
- Remember what we said about hotels a long way from the slopes. They might make for a cheap package but they are heavy on 'extras' like taxis.
- Ski-ing is hungry and thirsty work. The snacks provided on the slopes can be some of the most expensive you have ever had.
- Little extras can add up: the swimming pool, a welcome sauna or massage, buying extra equipment, a night out— they are expensive extras.

Just how much these things will cost depends on your individual extravagance. You can save money buying drink and groceries in the local store instead of in cafés. All in all, though, we do not feel it is an exaggeration to say:

- If you are on an all-in holiday, take in spending money 40 to 50 per cent of what your package cost you. If you are

on demi-pension, and have to pay for equipment rental and lift passes, then double that amount.

Lift prices

Lifts will be a major item in the cost of your ski-ing, whether paid for in advance or on the spot. It may sound obvious if we say the higher they go the more they will cost. What we mean is that it will cost more to go from 6,000 feet to 9,000 feet than it will to go from 4,000 to 7,000 feet.

There are usually two ways of paying for lifts:

1. An 'unlimited use pass', which has your photo on it and which enables you to use all the lifts in the resort. It is not transferable, and no money is refundable if you get fed up with ski-ing or you lose a day due to bad weather.

2. A point system. You purchase either a book or sheet of tickets (points). It may also be a card which the lift attendant will clip each time you use it. The shortest lift in the resort will 'cost' you one point. The longer and higher a lift the more points it will cost you. When you have used all your tickets, or the attendant has clipped every point on your card, you buy some more. If you have some left over at the end of your holiday you can always sell them. Anyone can use these, but there are no refunds.

No beginner is going to get full value from an unlimited use pass. Most books we have read have advised beginners not to buy them, yet we are not at all sure that we agree. If you are a vigorous beginner you might do well with a pass for the following reasons:

- If you are going on a package holiday your tour operator will almost certainly be able to offer you a lift pass at a much cheaper price than you could get it at the resort.
- The points system, even so, might be cheaper. But we do not think this is necessarily worth:
  (a) All the fumbling with tickets every time you use a lift. (The beginner has enough problems without this.)
  (b) The trouble of having to go and buy some more points every day or so.
  (c) The worry that you might have mis-budgeted, that you are going to run out of money, and spend the last days of your holiday as a penniless spectator.

If you do not go on a package holiday then an argument for considering the unlimited pass has less force.

There is one final point to watch on lift prices. If you are going to a resort where the ski slopes are reached by a long cable car journey up from the valley, then make sure that your lift pass includes this cable car. It usually will, but if it does not, there go a lot more extras.

THE SKI SCHOOL

For the beginner, and even the intermediate skier, the best resort is nothing without a good ski school. We believe that it is this which makes or breaks your first ski holidays.

Unfortunately it is our sad conclusion that ski schools are responsible for more first week drop-outs than the snow. One leading ski organizer told us of knowing of 50–60% abandoning courses after the first morning session. All too often the tone is set the first morning when the beginner finds himself in a bewildering mass of people with no clear idea where he should go. He has arrived probably on Saturday or Sunday, and has not been able to benefit from any briefing about equipment or classes. He may some time later find himself doing movements to no apparent purpose in a group of 15 or so people (12 is the desired maximum), all of different abilities and speaking different languages, with the instructor speaking only his own. He leads you out into the snow and explains as best he can what he is about to do and why. You then each have a go at it. There is a lot of standing about watching other people.

Some beginners are naturally more gifted than others. The more gifted are frustrated by the less gifted, and the less gifted feel guilty about holding the class back, and often give up in despair.

There are many exceptions to this depressing picture, notably in Austria and America. We remember with particular pleasure the first morning at Gargellen in Austria, when over a loud-speaker the assembled crowds were told to look to the top of the nursery slope. 'This', said the ski school head, 'is what we hope to teach the beginners this week. Join class 5 for this.' And down the slope, one after the other in perfect formation, came four instructors doing plough turns. 'And this is what we hope to teach those in class 4.' And, presto, four instructors doing a stem turn. Another announcement, and four instructors doing a stem christie. Another announcement, and four instructors doing a long parallel. Another announcement, and four instructors doing the wedel. The crowds split up. They were tested to see how good they were, and then sorted into ability and language groups. The classes were still too big, but everyone knew what he was doing and at what he was aiming.

Unfortunately travel agents' brochures have a tendency to portray resorts as all things to all men, and will usually include a glowing report on the ski school. If you phone up the agents and insist on talking with someone who actually organizes the ski-ing programme and has visited the resorts then you may get a franker answer.

Otherwise, as with the question of crowds, the only safe sources of information are your ski club or what your friends say. Ultimately everything depends upon the teacher. For this reason it is a good idea to avoid Christmas, when the teachers are overworked, and Easter, when they are not only overworked but have been teaching for several months, are more interested in their summer plans, and have a general tendency to be tetchy. Here are some detailed observations on this vital matter of the ski school.

Good and Bad Schools

How can you tell whether the school is good? So much depends on who is the director at a particular time. We have learned to be sceptical when the man in charge is a flashy young skier, and hopeful when it is a gnarled old man. We would certainly name the good and the bad schools we have been to if there was any guarantee that they would be the same when you went. It is just something you have to check when you get there. When you get to the resort you can form a good idea of the relative efficiency of the ski school, and how much you should rely on it, by a number of simple observations. The good ski school will:

- sort pupils into different classes by asking them to do a ski movement
- sort pupils into language groups
- never exceed 12 in a group!
- take especial care with children

A proper system of allocating skiers to groups, and, possibly, demonstrating what each group might achieve, can take all the first two hours. It is worth it, however. It saves time later in the holiday and it reduces the drop-out rate of confused or shattered beginners, put in wrong classes. The process of organization is aided if the ski school uses a loudspeaker, and a good school will carry, in its window or outside board, a picture of each instructor with his name, nationality, and background. The school in Pontresina, in Switzerland, did this effectively when we were there; it is obviously important to know who is your teacher.

If you find you have been allocated to a class of more than 12, you will get in very little ski-ing on the normal routine. If a class like this has first to watch the instructor for a series of exercises and then, one by one, do them, they may each get in only ten minutes' ski-ing in a two-hour session.

THE GOOD TEACHER
will work on one ski
movement at a time and
praise you when you get that
right. He knows that ski-ing is
60% confidence.

Will lead his group down the
slope doing the movement he
expects them to do. He will
always make it look simple.

Will be prepared to check
your equipment. He will
certainly carry a screwdriver
for adjusting ill-set bindings
(though in some countries
teachers are officially
discouraged because of the
legal risks.)

Will keep rotating the order
in which the group skis so
that the poorer skiers get a
chance to ski behind him.

Will vary the runs and the
routines and keep you in the
sunshine so that ski-ing is fun.

THE BAD TEACHER
will always be finding fault.

Will do parallel turns when
he is leading down a
beginners' group. He will
always be showing how
good he is.

Will let a frail girl beginner
ski on 200 cm skis, or, even
worse, will overtighten
bindings to keep beginners
on their skis.

Will let the weaker skiers be
the tail-end Charlies—
learning little and feeling
worse and worse.

Will spend a week on the
same things—and never
learn anybody's name.

Children in Classes

We urge parents to take great care with the allocation of their
children to groups. We are not very keen on children being
taken too young (under eight). The dice are loaded against
the parent enjoying the holiday or the child taking to ski-ing
for pleasure. But even older children can be put off ski-ing by
the idiocies of the poor ski schools. We have known children of
twelve and thirteen allocated to an advanced group without
any testing at all—and then left as stragglers on the mountainside to find their own way down! Some children get in the
wrong groups because parents leave it to them to tell the
organizers how good they are. It cannot be left to them to do
this properly. However confused the parents themselves are on
the first day, they should see to it that their children are in the
right group in a reasonable number, and with a teacher who
speaks their language. And they should know how to carry

skis and put them on.
All this is difficult for parents who have to join their own groups
at the same time—a factor most schools never consider. But it
must be done. Failure to do it can mean that the children hate
ski-ing and miss classes for the rest of the holiday.
Allocating children to their proper class levels is made more
difficult by the varied systems of dividing classes and the fact
that hulking teenagers would rather die than ski with nine-
year-olds. It is another area where a sensitive ski school can
help by using the first hour or so to permute ages/sexes/
abilities/languages. Parents must be sensible, too. Pride so
often tempts parents to push their children too hard—putting
them in a class for bronze badges or stars when they can barely
do a single turn. Kids—beware when Dad seeks ski-ing glory
through you.
If you go to a resort which teaches by graduating the length
of skis, there is a further complication. Short-ski resorts
generally teach younger children the traditional methods of
plough, stem and christie; but some children are allowed to
begin on short-skis and do the parallel from the beginning.
There is confusion about the dividing line. Sometimes it seems
to depend on the fact that all the rented short-skis are fitted
with bindings that suit adults and will not release easily
enough for the leverage produced by a child. Sometimes it
seems to depend on the number of teachers. Sometimes it
seems to depend on a judgement of a child's strength and
athletic abilities. The short-ski resorts will have to come up
with a clearer policy on this. All we would say is that short-ski
classes are more fun and, whatever the teaching method, you
should insist on your child renting skis which are no higher
than his chin.
There is need to worry, though, about children's equipment.
In very many resorts it is atrocious. We have found children
issued with skis without tracking grooves and with sharp bits
of metal protruding from a defective edge. Confronted with it
the ski shop confesses, 'Sorry, we didn't look . . .' Teachers who
are taking large parties of children to a resort should write
ahead, through the tour operator, and say that so many children are thinking of coming and they would like reassurance
on the equipment. At the same time they can ask the ski
school how it divides children. If you do not get an answer,
do not go.
What can you do if you find, from these observations, that
either the school or the teacher is bad—or, worse, you have a
weak teacher in a poorly organized school?
It would be really bad luck to have both a bad teacher and a
poor school. We have often found that, after the chaos of a

43

morning or two in a poor school, we are in a reasonable group with a good teacher. Do not pack your bags the first day simply because the school organization is weak. Use the tips we have given here to make the best of the bad job.

You can, conversely, end up with a weak teacher in a well organized school. If that happens, two or three of you can tell him that you would like the routine changed. Or you can attach yourself to another group. Or you can go to the school and ask them to do something. In a small resort this might be difficult. If you and a few others really are fed up with the teacher, we suggest you cut his classes. Scribble down a few exercises each day from this book and practice them among yourselves. It is better to do this, getting in a reasonable amount of ski-ing, than idling around in a large group with a poor teacher who does not speak the language. If you do this, return your ski school tickets and ask for your money back. Take the representative of the tour operator along with you. We believe the poor schools will survive while skiers meekly put up with third-rate service.

Classes

In traditional teaching ski school classes divide into about six main groupings. The numbers used to indicate the standard of each class vary from country to country. For instance, in Austria and France you begin in class 6 and hope to end up in class 1 (experts). In Switzerland the reverse system applies: you start in class 1 and hope to end up in class 6. In the United States classes are labelled A (beginners) through F (expert)[1].

Choosing the right class: If the school is so sloppy that it does not sort out itself, always assign yourself to a class conservatively. You are expected to stand by the post marked with a numeral according to grade (see below). It does your vanity good, perhaps, to stand in the better groups, but there is nothing worse than realizing you are out of your depth and having to go down a class. Equally, there is nothing nicer than being persuaded to go up after you have shown what you can do. It does no harm in the meantime to be a star of a class; perfect your side-slipping or traversing or stem christie or whatever it is that you consider rather below you. Here are the normal groupings:

Beginners: This is for those who have never been on skis before. You are taught to put the skis on, adjust the bindings and safety strap, hold the poles, walk, climb with side-step and

herringbone, fall, get up, kick turn, schuss. You may also begin the snowplough turn and traverse.

Improved Beginners: Beginners who have been on the dry slope may go here or improved beginners or 2nd-year beginners. You are assumed to know all the movements in the first class. You are taught the snowplough turn, traverse, and side-slipping.

Intermediates: Once you can snowplough well and control your speed, you move to the stem turn. This group will go on longer runs in different snows.

Improved Intermediates: For those who can do a stem turn on a slope of about 15 degrees and can stop and side-slip effectively. The concentration here is on the stem christie. There are less new techniques to learn now; your time will be taken up in practising and gaining experience. Most holiday skiers spend some time in this group, perhaps several seasons.

Advanced: You learn parallel turns. You are expected to be able to do 20° slopes with stem christie, but emphasis will be on eliminating the stem. Depending on the group, the snow and the instructor, this class may ski quite fast and tackle difficult (black) runs and off-piste ski-ing, but in a good school there will be a lot of exercises to improve movement.

Expert: Those who can do the long radius parallel turn learn to make shorter linked parallel turns—the wedel.

In a large resort there may be more than one class at each level —sometimes as many as half-a-dozen groups among beginners and intermediates. Language groupings are one division, but another is ability. If you are assigning yourself you can only ask or guess on the first day. Go where the skiers look like you do. (Be honest!)

Getting the best out of your ski class

If you do not enjoy it at first try not to despair. Classes tend to get better after two or three days. The more gifted skiers will have gone to another class, the less gifted will have dropped back a class, and there will be less disparity of ability. You yourself will begin to get some feeling of progress, and a certain rapport can arise from shared adversity and triumph between the members of the class. When a class is working well together with a good instructor it is an unforgettably happy experience.

When you are in a class, there are certain things to avoid. The first is not to be cast as the lame duck or even the willing sweeper at the end of a moving line following the instructor. It is all right to ski last in the line once in a while—somebody has to do it—but to do it regularly removes you too far from the instructor's movements. Rather than copying him you

---

[1]Schools and teachers who want to do better would benefit from studying *Ski Teaching* by John Shedden (John Jones Cardiff Ltd, 1974). Shedden is senior coach of the National Ski Federation of Great Britain.

may instead be following another learner, perhaps imitating his errors. You will certainly be delayed by somebody falling or ski-ing across your path. When you reach the line-up for the next session everybody will be impatient to move off, and you will have no time to recover. Undoubtedly the best position in the follow-my-leader line is next to the instructor. You will be astonished how much it helps to turn where he turns and to try to do what he is doing. Since there is competition for the spot—and it should be shared—the next choice should be to follow the best skier of the group. If that fails, try to ski without getting absorbed in the rhythm and the movements of the skier in front.

Finally, since you may well be taught in a foreign language, we have compiled a ski-ing vocabulary in German, French, and Italian (p. 246).

Tuition costs

It is easy enough to establish the cost of tuition. It is a rare travel agent indeed who will not sell you ski school tuition with your holiday package. There are no hidden extras here. On the contrary, if you pay for your lessons in advance, then it is as well to establish whether or not your tuition includes a lift pass. It sometimes does.

How many lessons?

The teaching package your travel agent sells you will usually be for group classes twice a day for the duration of your holiday. One lesson will be in the morning, the other in the afternoon. They usually last two hours each, and are so timed that, if you have the inclination and the energy, you should be able to get in an hour's ski-ing on your own before lunch after the morning one, and an hour again before the slopes close after your lesson in the afternoon.

You may well feel that one lesson a day will be the limit of your stamina and interest. This may be possible to arrange within the group lesson framework, but check that the people you are learning with are on the same system. Otherwise you will get left behind, and your morale may collapse.

Be warned, however! When we were learning we found it a great temptation to have just morning lessons and then play around in the afternoon. After all, lessons are rather boring at the best of times. And after three or four days we knew enough about ski-ing to be able to enjoy ourselves on our own. Ruefully we must report that for beginners this is a bad idea. In those afternoon play sessions we had a tendency to muddle through and pick up bad ski-ing habits. The result was that we were not only worse skiers than we would have been if we had had two lessons a day; we were also worse skiers than we

would have been if we had simply hung up our skis in the afternoon and read a book. By all means take an afternoon off if you are exhausted, depressed or simply fed up with lessons. Even play-ski a bit. After all, it *is* a holiday. *But do not make a regular habit of it.*

Private tuition

We often found that an hour's private tuition shared between two or three persons was only a little more expensive than a normal two-hour session in a ski shool. We also learned more. Other beginners we spoke to felt 'classes were more fun'. They liked the jolliness of all being in the same boat together, laughing at their own and each other's mistakes, striving to emulate the better pupils, and meeting new people. So a lot depends on how sociable and how impatient you are. Private tuition is clearly a more attractive proposition for the intermediate skier, who may only wish to have a few lessons and who wishes them to interfere with his ski-ing pleasure as little as possible. However, we believe that even the beginner who finds his rate of progress to be significantly faster or slower than the class as a whole should consider private tuition. If you have paid for your lessons in advance you might prefer to ask your instructor about the possibility of jumping up, or back, a class. Otherwise we suggest you recruit another person (or two) equally brilliant (or hopeless), and get a quotation for private tuition.

Orientation

When talking about ski classes we mentioned how confusing resorts can be to beginners.

We have always found ski resorts rather bewildering places when we have first arrived, even in our later years as veterans. There is a distinct air of well-oiled incoherence about them. Everyone is milling around with a rather unclear sense of purpose. Obviously the purpose is ski-ing: but why, for instance, is a particular piste so crowded in the morning, and utterly empty in the afternoon? Where has everybody *gone*? And how do you get to a particularly attractive-looking piste over the mountain? Your map shows it, alright; but there is no obvious way of getting there. Or, if there is, it is not sufficiently clear whether you have the ability to get there—or back.

All these problems can be clarified by talking to people. It is a good investment to spend your first hours in the resort talking to people who have already been there for some time. Ask them about the ski school, and exactly how it works, or about the snow conditions, and the runs. The best places to ski at different times of day. (That piste was suddenly empty in the afternoon because it is south facing and the snow is better then on the northern slopes.) Which are the cheaper restaurants, which the most expensive.

Things will seem a good deal less bewildering after that. You will be getting the 'feel' of the resort, and of the migratory urges of your fellow skiers.

Insurance

Insurance cover is essential. This is not because ski-ing is incredibly dangerous, but because your expenses in the event of an accident could be very high. As we have said, doctors' and hospital fees will be much higher than elsewhere, and you may also face charges (such as helicopter rescue) you would not normally expect. In our opinion *many tour operators offer inadequate insurance*. Perhaps they are frightened of scaring you off. In any event, we strongly advise consulting either an experienced insurance broker or your ski club for guidance on how much to insure yourself for. You should check that you have adequate cover for:

- Medical expenses; doctor's and hospital fees.
- Transport from the site of the accident to the hospital.
- Any additional travel and accommodation expenses for yourself and other members of the party. These might well include a scheduled air flight home for yourself as a stretcher case (in which case you may have to pay three or more times the normal air fair).
- Medicines: these are unlikely to be a major expense as a result of a ski accident, but if you can get cover for them as well, then why not? After all, you can be ill on a winter holiday just as you can any other time. (Sore throats, incidentally, are a common complaint—due to gulping dry high altitude air. Drink a lot—of anything—and suck a humbug.)
- Public liability insurance: in the event of your injuring another skier and being liable for damages.

Those are the essential risks against which to be insured. *Take your insurance policy with you.* You may feel happier if you are also covered for: loss of earnings, breakage or loss of skis, equipment, luggage, tickets and money. The small print is also worth attention. For instance, it may well exclude racing. 'Fair enough', you may feel, 'Me, race! I'll be glad if I can just *stand* on the things.' In which case think twice before you join in the ski school beginners' race.

Dry slopes

There is not the slightest doubt but that any ski-ing holiday benefits from a visit to a dry slope before you go. This is not just our opinion. It is the opinion of *every* person we have talked to with dry slope experience.

Dry slopes are made either of bristle or plastic. The result is rather like ski-ing across a lot of upturned scrubbing brushes. For the beginner the advantages are obvious. If he has dry slope tuition then he arrives at his resort with a head start. He has, in effect, given himself a few days' extra holiday. It is also a good opportunity to try out (albeit not in full combat conditions) whatever equipment he may have bought—notably to detect ill-fitting boots. It also gets the ski-ing muscles working.

There is one use the dry slope does *not* have for the beginner. It is a most unreliable guide to the question 'will I like ski-ing?' Frankly, dry slopes are not much fun. They are harder work and nastier to fall on than real snow. It would be a mistake to judge ski-ing by your dry slope experiences.

Even though we are now no longer beginners, we still try to visit a dry slope just before our ski-ing holidays, as it can still give us an extra day or two of holiday. The first few days are always spent 'recapping' before we can ski as well as at the end of our previous holiday. Some (but not all) of this recapping can be done on the dry slopes. We also have just as much need to tone up our muscles and check any new equipment as we did when we were beginners.

Dry slope tuition fees usually include the hire of equipment. No special clothing is needed. In fact, it is advisable *not* to wear your best ski-ing gear in case it is torn when you fall on the hard slope. Any old clothes which allow freedom of movement will do, plus *gloves*—whatever the time of year. It is a natural instinct to break a fall with your hands, and on a dry slope this can be painful without gloves. If you have skis, there is no point in taking them. There will be others better suited to the artificial surface available at the slope.

Up-to-date information about dry slopes, their whereabouts and their charges can be obtained from your ski club. In Britain you should contact: The Secretary, The National Ski Federation of Great Britain, 118 Eaton Sq, London SW1.

Guide books

In America, in addition to Berry's book and resort brochures (p. 23), budget skiers will find help in *Ski America Cheaply*, by James A. Mokres (Little Brown and Co.), and *The Complete Skier*, by Curtis W. Casewit (Popular Library). There is also *The New York Times Guide to Ski Areas in the USA*, by Michael Strauss (Quadrangle $4.95, 1972), and periodic reports by ski magazines. For Europe, we recommend *The Avis Guide* (FMP Publications), and Abby Rand's *Ski Guide to Europe* (Scribner Emblem Edition $4.95, 1970).

NORDIC SKI-ING

This book is about Alpine, 'slalom' or 'downhill' ski-ing, as it is variously called. In this you ski down manicured pistes wearing boots that are rigidly bound to your skis. But this is not the only kind of ski-ing, and it is certainly not how ski-ing began.

The origins of modern ski-ing as we know it today in Central Europe and North America are rooted in the folklore of another civilization far removed from the bustling slopes of the Alps. Rock carvings in arctic Norway four thousand years ago show that, even then, man had discovered how to ski. To some people this 'Nordic ski-ing'—which man introduced into America and Europe and modified to suit Alpine conditions in the latter half of the 19th century—is still the real sport. Using the word 'sport', though, obscures its origins and some of its charm. Nordic ski-ing is natural. It was a way of getting about before it was a way of having fun. Today it is an enchanting way of enjoying the countryside in winter. If you enjoy mountain rambles then you will enjoy Nordic ski-ing; and will be able to do it too, since its movements are not very different from walking. In fact, we have found that knowledge of downhill ski-ing is a positive handicap when it comes to learning Nordic ski-ing. The walker enjoys a distinct advantage, since he has no preconceived ideas about what he should be doing with his skis.

Nordic *touring* however, as opposed to racing, is what most visitors mean when they talk of ski-ing Nordic style. Touring is certainly a more accurate term. Uphill, downhill, on the flat; across frozen lakes; along ski trails sneaking through forests of pine and birch—where there is snow there is nowhere a pair of Nordic skis cannot go. Nordic is still the most common form of ski-ing in Scandinavia, but most Alpine resorts feature it also. But what they offer is not, strictly speaking, cross-country or touring ski-ing. What the Germans call *langlauf* and the French *ski de fond* uses the same equipment and techniques as Nordic ski-ing, but the ski-ing is done along marked trails. The Alps are just too treacherous for amateurs to head off over the horizon. Here, then, is a summary of ski-ing the Nordic way. For further reading we recommend *Ski Touring for the Fun of it* by Steve Rieschl (Little Brown). The dedicated Alpine skier may find a year off in Scandinavia or ski touring in the Rockies a refreshing change, and more elderly beginners and those without a taste for speed may prefer Nordic from the start.

Watched (by a would-be-hot-dogger?), Colorado cross-country skiers blaze fresh trails through the aspens

Equipment for Nordic ski-ing is designed for four different purposes: mountain use, 'general' and 'light' touring, and racing. To anyone accustomed to heavy Alpine gear, the difference in Nordic equipment is amazing. Not only is the entire weight of the lightest pair of Nordic boots and skis (for racing) a mere fifth that of the Alpine equivalent, but their appearance is vastly changed, too.

Nordic boots: Touring *(top)*, Light touring *(centre)* and Langrenn

Boots

Those most commonly in use look like a cross between a hiking boot and a football boot. For mountains and general touring they are semi-padded, with double-tonguing or lacing to keep them watertight. Light-touring specialists prefer an even lighter 'shoe', cut just above the ankle. Langrenn boots, cut below the ankle like track shoes, are even more pliant, light and flexible. A pair of man's size 9 Langrenn boots, for example, can weigh a mere 1 lb 10 oz compared with the 7 lb 4 oz of similarly-sized Alpine boots.

Skis

A similar difference in weight applies here, too. A pair of Nordic racing skis (6 ft 9 ins) weigh as little as 2 lb 11 oz compared with the wooden Alpine equivalent of 9 lb 13 oz. Nordic skis in this narrowest and lightest form are as much as $1\frac{3}{4}$ in slimmer than Alpine.

The basic rule in Nordic ski-ing is that the thinner the skis the faster they are. They are normally made of laminated wood, and, with the possible exception of some mountain skis, do not have hard steel edges—only hard wood. The beginner, amateur or holiday-maker would be best advised to pick a pair fit for general touring as perhaps the best compromise.

Bindings

These again bear little resemblance to those we will describe in Chapter 3. For mountain ski-ing and general touring the foot is attached to the ski by a toe-clip which clamps over a front lip on the boot. For extra security a cable runs from the toe-clip around the heel. Light-touring and racing skiers use only a toe-clip binding, however, for only the ball of the foot need be on the skis at certain times.

This is, in fact, the crucial difference between the two types of ski-ing. Whereas Alpine ski-ing demands rigid bindings, feet clamped firmly to skis, in the Nordic style the heels rise completely off the skis and the bindings give maximum freedom of movement to the feet. The accent is on flexibility.

Nordic bindings are fixed at the toe only, allowing maximum freedom of movement

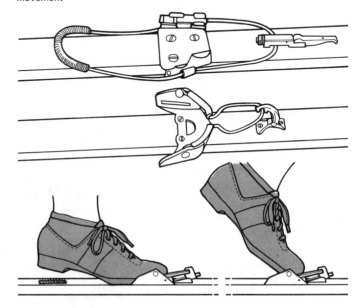

Poles

The difference this time is only slight and for the novice relatively unimportant. Nordic ski poles have slightly angled tips. The reason for this will be clear when we explain technique: the poles are seldom plunged straight down into the snow, as in Alpine ski-ing, but are swung forward alternatively, like pendulums. The angled tips help to guide the poles into the snow and give good setting.

Glide-grip, every trip

The lightweight equipment we have described is needed to enable skiers to travel uphill as well as down. But the secret of Nordic ski-ing lies in another form of preparation: waxing. In Alpine conditions, waxing and the mystique which surrounds it need be of little concern to the beginner, for he can rely on his momentum to propel him downhill. In Nordic ski-ing, however, waxing is essential: it provides not only the glide needed for forward movement but also the grip which is vital on inclines.

Snow ('atmospheric vapour frozen into ice crystals'. OED) is something most Europeans are familiar with—or, rather, think they are. But as we show, there is more than one kind of snow. New snow, or falling snow; settled snow; changed snow (ie ice, slush, pack). In each case it can be very dry, powdery, wet, slushy or transitional, from dry to wet.

Ski wax is made to suit all these varying snows. Each manufacturer produces a wide range of hard, soft and fluid waxes (the difference is denoted by colour) and corresponding waxing charts to accompany them. For the Nordic skier who must match wax with snow correctly such guidance is vital. What happens when a Nordic ski is waxed? Briefly, the irregu-larities of the waxed surface fit like a cog-wheel into the irregularities in the snow created by the jumbled snow crystals, so that this microscopic interlocking acts as a brake on a motionless weighted ski. The ski grips the surface, preventing the climbing skier from sliding backwards. On the other hand, when a skier wants to go downhill or cross flat ground, the moving ski, even when fully weighted, will be able to glide. Properly waxed, skis will glide as long as they are in motion. Once the gliding stops they will stick, and must be un-weighted before the skier can move forward again. If the waxing is too hard, snow will not penetrate, and the skis will not grip; yet, if the wax is too soft, snow will bite into the skis and form into a pack. This will cause the skis to stick even when you want them to slide forwards.

Technique: balance, rhythm and pace

From this it is easy to see how Nordic technique has evolved. The basic movement is exactly like walking, and has a rhythmic stride: a kick-off with one foot and a gliding step (or skate) with the other. The resulting kick-glide, kick-glide alternation, rather like the smooth movements of a skater, can be increased in tempo for racing. Arms and legs work alternately, as in walking. As you kick off with your right foot you give an extra push with your left pole. The good Nordic skier quickly develops a relaxed, easy glide, with his weight balanced entirely on first the one ski, then the other.

The most easily learned method of turning on the flat is to use the skating technique explained in Chapter 12.

For downhill runs the most commonly used turn is the Stem Christie, explained in Chapter 16.

The basic Nordic stride — a kick-glide movement with arms and legs working alternately. Demonstrated by Steve Rieschl.

2 WHAT TO WEAR

It is tempting for the new skier to dismiss all those ski pants and goggles and gloves and jackets as so much high fashion. It is true the models get up to some ski poses, in the fashion photographs, that would do them a severe mischief if there were any snow around. But a pair of old jeans and woollen mitts will not do. There is, to be sure, a touch of nice bravado in ski-ing in jeans. The implication is, 'I never fall'. But if you do fall in jeans they will soon be soaking and perhaps frozen. From our own experience we urge you not to underestimate the apparently trivial pieces of clothing or equipment. Here is the completely kitted skier. We deal with clothing, including boots, in this chapter and skis, bindings and poles in the next.

Rent or Buy?

Ski-ing cost a lot of money. You can cut costs by hiring skis and poles of course—but also boots, anoraks and ski pants. The cost of renting the clothes comes out at between 10 and 50 per cent of the purchase price for a fortnight, depending on whether used or new clothes are rented. In some stores you can deduct the rental fee from the purchase price if you decide to keep them. Most people invest in pants and jacket, choosing something if they are wise which can be worn at home without causing a breach of the peace. But it is a good idea to rent children's clothing.

Once we had decided we enjoyed ski-ing, boots went straight on to our purchase list. We had several reasons for this: first, we had a reasonable expectation of being able to wear the same pair of boots for much of our ski-ing lives, whatever our future abilities. The second is the agony that some of us experienced in hired boots. It is easier to wear a friend's shirt than to wear his boots. Before the new kinds of boots came out there was still something to be said for hiring boots. Hired boots had been broken in so that they might be more comfortable than a new, unbroken pair. But the new kinds of boot are made to mould to your feet (see below), and generally you can get a new boot which is comfortable. The third reason for putting boots on the priority purchase list is that what you buy is likely to be more efficient as a ski 'lever'—and that is what it is—than an old hired boot.

Skis, poles and bindings should be rented the first year (bindings hold the special ski boot, and hence us, on skis). Certainly nobody should buy skis who may be going to learn by the short ski length method (described in Chapter 18).

You are likely to need three different lengths of skis in your first fortnight. In the second year or later, of course, it is well worth considering buying skis and poles—again, except for children.

Where to Rent?

Rent skis and poles at the resort. If you rent at home, you have most of the drawbacks of ownership (notably carrying them out) and none of the benefits. We found it comforting to ski in the knowledge that, if the skis turned out to be ill-fitting, unsuitable or defective in any way, then we could take them straight back: never hesitate to do this.

For boots, there is a lot to be said for home rental. They are not too bad to carry, especially if a carrying frame goes with the hire. (If you rent skis at home and create excess baggage, airlines charge only for two kilos on the skis.) Hiring boots at home avoids the horror of arriving at the resort and finding there is none your size left. This has never happened to us, but we have seen it happen to others. We have also seen some fair panics as bootless beginners scamper from shop to shop in the resort for a suitable boot, wasting valuable holiday time. If you rent them at home you avoid this risk and you can wear your boots around the house for a few days before you go. This can warn you of any obvious discomfort. The real test of a good fit, of course, is not at home in the kitchen but when you are on the slopes ski-ing, and then it is too late to take back boots hired at home. You will then have to hire locally and may well be obliged to settle for a boot which is something less than the embodiment of all the virtues we shall be describing. If so, put comfort first, however old and battered the boots you end up with. This means extra cost, and you will have to balance the risk of this due to renting at home against the risk of a boot famine at the resort. Check with the agency and at peak times err on the side of security rather than economy: rent at home.

Where to Buy?

Buy most things at home. Buy goggles at the resort, because you can step out of the shop and test them on the spot against sun and snow. Buying the other clothes at home, however, gives you more time to compare and choose. It will also probably save you money, since stores at ski resorts tend to profiteer.

The vital thing is to *make your purchases at a specialist shop or store*, and not in a small town or suburban sports shop that happens to have a few pieces of ski-ing equipment. We hope to tell you enough about the things you need to give you some protection against the ignorant or misleading salesman. But if a shop does not have the best equipment for your needs there will always be the risk of getting fobbed off with second-best. It is worth a trip to your nearest big city.

BOOTS

Ski boots are specially designed to fit a ski binding which holds boot to ski. Any old army boot will not fit the binding. Ski boots are what all too many of us remember our ski-ing by. Ask a friend how he enjoyed his ski-ing holiday and he may simply snarl: 'My boots hurt!'

There is an element of contradiction in what we ask of boots.

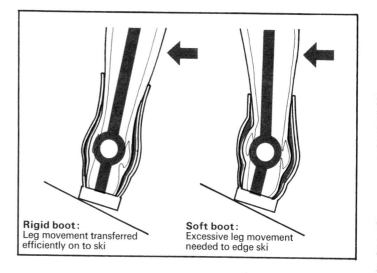

Rigid boot:
Leg movement transferred efficiently on to ski

Soft boot:
Excessive leg movement needed to edge ski

The more rigid they are, the more positive the transmission between leg and ski. A rigid boot makes it easier to turn the ski on its edge, an essential movement you will learn for controlling your speed. Sideways (lateral) movement of your ankles will reduce the amount you can edge. It has no place in ski-ing. The whole calf and foot should roll sideways from the knee as one. This sets the ski on its edges. If your boots are too soft, and you retain lateral movement in your ankles, you will roll your legs to little effect.

Making rigid boots is no problem; making rigid boots that give a perfect fit is no problem; making rigid boots with a perfect fit that are comfortable is. And comfort must be your first priority. From our own experience, and having seen hundreds of others take up ski-ing, we would say tolerating inefficiency in the boot is better than coping with discomfort. You will ski less well in a boot which is too soft to enable you to edge properly. You will not ski at all in a boot that hurts.

A typical boot for
intermediate skiers

Rear entry boots are
kinder to the shins

The qualities of a boot

Ideally, of course, you will want boots which are both comfort-able *and* efficient. We certainly do. This is the secret ingredient which sets good boots apart from mediocre ones, distinguishes those made for experts from those which are perfectly adequate for beginners, and which, more often than not, accounts for one pair of boots being much more expensive than another seemingly quite similar pair. The less the compromises which have been made between comfort and efficiency the better the boots. When we refer to comfort we mean absence of pain. A good boot, since it gives a firm grip, will always be a pleasure to take off.

We have already mentioned rigidity or 'flex', and seen that sideways flex is undesirable. Some degree of forward flex is, however, essential. All ski-ing movements, as you yourself will discover and it sometimes seems that many teachers have for-gotten, including upper body ones, have but one purpose and that is to regulate the contact your skis make with the snow. Boots and bindings transmit these movements, but also func-tion as shock absorbers for our legs.

Ill-fitting or inferior boots will hurt in all the places and for all the reasons that a bad pair of shoes will: plus and especially at the ankles. We wear boots rather than shoes for ski-ing because we need their support at the ankle to transmit those knee move-ments so essential to achieve that sideways roll from one edge to the other and keep the weight forward. That's impossible with straight legs: hence the classic cry which we repeat —'Bend the knees!' You will find the benevolent effect of all these manoeuvres on the ski's behaviour explained in Chapter 9; but all too often the most immediately noticeable result is painful shins. The shin bone is close to the surface of the skin. There is no fleshy cushioning. And it is simply not used to this kind of treatment.

The amount of resistance the boot offers to forward pressure is its 'forward flex'. All boots have some and it is provided by a variety of mechanisms all of which create some form of hingeing movement at the ankle. Plenty of forward flex, or a 'soft' boot minimises the likelihood of sore shins. It is also a desirable quality for beginners. When learning we tend to be unsteady on our feet and it's as well that every wobble is not faithfully transmitted to our skis. A soft boot can easily be made comfort-able and hence is cheap.

Heavier skiers, however will need the extra support of stiffer boots, and experts, whatever their weight, will want them for the more positive transmission of knee movements. But they still need *some* forward flex, if only to act as a shock absorber when travelling at speed. Backward flex should be minimal: just enough to avoid discomfort on those occasions when you want weight back: some of the more advanced turns and deep soft snow require this. To make these stiff boots comfortable, however, is difficult and expensive.

The shell

The most obvious outward sign of the quest for comfort at the shin is the 'rear entry' boot. All ski boots have two main com-

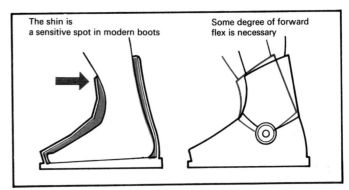

The shin is
a sensitive spot in modern boots

Some degree of forward
flex is necessary

ponents. A hard moulded waterproof outer shell made of polyurethane, or one of its derivatives; and a soft removable inner boot. Most of the engineering which ensures a comfortable fit takes place in the inner except for those boots which open at the rear. The rationale for the rear entry boot is that without a tongue or any other irregularity to rub against the shin, the chances of discomfort will be less. But you still need to test rear entry boots. They can hurt elsewhere as we've discovered.

The other obvious quality of a boot's shell is the number and type of buckles it has. All rear entry boots have fewer buckles. But otherwise the more buckles there are the more expensive the boot and the more advanced the skier it is designed for. The more finely the buckles can be adjusted the better the chances of holding the foot firmly yet comfortably in the boot. In our experience buckles with only a few settings often mean the misery of choosing between a setting which is tight but painful or one which is comfortable but sloppy. Some boots, notably the Salomon range, have mechanisms which grip the foot *inside* the boot.

Some boots have further adjustments which can be made to their shell. The angle of forward lean at the ankle can often be changed. The average boot has a forward lean of approximately 18 degrees from the vertical. In some circumstances, such as ski-ing bumpy terrain at speed, a skier might prefer less, a racer would certainly want more: perhaps as much as 23 degrees. On more expensive boots both the angle of forward lean and the amount of forward flex are usually adjustable. Some also have adjustable canting or wedging (See pp. 61-63 for more on this.) And most men's boots are slightly canted to compensate for the male tendency to bow leggedness. This is one good reason why men's and women's boots are not interchangeable. Another is that they are designed to take into account differences between the shape of the average male foot and the average female foot. Boots are made for ski-ing—but sometimes we have to walk in them, awkwardly, like men from Mars. Boots which stay on even when the buckles are released are a comfort. Boots with replaceable soles at the toe and heel are another bonus, since this is where boots tend to wear out first. It also means manufacturers can use a soft high-grip material on the heels, minimising the chance of a nasty fall when walking on ice and snow.

The inner boot

The inner boots are filled with a variety of materials, depending on their model and make. It is the familiar problem: it is easy

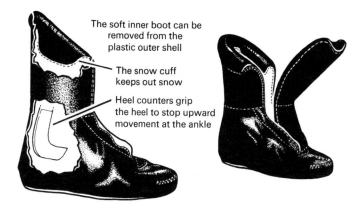

The soft inner boot can be removed from the plastic outer shell

The snow cuff keeps out snow

Heel counters grip the heel to stop upward movement at the ankle

to make nice comfortable inners but they will be like ski-ing in a pillow. To be good they need to be made of firmer material and so more care must be taken to ensure that they fit properly or they will hurt. Remember that no material is so wonderful that it can compensate for a bad fit. However, most inners, except stitched ones, can be ground to relieve pressure points. It is a wise precaution to wear your boots around the house for a few hours over a week or so after purchase, so that these can be revealed. A good shop will give assurances in advance on their readiness to exchange or remedy the fit of un-skied-on boots. 'Boot doctoring' is now quite an advanced art and in good resorts you can have pressure points eased by machine. It's vital before you take the boot in to note exactly where it hurts—mark it with sticky tape if you can.

Because boot shells can easily be damaged by heat we always remove the inners when they need drying. They can be placed somewhere warm (*never* in direct heat) overnight, and the interior of the shells dried with a cloth; and, however exhausted, we try to fasten all the clips on the empty boots. It helps to keep their shape.

The boots to get

- Comfort is your top priority.
- Beginners should rent, not buy, and choose from the cheaper models.
- But once you have been ski-ing, and know you enjoy it, optimism is justifiable. Your ski-ing is going to improve during the lifetime of your boots. Go for the best and most comfortable you can afford. But be realistic too: few of us ever progress to the point where we need a top of the range model.
- Children should always be given soft boots. You will never convince them that there is any point in being uncomfortable. They will just refuse to ski.

Getting a good fit

We urge you not to underestimate the importance of this. Avoid a rush selection in the lunch-hour or in five minutes at the resort. Here are the stages of boot selection:

1. Wear your ski socks and trousers.

2. Boot selection is limited when renting. But purchase calls for dialogue. Make your abilities and budget clear. Question staff about the qualities of boots they suggest. You need plenty of time and you may tax the patience of the shop. Don't be bullied! It's you who will be at risk of pain on the slopes.

3. Ask first for your normal shoe size, and try that. Here is a conversion table for those renting in Europe.

France Italy Spain Norway Austria		34	35	36	37	38	39	40	41	42	43	44	45	46
United Kingdom Switzerland		2/2½	3/3½	4	4½	5/5½	6	6½/7	7½	8	9	9½/10	10½	11½
United States New Zealand Australia	Mens	–	–	–	–	6/6½	6½	7/7½	8	8½	9½	10½	11/11½	12/12½
	Womens	4½	5/5½	6	6½	7/7½	8	9	9½/10	10½	11½	12	–	–

4. With the boot still open, press your ankle forward. There should be room at this stage to insert a finger between the back of the ankle and the boot.

5. Do up the buckles. A bit tighter than the loosest setting is best. They will need to be done up tighter with wear since they effectively expand as the inner sole compresses. But if renting they *must* close easily when you try them in the shop.

6. How tight is the fit? A boot that is excessively tight will be uncomfortable—and cold, because there will be less insulating air between your skin and the boot surface. But too loose a fit is inefficient and invites abrasion. The boot should grip tightly, but comfortably, at the instep, ankle, heel, and ball of the foot. Try these tests:

(a) Can you lift your heels up and down inside the boots? Yes? Then the boot is too loose.

(b) Can you wiggle your toes? No? Then the boot is too tight at the toes.

(c) Can you stand on your toes without the toes pressing hard against the end of the boot? You should be able to do that without discomfort.

(d) If you are a parallel skier, look for a tight grip at the ankles but which allows a slight flexing of the legs. If you are a beginner/intermediate you can be less concerned about ankle grip—and worry more about the absence of pressure points. Bend your ankle forward and back. How does it feel? A small pressure in the shop can become agony on the slope, as you force the ankle time and again against the boot.

7. If you cannot find the ideal fit, choose one that is too large rather than too tight. Socks or crepe bandaging can fill out the extra space. It will not be as efficient for ski leverage, but comfort comes first.

After selection of the boot, adopt another precaution however comfortable they are before ski-ing. Pack:

(a) Extra socks. Quality silk socks are often a boon, warm and smooth to wear next to the skin with a woollen sock over.

(b) Latex foam. You can buy latex foam ankle pads. Buy these pads and a piece of thin foam which you can cut for tender spots. (One of us with skinny ankles and big toes has had a special pair of thick-ankled toeless socks made for him.)

(c) sticking plaster.

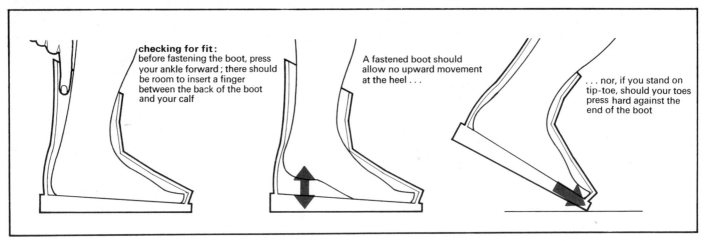

checking for fit:
before fastening the boot, press your ankle forward; there should be room to insert a finger between the back of the boot and your calf

A fastened boot should allow no upward movement at the heel . . .

. . . nor, if you stand on tip-toe, should your toes press hard against the end of the boot

How to look after your boots
- Never dry ski boots with fierce heat. Close to a radiator is all right. Near a fire is *not*.
- Treat leather boots like ordinary shoes and polish with a shoe cream. Plastic boots simply need to be wiped clean with a damp cloth.

Boots made for walking
Ski boots are not made for walking. They are hard work when you are not wearing skis. You feel like a stranded spaceman. So the only piece of advice on *après-ski* wear we intend to give you is to take a pair of boots suitable for walking in snow and on ice. They should be water resistant, warm, and they must have supple *non-slip* soles. Ski shops sell them. Wellington boots will not do; apart from fashion reasons, they have poor insulating qualities and tend to slip. Nor will cowboy boots do. They also slip on snow and ice. We have had some painful falls, and no skier likes to have to potter forward in the manner of an elderly invalid. Fashion boots will not last a day.

CLOTHING
Put function before fashion. This does not mean padding yourself with lots of clothes regardless of your appearance. Warmth is not the only consideration when you go ski-ing —too much padding will make you ungainly.

Besides, air temperature is not a reliable guide to how cold you will feel when ski-ing. What matters are wind, dampness, and how much energy you are burning. You also need to consider what happens when you fall.

Wind: A sudden increase in wind can make the apparent temperature plunge dramatically. A warm day can be turned into a bitterly cold one, even though the thermometer remains steady. When you ski you encounter wind. This does much to dispel the extra heat you generate when ski-ing. It can dispel it entirely if you are wearing no windproof clothing. (Riding tows up the mountain, when you are generating no heat, but encountering air movement, can be coldest of all.)

Energy: When you ski you have bouts of intense energy burns followed by periods of inactivity. You generate heat when ski-ing, or climbing a short slope. You lose it rapidly when riding a lift, or waiting for one. So, the wind-proof jacket that can exclude air should also be easy to open to let ventilation in when you have generated a lot of heat.

Dampness: You are also in contact with snow. And if it is not damp when you fall in it, or it falls on you, your body heat will soon make it so. Also, water is an excellent heat conductor. Damp clothes feel colder than dry ones. *Much* colder. This means you will want something water-resistant. The reason we say resistant and not waterproof will be appreciated by anybody who has worn a plastic mac or waterproof shoes. For you can get just as wet keeping your body moisture in as you can from failing to keep the elements out. Your ski clothes, like your shoes, need to breath.

Safety: When you fall, you want to stay where you are, not continue on downwards. A few seasons ago shiny 'wet look' ski suits were all the rage, but unfortunately the material proved to be so slippery that when you fell you continued sliding down the hill. As a result of some nasty accidents several ski resorts banned the 'wet look'. Nowadays ski wear manufacturers are aware of the need to design clothes that are practical as well as pretty, but if you are going in an old anorak examine it for potential slipperiness. Some nylon jackets slip very badly.

Jackets
The requirements are: (**a**) water-resistant (**b**) wind-proof (**c**) snow-proof (**d**) non-slip (**e**) good insulation. A ski anorak —or, as the Americans call it, a 'parka'—with thermal filling and made in 'anti-gliss' material meets these needs. 'Anti-gliss' stops you sliding too far when you fall. If you are to ski in really cold places, such as mid-winter in Norway or in the Eastern United States, look for a jacket with maximum thermal quilting but with a minimum of stitchwork. Every hole a needle has been through the wind can go through also. If you will be ski-ing in extreme cold, it is worth considering a down-filled jacket. This will be more expensive than one with a synthetic filling, and will not dry out as quickly nor wear as well. But, weight for weight, down is the most effective clothing insulator there is. It has a high 'loft', or thickness, trapping the maximum amount of air for its weight. The more 'loft' the better. Down also allows excess body moisture to escape more freely than do the synthetic fillings. An extra point to bear in mind when choosing a down-filled jacket is its resilience. If you crumple it up it should spring right back to its original thickness.

The jacket should also be long enough to cover your bottom. 'Snow-proof' means the jacket should have zipped pockets, close fitting cuffs, bottom, and neck to keep out the snow in a tumble. Bonuses are:
- A two-way zip which opens from both bottom and top.
- Capacious pockets.
- A hood which is stored *inside* the neck of the jacket: if it hangs permanently outside the jacket it can fill with

snow. When the hood is worn, the collar, which may be wet, should be outside it—and choose a jacket with a good high collar (see above right).

- A plastic window for the ski pass. This saves a lot of fumbling at lifts.
- Square pockets. There is a fashion for diagonal pockets. They are usually useless. If you fail to zip up, you are sure to lose something from a diagonal pocket. They are also often too shallow. Insist on big square pockets with a horizontal zip and/or buttoning. It is time to wage war on the fashion freaks.

Trousers

Old-timers, not so long ago, bewailed the fashion for skin-tight stretch pants. This, they said, was a slavish imitation of the racers of the '60s who wore them to cut down wind resistance. They did not, they argued, give the holiday skier the warmth he needed.

We have found tight pants like this all right—provided they are water-resistant and have zipped pockets. But we would always pack a pair of long johns or tights for extra warmth since we tend to ski woodenly when our knees are cold.

Trousers like this are worn *over* the socks. They also have an elastic retaining strap which goes under the arch of the foot to stop them riding up. If the strap is narrow, or badly sewn with bumpy seams, it will become uncomfortable during the day's ski-ing. It bites into the foot. A smooth, broad strap (one and a half inches minimum) is essential.

Nowadays the fashion is for trousers *over* the boot. This is a practical improvement. It lessens the chances of getting snow in your boots. It also looks better. Some have thermal linings

for extra warmth. *But*, bear in mind that if you have chosen or bought your boots while wearing trousers *inside* the boot, these boots will now be looser around the ankle.

Now the racers are wearing a descendant of the old skin-tight pants worn inside the boot. They are skin-tight but outside the boot. They zip around the ankle and there are holes for the boot clips. They look good but have one snag: they tend to ride practically up to the knee once you undo them or remove your boots.

Salopettes

This is a French word for overalls (not to be confused with the French word "salope" meaning an improper woman or tart). We like them, worn with a good ski jacket. They do not constrict the middle. They are light. They can look good, especially on women. The usual material is quilting or corduroy (which has excellent non-skid qualities). But watch these points:

- Shoulder strap buckles. Many of them are incapable of taking the strain or easily being adjusted. Strong buttoning is good.
- Kidney cover. Some salopettes are too low and offer a loose snow pocket at the back. The back part of a good salopette should be inches higher than the waist. Repeat: inches higher.
- They must have snow traps inside which grip tight around the boot. Otherwise those beautiful bell bottoms will become snow scoops every time you fall. The same is true of all flared trousers.

There is one practical drawback to any quilted trousers. They tear more easily. The beginner, who is liable to fall more often, might be better off with another material.

Trying them on

Always test trousers both by sitting on your heels in them and by going into a splits position. Are they comfortable in these maximum stretch positions?

Always try the clothing on all together. The jacket should be tried with the trousers (is there a gap at the waist when you are bent over double?), the gloves with the jacket (is there a gap at the wrist?). And the trousers must be tried with the boots, especially if they go inside them.

Warm-up pants

When function is more important than elegance these are worn over ordinary ski pants. They are waterproof and are used in exceptionally slushy or cold conditions. Not a standard item in the average skier's luggage, but an investment worth considering if you find yourself ski-ing in the wet, or believe you are likely to.

Zips

Zips are an essential feature of trousers and jackets. *And they must be tough.* They are likely to be the first thing to go, so, unless they can be replaced, the clothing is at once useless. Not so long ago metal was the automatic choice for zips, but the design of nylon and plastic zips has now improved. They are better: they do not conduct heat (and so do not let in the cold) and they do not corrode. They are also more expensive. *Big* zips that you can handle with gloved fingers are best.

Gloves

These complete our essential outer defences. Hands are nearly always the first part of your body to get cold. They are also the part of your body which has the most contact with the snow.

Mittens have a smaller surface area than gloves, and are therefore warmer and more resistant to water. Ask anybody who rides a motorbike. Wet mittens are also warmer than wet gloves. The advantage of gloves is that they make it much easier to grip the poles, and they give a greater freedom of movement.

The beginner who is not sure which to wear will do best to take mittens. No niceties of pole handling are called for in the early days, whilst it is the beginners who are always finding their hands in the snow.

Intermediate skiers and above can wear gloves, but in extreme cold they should have a pair of mittens with them.

Gloves and mittens come in three basic materials. Water-resistant nylon or leather; a variety of plastics such as vinyl; or a combination of these materials.

You get what you pay for. Leather is best. Plastic worst. But once again the beginner should not necessarily get the best. Like all ski-ing clothing, gloves are water-resistant, not waterproof. Gloves that are constantly brought into contact with the snow will get wet, though, and, as drying out wears them, a beginner will quite quickly destroy a pair of expensive leather gloves. A cheaper pair of plastic or synthetic mittens is all right; we found that the thinner plastics were better than the thicker ones.

The intermediate skier will prefer leather. Ordinary leather gloves will *not* do. They must be specially treated ones designed for ski-ing. We found silk gloves under an outer leather pair excellent for protection and nimbleness.

Do not get tight gloves or mittens. Without the air trapped between your hand and the gloves they will be cold, and they will restrict your fingers. All gloves and mittens should have a firm and preferably long grip around the wrist to keep out snow.

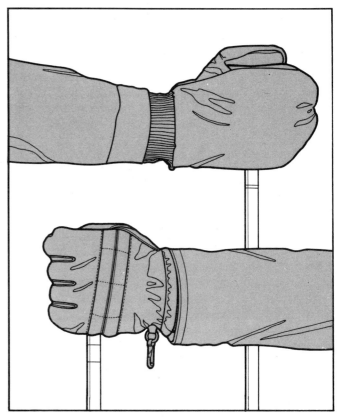

Mittens *(top)* are best in the cold; but gloves allow greater freedom of movement

Head gear

Why is it that some of us wear hats and others do not? Nobody seems to know—least of all the hat wearers. It is much the same with ski-ing. There are hat people (us), and there are no-hat people. The reason we are hat people, even in relatively warm conditions, is that, strange as it may sound, we have found that a hat can be an excellent remedy for cold feet (as is munching a bar of chocolate!). Since blood circulates, loss of heat in one part of your body can affect the rest of it. Conversely, removing your headgear is the first step in cooling down if you are too hot. (The second is unzipping your jacket.) When it is cold, however, *all* skiers are hat people. The reason is simple: their ears are freezing.

If you have a jacket hood, it will provide excellent head and ear insulation. It should have a cord to pull the hood tight around your face. But we all felt uncomfortable ski-ing for long with the hood up. We felt it limited our sideways vision. Ear muffs will do, but it can be difficult to hear if you are wearing them. A head band is cheap and good for cold ears. We preferred a woollen hat which kept the head warm and could be pulled down over the ears.

Socks

Everyone used to wear thick oiled socks. They were meant to be water-resistant. And they were—until you washed them in detergent—and the oil dissolved. We used to wear lots of socks, as insulation and to pad out loose boots. Now our boots fit better. Those of us with foamed boots wear silk socks plus one pair of medium weight washable socks. We can ski in these boots without any socks at all. The best socks, we think, are made of a substance like towelling—smooth outside and curly inside. Some people have proportionately thicker ankles than feet, and this is useful for those with tender ankles.

Our advice to beginners is to pack several different kinds of socks and try them out.

Under garments

By this we mean anything worn under jacket and pants. Air is one of the best insulators. You need clothes underneath which trap air. It is the number of layers that you vary according to the temperature. (If we got hot we would discard our top layer during the day, but we never went out without our outer jacket, because weather can change in minutes.)

These under-layers should not be nylon or any other synthetic. Because synthetics are excellent heat conductors they will refrigerate rather than warm the skier. Neither do they absorb moisture and so, in exercise, they make you feel clammy.

We advise packing:

- light high-necked sweater made of cotton or wool;
- a medium weight sweater or second light one;
- heavy woollen sweater;
- long woollen underpants or tights;
- ordinary underpants/shorts;
- vest or undershirt (some skiers swear by string vests. We have never been particularly impressed by them);
- cotton sports shirts.

You are likely to wear your clothing and to peel off, in layers. So all the sweaters should not be high-necked, only the lighter ones. Several light and medium layers of clothing are better than a couple of heavyweight ones. But do pack enough —and always err on setting off up the mountain with more than you need. It is easy enough, if you are too hot, to take off a sweater and tie it round your waist.

Do not be seduced by all those wonderful photos you have seen of skiers in swimming costumes. On hot sunny days it *is* quite possible to ski *en déshabillé*, if you do not venture too far from base. But you are likely to take at least a thin layer of outer skin off in an ordinary fall, perhaps more if you hit a bare patch of piste. We were too chicken for that sort of thing. And *never ski without gloves*, or in a short-sleeved shirt.

Goggles and glasses

You need eye protection most of the time. If you ski at any speed at all you will want to stop them watering. If it is snowing you will want to keep the snow out. If the sun is shining you will want protection from the fierce high altitude ultra-violet rays and snow-glare. You will receive about as much again in reflection from the snow as you will from the sun direct. Hence those rapid tans you get when ski-ing—but hence also the need for glasses or goggles. Snow blindness is not unknown among holiday-makers going without protection. We have seen it happen (the eyes recovered after a few days, but it is a nasty experience).

Finally, in some light conditions, you will need something to improve your vision.

Whatever you wear, two lenses (at least) are advisable: a dark filter lens to keep out the sun, and a special lens (usually yellow) to help in poor light. It is often difficult, especially when it is snowing, to pick out the contours of the ski-ing surface. The first time this happened to us was memorable for the rapid disintegration of our morale. All we could see ahead was an expanse of white, but it concealed heart-stopping bumps and dips. In a full 'white out', all we could do was to creep slowly down to increase our chances of seeing a bump before we hit it, and to minimize the consequences if we did not.

Yellow 'fogstop' lenses (some are red) make a major improvement. Some glasses and goggles have lenses which are said to be light sensitive, changing colour according to the outside light. In our experience they never worked properly.

Glasses or goggles? We now take one of each—yellow (or red) lensed goggles for bad light, sunglasses for strong glare when goggles are too hot. People who wear glasses can get goggles with enough room for glasses underneath. And goggles are much better than glasses when it is snowing. Both goggles and glasses are available with interchangeable lenses. One need have only one pair of each.

Goggles should have a system to stop them steaming up. Some expensive ones have a lens polarized against misting. Others have air vents. Lots of people have patent remedies to stop misting. We just took them off and wiped them. When we did not want to use our goggles we carried them on our arms (see illustration).

Glasses should be purpose-built. Some kind of wrap-round protection or side flaps improves them. A hole at the end of each side behind the ear is a help. You can then put a loop of string through each hole, so that if the glasses come off you do not lose them. Otherwise metal frames are best. These can be bent in the shop to get a tight fit. Plastic or shock-proof lenses are a wise safety precaution. If for some reason you insist on using ordinary sunglasses, then it should be remembered that cheap ones will provide inadequate anti-glare protection.

Skin protection

The fierceness of the mountain sun makes skin protection essential. Half an hour on a high mountain in spring is quite enough to give a nasty burn to sun-starved unprotected city wintertime flesh. Even suntan oil is a risky prospect for the first days. Buy a *total barrier* cream—available at any ski shop. A barrier cream for the lips is essential: whatever the weather the lips need protection from wind and exposure. Ordinary lip salve or skin cream is enough when there is no sun. Special barrier lip-sticks can be bought for sun. Those with dry skin may also find they need a cream to protect the face against wind.

Bags

'Bum Bags', or bananas, as the French more elegantly call them, are useful. For all except the cross-country skier they are the only practical form of holdall. In ours we stored: elastic ski grippers, lip salve, sun cream, penknife with screwdriver attachment, sweets or fruit, piste map, ski wax, and sometimes we stuffed in our woollen hat or sweater.

Photographs

Finally, you need a couple of photographs of yourself for lift passes (you need a couple because you may buy more than one pass during your holiday). These should be head and shoulders shots of passport size or smaller. The ones produced by automatic machines in department stores and on railway stations are ideal. Most resorts have these machines, but you cannot depend on it.

Goggles *(below left)* are best during falling snow or 'white-outs' and can be worn on the arm *(centre)* when not in use. Sunglasses *(top left)* should be close-fitting and feature a safety strap.
'Bum Bags' *(below)* are useful for small items

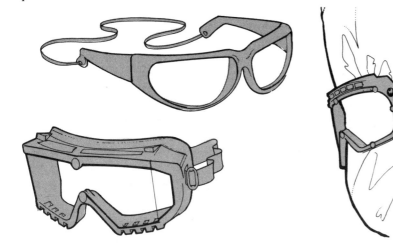

3 SKIS AND BINDINGS

Most ski schools and teachers will not care a fig about your skis and poles. Almost none of them will have heard of wedging (of which more in a moment), although it can transform your ski-ing. Some rental shops will still insist on giving you a ski which is too long. The result is that most skiers do worse than they ought; or, to put it the brighter way round, most people would ski far better if they had the right attention paid to their equipment. There are people who could ski parallel—a highly desired objective, as you will discover later—but who never will, because nobody has ever worked out the proper relationship of skier to skis. There are people who could become proficient holiday skiers who will give up after the first year convinced they are hopeless, when in truth it is their equipment which has let them down. There will certainly be improvements in ski schools and ski and boot manufacture which will redress this, but it will happen too slowly. Self-help is required, as much as a campaign, and self-help must begin with the ordinary skier learning about his equipment. Knowledge gives confidence. Many skiers who have suspected something wrong have felt ashamed to inquire or been afraid of inviting the reply that a bad workman blames his tools. The answer is that bad workmen may do that, but a good workman knows what good tools are and sees that he gets them because they allow him to realize his skills. Bad equipment particularly affects the beginner and the intermediate skier, whose confidence can be easily undermined.

We had come to these conclusions from several years of experience and observation. When we made the points in conversation at the average ski school we noted a tendency to regard them as some kind of fussiness or special pleading for 'softies' from the cities. Self-doubt did not set in because the personal experience was vivid, and we have been reinforced in our convictions by a remarkable ski teacher, Warren Witherell, director of the Burke Mountain Alpine Training Centre in East Burke, Vermont, USA.

While we were learning in Europe about the importance of correct skis, edges and wedges for holiday skiers, Witherell was publishing a book about racing skiers: ten young racers from his centre have earned places in the US ski team. Witherell's book* is about racers, and his observations are based on experience in America. Nonetheless, his conclusions emphatically endorse our own as holiday skiers in Europe.

*How the Racers Ski, published by W. M. Norton & Co, New York, 1972

'I don't know of any snow skis available today that are ready to be skied on as delivered by a retail shop. Nor do I know of any manufacturer or retail shop that publicly admits this to the ski purchaser. Keeping this secret has greatly reduced the pleasures people can derive from ski-ing.

'There are thousands of perpetual stem turners in America—people who have taken lessons for years with hopes of becoming parallel skiers. Many of these people don't need lessons; they need wedges to flatten their skis in a natural stance.

'Most ski schools accept the equipment limitations of their customers. This limits the progress each customer can make regardless of the calibre of on-snow instructions provided.'

There are four questions every skier should be able to answer for himself about his skis, hired or bought, first year or tenth year:

- Are the skis the right length for me?
- Do I stand flat on both skis?
- Are my running surfaces right?
- Are my ski edges right?

There is more to choosing a ski than this, but we urge you to concentrate on these four, especially if a beginner or intermediate skier.

Ski length

What a revolution there has been. When we published the first edition of this book we said that most people were made to learn on skis far too long for them. The victim – for such he was – used to have to wrestle with skis that reached up above his head as high as the wrist of a raised hand. Skis that long are harder for the learner to turn; hence thousands of people gave up trying.

It would be nice to think our condemnation of the practice, and our advice that beginners insisted on shorter skis, had something to do with what has happened: certainly hundreds of readers did cause consternation in ski shops in several resorts we know. But when we said it a lot of people in the sport, and especially the manufacturers, had reached the same conclusion. Today it is easy for the beginner to follow this essential advice: *Never accept a pair of skis taller than yourself.*

All this, of course, is on the assumption that you are being taught traditionally and not by the mini-ski method discussed in chapter 18. That kind of short ski – as short as 100cm – is very different. Don't imagine there is any virtue in trying to get a ski as short as that, unless you are firmly in a mini-ski resort (and there are not many in Europe). We will have to be more precise about the length of ski we advise for each individual. It needs to be preceded by a discussion of the types of ski there are (Chapter 9 will go into what the ski will do for you on snow), and we make no excuse for a simplified technical sortie. We have never heard a ski school explain what the ski will do for you or why it is built the way it is, and we think they should. Just consider length, which is the most obvious and has the most predictable influence on what happens to the ski with you on it.

What do we know? Briefly that, all other factors being equal, a long ski is more stable at speed than a short ski, gives better support on soft snow, a better grip on ice, and is faster. But it is also more likely to cause an injury since the lever which wrenches a leg in a fall is longer and hence exerts more force. It is also *much* harder to turn, and this is the factor which outweighs all other considerations not only for beginners but for the average recreational skier who perhaps is lucky to get in a fortnight's ski-ing a year. Much of the effort, skill and struggle of ski-ing goes into performing turns with muscles whose existence the beginner never knew were there. A ski which will turn easily is thus highly desirable, especially on today's crowded slopes.

But what about the snags? For most of us, certainly all beginners, these do not matter. The fact that shorter skis are slow is a psychological bonus. Beginners expend much of their energy (and a good deal of their reserves of courage) in the struggle to keep speed down. A first-time skier rarely exceeds 8mph (13kmph) by choice, although we were all

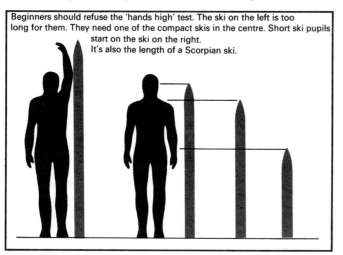

Beginners should refuse the 'hands high' test. The ski on the left is too long for them. They need one of the compact skis in the centre. Short ski pupils start on the ski on the right.
It's also the length of a Scorpian ski.

convinced we were doing at least three times that speed. Even a moderately competent holiday skier rarely tops 20mph (32kmph).

At speeds like this the modern shorter ski 'tracks' (i.e. holds the road) quite satisfactorily. It also provides enough support (most are broader than full-length skis) for occasional forays off today's firm well-packed pistes. Granted the dedicated off-piste skier will want a more specialist ski, but for most people the only significant drawback of the average shorter ski is that, all other design factors being equal, it will have less of a grip on ice than a longer one. Just keep your edges sharp (see page 64) – and your knees into the hill.

None of this changes the fact that long skis are more efficient than short ones on the feet of *those who are capable of using them*. Racers are. But they use long skis because they are expert; they are not expert because they wear long skis. There is more than one way of measuring the length of a ski. Neither beginners nor the average holiday skier need concern themselves with the distinction. But it is worth knowing that

● material or nominal length is the reading you would get from running a tape measure from tip to tail of the ski along its underside. Most manufacturers use this.

● the chord length is that of a straight line from tip to tail. On any given ski it will be shorter than the material length, usually by a matter of two or three centimetres. A few manufacturers stamp this length on their skis.

● the contact length is the amount of ski that is in contact with a flat surface (e.g. snow) when in use. It is never used to describe the length of a ski, but it is the statistic which has the most predictable bearing on ski behaviour, and is hence invariably given in ski tests or in technical data.

The net result of all these variables is that there can be a difference of up to 10cm between the contact lengths of two skis both described as being the same length. Thus the more adventurous skier juggling with different makes and lengths of skis may wonder why an apparently longer ski does not behave like a longer one. The answer could well be that he is not comparing like with like.

We will give more precise guidance on the length of ski you should choose once we have looked at the other qualities of a ski.

2. Do you stand flat on both skis?

Most of us do not stand flat on our skis. Look at the bottom of your ordinary shoes. It is unlikely that they will be worn evenly all over. Most of us walk more on the outside. This means that when we put skis on we are putting most pressure on the outside of the skis. This has profound importance on the way we ski. Efficient ski-ing requires us to stand flat on both skis and to be able to roll over each ski (edge it) to the same angle. To do that most of us need to some varying degree to have wedges of plastic or metal between boot and ski to compensate for our natural stance. Yet most resorts have barely heard of wedges, and they are almost universally ignored in textbooks on ski-ing.

The beginner can do very little about wedging (we prefer that term to the term 'canting' more knowledgeable British skiers have been using for some years). To fit wedges requires taking off the bindings and fitting the wedges underneath heel and toe. That will not be practical for the graduated length skis, which are changed during the week, and the beginner who rents skis will hardly be able to get the advice and help needed. Nor should he worry much on his first holiday. Checking your wedging needs is vital after that, but in your conventional first year you can enjoy learning the plough and stem and other movements. Those turns need little refinement in edge control and if you have soft, loose boots you will provide correction yourself by ankle movement.

Not until one of us had been ski-ing for three years, with a lot of private lessons in Austria, Switzerland, and the United States, did a teacher—Romano Bossi, at Davos in Switzerland —notice anything vital. 'You are not,' he said, 'standing flat on your skis. You are standing on your outside edge.' (We will be dealing in detail later on about how a ski turns, but, roughly, a good skier makes the skis turn by rolling the skis on to their edges—the metal strips along left and right of each ski—and then applying pressure. The turn is smoother and more efficient when the skis are edged simultaneously and to the same degree.)

To prove his point the instructor found a patch of flat, unmarked snow where one of us stood as flat as he could, yet there in the snow was the trace of a metal edge at the far left of one ski and one at the far right of the other. Next he found a hillside where it was possible to traverse (ski across rather than down the slope), with the teacher observing the angle of the ski. One ski was edged more than the other. Try as we might, we could not get both skis to be edged the same amount. 'That is why,' said this perceptive instructor, 'you are having difficulty with the parallel turn.' And he was right. But spare your sympathetic murmur, dear reader, for this is almost certainly true of you, too. You may not be quite like that, but Witherell estimates that 80% of skiers stand on outside or inside edges. We are divided into bow-legged cowboys (majority), and knock-kneed Charlie Chaplins

(minority), but we do not notice it until we put on skis. A few do stand flat, of course. Their legs are made that way. For the rest of us the injunction to stand flat or on equal edges is a waste of time. Our bones will not allow it. Yet if you try to raise all this at an average resort you will be met with incredibility or giggles. But listen again to Witherell, referring here to the need to recheck the need for wedges when boots are worn-in:

'I have seen skiers in my own programme winning races in December, then falling behind in January. A simple change of one degree in wedges has put these racers back on the winner's circle. . . . The improved efficiency in balance, economy of motion and precision and ski-control are much greater than anyone expects.'

If you are still in doubt, one of us had wedges fitted to flatten his skis in the snow. After the initial strangeness of not having to try and compensate for being on the outside edges, he found it transformed his performance. The drawings opposite show you what many skiers are up against.

When a bow-legged skier turns he risks catching an outside edge in the snow: a fall results. Mostly he compensates by opening (or stemming) one ski away from the other or by hopping off the ground with both feet. Neither of the moves— as we see later—is correct. When the skier turns the skis are unequally edged. The degree of edging determines the arc of the turn, so the two skis are not following the same track. This again causes great difficulty for the skier, less for a girl than a man because of the way girls use their knees and hips.

The wedges, strips of plastic or metal, are thicker at one end than another. They are generally screwed into the ski under the binding which holds the boot to the ski.

The Head Ski Co. makes a form of plastic wedging which is even more easily inserted between the foot and the ski. It is a clip-on wedge and is better than the screw-type wedges because these are prone to come apart in difficult conditions. One of us had the wedge and binding work loose halfway up a mountain in Zürs.

There are two machines which compute the degree of wedging the skier needs—the Kennedy Computer and the CB Sports Edge Exactor. One ski may need no wedging or more wedging than another. It is a tricky business using these machines and you must not assume that the reading given for you, in your ski boots, is necessarily correct for you. You must continue to observe the way you ski—are you catching a lot of inside edges? Are you having more difficulty with the turn one side than another? Are you, indeed, edging one ski more than another, despite the alteration?

It is worth your while if you fuss about this sort of adjustment because it will force you to concentrate on what is happening between your foot and the ski. This in itself is a good argument for writing about wedging. Some instructors tell us they wish they had never heard of the word. It would certainly be a pity if wedging difficulties became an excuse for poor technique. But at the moment there is so much ignorance among skiers on this subject that we happily run the risk of over-emphasis.

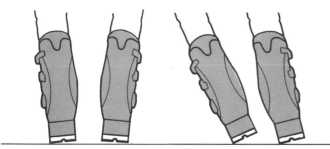

A bow legged skier cannot flatten his skis properly *(left)* and will tend to edge one ski more than the other *(right)* . . .

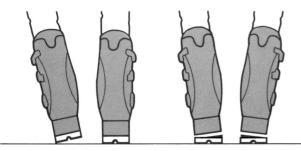

. . . As he releases his edges, one ski flattens before the other *(left)*. Wedges *(right)* correct this

You can give yourself several tests to see if you need wedges. Stand in your stockinged feet on a hard surface. Do your ankles and knees touch simultaneously? Yes? Then your legs are straight. But many ski boots are deliberately canted inside—the thick side on the inside to increase the edging of the lower ski—and often soles are accidentally uneven. So you should also test your boots. Check the flatness of the soles. Test again by standing in ski boots on a flat table and get someone to see if they can see light under the boot. If they can, you need wedges. You may be able to feel whether you are standing on your outer edges. Roll your knees—only your knees—so that you are poised at about twenty degrees on the edge of your boots. Get your friend to say whether both boots are edged over at the same angle. If not, you need

wedges. Now flatten your boots. Do they both flatten simultaneously? If not, again you need wedges.

Another good test, home life permitting, is to stand in your skis on a soft rug or carpet. An uneven stance is then very easy to see. And you can test yourself in snow. Can you edge the skis identically? Believe us, it is worth this bit of fuss.

The degree of wedging to correct any imbalance can only be gauged by trial and error. Witherell recognized that girls, because of differences in their joints, should be wedged so that they have $\frac{1}{2}$ to 1 degree on the outside edge.

If you need wedges but cannot get them fitted, you can, if hiring, try different boots. 'Canted' boots, as they are called, are usually designed to help the bow-legged skier. The knock-kneed minority should therefore make sure they are not buying canted boots which will merely accentuate their problem. Foaming may help a bit, since a good foaming technician takes care to see that your legs are perpendicular to the ground. But the best answer for anyone beyond their first year who has a serious edging problem is to buy skis and to have wedges fitted to them. Test them, of course, with the boot you are using. If you change boots check again to see if you still need wedges.

3. Are your running surfaces right?

We skied in blissful ignorance on badly gouged skis with no ill effects. But there is no doubt it is easier to turn if your skis are in good shape. There are four points about the running surface:

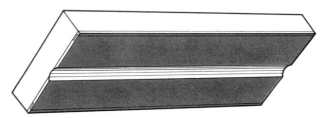

Turn a ski upside down and there is a groove running down the entire surface. This keeps you on your tracks, rather like a tyre tread. Without it, you would slide all over the place. A groove with a deep sharp edge tracks best. A downhill skier will look for this. A ski with a shallow rounded groove is easier to turn. A slalom skier (ie one who skis through gates) will grant this. That is more like what a recreational skier will want, but basically all we need to be sure of is that the groove is there and is not in any way blocked up or damaged. The groove *must be dead straight*. Check by peering along it with one eye.

Apart from the groove, the bottom of the ski should be flat and smooth. Many rented skis tend to have bottoms which slope in from the hard steel edges. They are concave. These skis will turn more jerkily or not at all. They are running too much on the steel edges. Get the ski shaved flat with a file, especially if there is an immediate slope from the edge. You need at least half an inch of flatness inwards from the edge before you can hope to turn smoothly on the ski.

Before skis had plastic running surfaces, waxing was important. It still is to the racer. He takes infinite care to choose the right wax for the conditions. It could save as much as two or three seconds in a race.

The odd second or two is no concern to most of us. The only time we really need to think about waxing is when the snow is wet and sticky. At first we were none too worried to discover that we went slower in these conditions. Then we realized that, though ski-ing on sticky skis might be slower, it was also a lot harder to turn the skis, and more dangerous if we got stuck.

So we tried waxing. All ski shops sell wax. The different types are colour-coded according to the snow conditions in which they should be used. Yellow, for instance, is the usual colour for wax suited to very wet conditions, red for drier conditions. But we found carting a lot of different waxes around with us an unnecessary complication. If we carry any wax at all, it is the silver all-purpose variety. We rub the wax block roughly over the running surface of the ski, taking care to get none on the metal edges. It usually gives the smooth ride you will want. The wax rubs off all too quickly in use. The only time you need to scrape skis clean of wax is when you are applying a different type of wax, or when storing your skis for the summer (when the metal running edges should also be cleaned and covered with paraffin wax to prevent rust).

You may see some skiers melting wax in a pot over a flame before applying it in an even film over the running surface of their skis. These are racers, or would-be racers, to whom the right choice of wax is all-important. They are brewing up a blend of waxes to get the recipe just right. Shops will perform this service. A hot waxing lasts longer, and some holiday skiers like to have their skis treated with an all-purpose wax in this way. New skis should have this treatment before they are first used.

Gouges: The wax for repairing gouges comes in two forms: either in an aerosol can or as a candle. These must contain the same material in the same colour as the running surface of the ski (most are now made of P-Tex, others, usually older

skis, are Kofix). Light the candle and drip the melting material into the gouges. Do it just as you would drip wax from an ordinary candle to fix it to a plate.

If you are using aerosol you simply spray on the mixture. You then scrape off the surplus material (special scrapers, like the wax, can be bought at most resorts) until the entire surface of the ski is flat. If you rent skis this is the hirers' problem, not yours. Unfortunately it is one to which they rarely attend. Gouges at the tip of the skis do not matter.

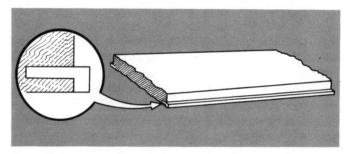

Cheap skis have screw-on metal edges, good skis have edges like this

Edges

These are the steel rails running along the edge of each ski. They should be sharp and right-angled. The bottom edges should be sparkling. In principle, the sharper the better because this gives a firmer grip on the snow. In practice the beginner should not bother with razor-sharp edges—he might cut himself—but just ensure they are reasonably keen. This is important if you are to ski on ice or hard snow. If your edges are blunt you will have a job staying upright. The expert skiers sharpen their edges daily. They want a straight, smooth edge with no pitted or blunted spots. Seven daily sharpenings are far less trouble than one weekly one. A special right-angled file can be bought for the job, but most skiers prefer something more ordinary. We suggest you refrain from sharpening your edges until an expert has shown you how. It is easy to make a terrible mess without a practical demonstration first.

We realize that all these preparations must sound exhaustive and pernickety. So let us confess that we skied in total ignorance of their desirability for a season or two. You *can* bumble around on deeply gouged, blunt-edged skis with no ill effect; just as an ill-tuned car makes a satisfactory family runabout. In fact, the difference you will notice in your skis if you care for them in this way is precisely the difference you will notice in your car when it has been newly tuned. Not essential, but it makes you wonder why you never bothered before.

THE OTHER QUALITIES OF SKIS

'After all, they *are* just two planks, aren't they?' one very knowledgeable skier observed to us. Well, no. The beginner or intermediate skier should concern himself with the four main points we have just discussed. All the same, it can help to know something of the other qualities of skis. If you are buying skis it at least enables you to check on the salesman. And you perceive something of the secret of turns in the way the ski is made.

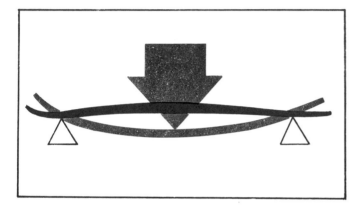

Camber

If you place a ski on the ground, it arches in the middle. This is its 'camber'. The camber distributes your weight along the length of the ski. It puts some of your weight on the tips and tails. You use this weight—or the sudden absence of it in a movement called 'unweighting'—to manoeuvre your skis. 'Reverse camber' is when weight in the centre of the ski bends it in an arc with tip and tail up at both ends. (Reverse camber can help you turn, as we describe later in the chapter on what the ski will do.)

Check the camber of skis by placing a pair together, running surface to running surface. On two-metre skis they should be 17 to 32 mm (2/3 inch to 1-1/4 inches) apart. On 170 cm skis 12 to 24 mm (1/2 to one inch). Too much camber makes a ski difficult to turn. (One of the reasons why modern skis are so much easier to turn than their predecessors is that manufacturers can now produce a ski with a relatively small camber without sacrificing any weight-distributing qualities.) Reverse camber too should be checked. This can be done by placing the ski between two chairs, the tip on one, the tail on the other, and pressing down hard between the bindings. The ski should not creak when bent in this way. And it should bend into a smooth arc with no flat spots.

Resilience

Resilience is the quality that makes a ski revert to its cambered shape when it is unweighted again. It is highly desirable, and the sharper a ski springs back the better. Resilience is what makes a good ski feel so responsive.

The side-cut

Look closely at a ski and you will see that the sides are not parallel, but curved. This is what is called the 'side-cut', and affects the turning qualities of a ski (as we explain in Chapter 9). The more pronounced the side-cut the more suited the ski is to short rapid turns. The less 'waisted' the ski, the more suited it is to straight downhill runs.

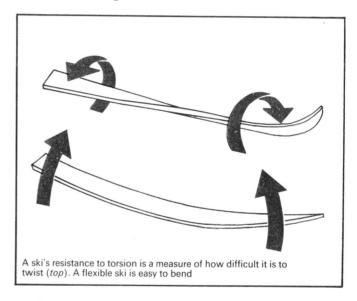

A ski's resistance to torsion is a measure of how difficult it is to twist (*top*). A flexible ski is easy to bend

Torsion and flexibility

Frankly, you can forget about these (apart from the flexibility test on page 68). Modern ski construction and tended slopes have rendered the if's and but's of torsion and flexibility academic for all but the most expert skier.

Briefly, they relate to the behaviour of a ski under stress. A ski with a high resistance to torsion is difficult to twist. An inflexible (or 'hard') ski is difficult to bend. It is also harder to turn than a 'soft' ski, and more liable to get bogged down in deep, soft snow. A ski that is ideal for icy conditions is therefore less than ideal for deep snow. And vice versa.

However, the modern ski is much more of an all-purpose job than its wooden predecessors. For instance, manufacturers can now produce a soft ski with a high resistance to torsion. In other words the ski is easy to turn, provides a smooth 'ride' on bumpy terrain (because it is soft) and yet, because of its high resistance to torsion, grips the snow well at the end of the turn, even on ice. The tail can now also be made stiffer than the tip to increase this grip. So the agonizing choice between flexibility and resistance to torsion is now a thing of the past for most of us.

The modern ski in the average store is an embodiment of all these compromises. And you are not likely to encounter conditions on the modern well-maintained slope that these skis cannot overcome. Only the expert—who wants the perfect ski for every occasion—and the dedicated off-piste skier need concern themselves with flexibility and torsion. The off-piste skier will look for a relatively 'soft' ski, the tips of which will plane on the snow like the bow of a speedboat.

CHOOSING A SKI

The choice of skis is bewilderingly wide. There are literally hundreds of models to choose from and, wherever you go, you are likely to be confronted with a wider range than you need.

But although different manufacturers employ different terminologies, and often quite different design approaches to the same problem, it is unlikely that you will come across a ski which does not fit into one of a number of basic categories. These are:

Regular skis

Sometimes called 'standard', full-length' or 'competition' skis these range in length from 170 to 210cm. The shorter lengths are designed for lightweight people (women and teenagers) and are *not* suitable for an adult male skier of average weight. They should thus not be confused with the other, shorter, types of skis described below.

Regular skis are for proficient, fast, aggressive skiers. They are also the best skis for high-speed carved, as opposed to skidded, turns. All skiers hope to use them one day. It is worth knowing how they are designed, since all other skis have evolved from regular ones. There are three types of regular ski. *Downhills* tend to be soft and with minimal side cut, and are for downhill racing only. The emphasis is on speed rather than turning so they are of no interest to the recreational skier. The giant *slalom ski*, since it is designed for a combination of downhill and slalom work, is, or should be, the most advanced and efficient recreational ski available. It usually has a pronounced sidecut and, like all regular skis, a narrow waist – 67mm is about average – which makes for efficient edge work. The more you ski the more you think

about using the edges. The narrower the ski the more rapidly and precisely it can be rolled from edge to edge – but the harder the inexperienced skier will find it to stand on. The third type of regular ski, the *slalom*, usually has a softer tip than the giant slalom. This helps to trigger those short sharp turns down the fall line (see page 92) for which it has been designed.

Shorts

Sometimes called 'compacts' – though some manufacturers call any ski which is not regular a 'compact' – they are 150-190cm, but they are not only relatively short but are broader than regular skis. Many recreational skiers never feel the need for skis with better performance than these. The wider shorts (around 73mm at the waist) give more stability and hence are more suited to beginners. Intermediates will prefer the narrower ones (perhaps 70mm at the waist) for their better edge control. Many shorts have rounded tips. These don't do anything ordinary tips cannot do, but are a distinguishing mark of a short.

Mids

Mid-length or sport skis, usually 160-200cm in length, are the obvious choice for an advanced intermediate who wants something livelier than a short. Both their width (68cm at the waist is a fair average) and their sidecut (moderate) represent a compromise between the short and regular/giant slalom ski. A soft tip to trigger turns and dampen bumps at speed is more or less standard, but manufacturers seem divided between the virtues of stiff tails (to accelerate out of turns and carve) and soft ones (for an easier ride). A flat chiselled tip is a sure sign of a mid. More sophisticated in construction, and hence more expensive, than the average short and is skied on longer lengths.

Freestyle

Length 150-195cm. There has been a lot of confusion about these. There are three kinds of free-style ski-ing. These are ballet, aerial and mogul ski-ing, all of which also get lumped together as 'hot-dogging'. The confusion has arisen from manufacturers cashing in on the glamour of hot-doggers and afixing both the distinctive tapered and turned-up tail of the free-style ski and its terminology (the 'Hot Shot' etc) to skis which are nothing more than shorts. Doubtless the confusion will continue. You will find few genuine freestyle skis in the shops and these will probably be mogul ones (ballet skis being of little use to the recreational skier). They are designed primarily for pivot turns atop moguls. They have a deeper sidecut than shorts and most mids, and are around the same width at the waist as mids. Intermediates attempting to conquer a fantastic mogulfield could do worse than rent a pair for a day or two to see what happens.

The Scorpian

This is good news. The Scorpian is a newly-patented American invention, available in Europe since 1979. It happens to be 106 cm but it is not just a short ski, and it has now been designed as a short ski from which a learner graduates to a regular ski, as in the graduated length method in the United States and ski-évolutif in France. It is a broad ski with a sidecut that tapers from 10.1 cms at the front to 8.2 cms at the tail with bindings mounted so that the back of the heel of the boot is 16.5 cms from the tail of the ski. It is designed for all classes, beginner to advanced, and all sizes of skiers. Side wall and the bottom have positive carving arcs so that the Scorpian turns fast and easily. Thousands of people are now having great fun on Scorpians: Harold Evans wrote in *The Sunday Times* and *Times* about his happy experience with them and received a flood of testimony, most particularly but not exclusively from the older, the stalled and the beginner. The former English racing skiers Gina Hathorn and Divina Galica, who can leave most of the machos standing on the slopes, have lent their names to the skis and Tom Williams, director of Aspen Highlands, Colorado writes: 'Scorpian is the best ski available for probably 70 per cent of all skiers. For intermediates there is no better way to master the moguls. For experts, like myself, the ski opens up new areas of skiing challenge.' There are some drawbacks. They are not on hire much anywhere. You have to buy and add your bindings. They do not go as fast on a schuss (so sometimes on a run-out you may have to step up a hill). Some people worry about the tips wandering as in a car wheel wobble. Off-piste and in porridge the heels sink in and that can make turning more tiring. But these are minor matters. 'I enjoyed my ski-ing more so I learnt faster and everyone marvelled at my progress,' reports a 28-year-old beginner. A 46-year-old: 'Heavy mogul fields and gun barrels are now a piece of cake.'

'I am a 37-year-old with total lack of interest in anything athletic. I have, however, become obsessional about skiing because of my success with Scorpians. Whereas my lack of co-ordination on compact skis discouraged me from making progress I am now a parallel skier on Scorpians ready to tackle any difficulty of slope with reasonable aplomb.' Finally, Major J.H. Dyas, over 75 and six feet tall who has skied for over 35 years, says he took a pair (easy to carry at only 4.4 lbs without

bindings) and concludes: 'Remembering the reluctance to accept and use safety bindings in ski schools etc. I have no doubt that Scorpian will eventually be generally acceptable. The sooner the better!'

There is, it has to be said, great suspicion and hostility in many quarters to the Scorpian. Many people regard anything which makes ski-ing easier as effeminate; and the idea that anybody can ski well on a short ski is an assault on the manhood of guides and instructors throughout the Alps and numerous citybound shopkeepers, too. But who cares? Scorpians give fun to skiing and that's what counts. For those who worry about giggles and gazes, carry a pair of 220 Kneissel White Stars up the lift and only use the Scorpian for ski-ing . . .

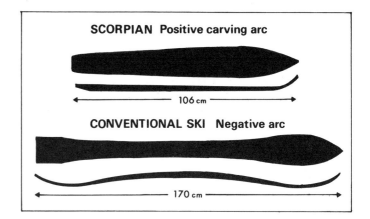

How to choose

The beginner should go for one of the wider shorts from a reputable manufacturer or the Scorpian. Just what it is that makes one ski better than another is an elusive quality. We have shown that any ski is to some extent a compromise between the desirable but often conflicting demands for ease of turning, speed, good tracking and satisfactory behaviour both on ice and deep soft snow. A good ski is one which achieves the most whilst compromising the least, and if a manufacturer is reputable it is because he has a good record at achieving this. The wider conventional shorts also tend to be the cheapest skis because they are the least sophisticated. Although we would never advocate a defeatist approach, it is clearly good sense not to invest too much money in a sport until you are sure you will enjoy it. So it is also best at first to rent rather than buy. For quite different reasons there is also an argument in favour of more proficient skiers renting rather than buying. They will be able to use the skis most appropriate to their inclinations and the conditions of the day without major outlay on several pairs.

As your ski-ing improves, so will your aspirations. It is difficult to generalise, but by your second ski-ing holiday you will probably appreciate the superior qualities of narrower shorts without being troubled by their less sedate behaviour. By the time you are doing parallel turns your thoughts can be turning to mids.

The length of ski you need will depend, as we have already indicated, on the type of ski you are using as well as on your ability, weight, age and strength and general fitness. Your weight matters because the flexibility and camber of a given ski have been designed to perform best within a given weight range.

This is one of the reasons it is difficult to give a hard and fast rule for ski lengths. Manufacturer X, for instance, may have a different design philosophy from manufacturer Y, and his 170cm shorts may have been designed with a heavier (or lighter) skier in mind than Y's 170cm shorts. The difference will be small, and probably undetectable for the average beginner or intermediate. But it is a good reason for following the manufacturer's own recommendations when buying or renting.

Ability is another major determinant of ski length. The more proficient skier, as we have explained, will prefer and be able to use longer skis. Beginners need shorter ones. A mid of 185cm will, as likely as not, have been designed to carry a skier of the same weight as a 170cm short, or a 200cm regular. Thus as your ability improves you will go up the ladder towards both more sophisticated and longer skis. (If those of you who have or are planning to learn by the short ski method notice an uncanny familiarity about this process you are right. The innovation of the short ski method was directly responsible for the big manufacturers imitating it with their broad short-narrow short-mid-regular graduation.) There is, of course, no need to make the big jump from short to mid if you don't want to. As your ability improves you may well find that going up a length in shorts, or changing from broad to narrow shorts, gives you all the extra excitement you can handle for the time being.

Fitness has a direct bearing on length because a less than averagely fit skier needs a shorter, more easily turned ski than his weight and ability might otherwise indicate. Older skiers (and this means those over 30) should also go for the shorter lengths, not only because they are less likely to be as fit as younger skiers, but because they are also more prone to muscular damage in a fall. Although we hear a lot about broken bones a ruptured tendon can be a more painful and,

Short	Freestyle	Mid	Competition
190	195	203	210
190	195	203	207
180	190	200	207
180	185	195	203
170	180	190	203
170	180	185	200
160	175	180	195
160	170	175	190
160	160	175	185
150	160	170	180 175

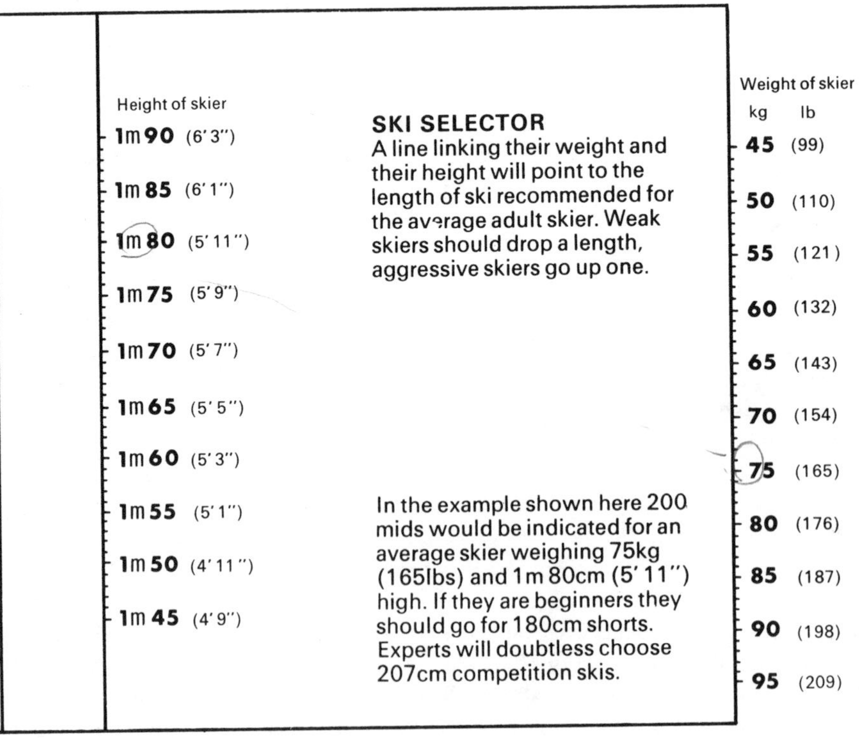

SKI LENGTHS IN CMS

Height of skier

- 1m 90 (6' 3")
- 1m 85 (6' 1")
- 1m 80 (5' 11")
- 1m 75 (5' 9")
- 1m 70 (5' 7")
- 1m 65 (5' 5")
- 1m 60 (5' 3")
- 1m 55 (5' 1")
- 1m 50 (4' 11")
- 1m 45 (4' 9")

SKI SELECTOR
A line linking their weight and their height will point to the length of ski recommended for the average adult skier. Weak skiers should drop a length, aggressive skiers go up one.

In the example shown here 200 mids would be indicated for an average skier weighing 75kg (165lbs) and 1m 80cm (5' 11") high. If they are beginners they should go for 180cm shorts. Experts will doubtless choose 207cm competition skis.

Weight of skier

kg	lb
45	(99)
50	(110)
55	(121)
60	(132)
65	(143)
70	(154)
75	(165)
80	(176)
85	(187)
90	(198)
95	(209)

in the long run, a more serious injury. A shorter ski diminishes the chance of injury.

Let us emphasise – it is best to follow the manufacturer's recommendations on length. Overleaf we illustrate Rossignol's for their own range because it gives some indication of how the average skier may expect to progress.

In the case of a 10 stone three pound (65kg or 143lbs) person, five foot nine inches (1m 75cm) high the ideal lengths would be:

1 A 170cm broad short to begin with. Our skier has dropped a length or two on grounds of inexperience and suspected unfitness.

2 170cm narrow short, perhaps on the next holiday. Our skier still qualifies as a novice, but can now expect to enjoy the narrower shorts.

3 180cm narrow shorts next. Our skier is now an intermediate-plus tackling parallel turns with some success. He may well choose to stay on these skis for the rest of his ski-ing career (you will note that these are anyway still recommended for the strong skiers). A good but prudent skier might well drop a length back to 170cm as he – or she – gets older and more vulnerable.

4 For the more gifted and keener skier experiment with 195cm mids is now indicated. No harm in 190's if that seems too big a jump.

5 With the parallel now perfected and our skier tackling carved turns they should now be on 200cm mids and even perhaps eyeing. . . .

6 207cm regular skis (well, 203cm ones then).

Which ski? For a beginner a low to medium priced ski will do. Anything more sophisticated will be a waste of money. You do not need an expensive car to learn to drive. If you feel like spending money, we insist you save it for your bindings (next section).

The expert will do a lot of twisting and flexing of skis before he uses them. There is no substitute for his experience. Only *he* knows the 'feel' that is right for him. But there are still a few basic tests that any skier can perform to make sure that his skis are sufficiently flexible and resilient.

1. The only absolute thing that can be said about flexibility and camber is that both skis should be flat on the ground with the skier's weight on them. Since you are never likely to encounter skis which fail this test, you should perform a more sensitive one.

Place the tails of the skis on the floor. Place the skis running surface to running surface. With your thumb and two fingers squeeze the skis where your foot would be if you were wearing the skis. Can you close them tight? You should be able to do so. Obviously you must test your own skis, not someone else's. There is no point in a 6 ft 6 ins muscular giant performing this test on the potential skis his tiny wife might use.

While the skis are pressed tight together, check that they match perfectly. Are they exactly the same shape, the same width and length? If you are buying skis, look specially at the metal edge at the side of the running surface. If the metal bottom is nearly flush with the side of the ski, its effective life is limited by the number of times you can sharpen this metal edge.

2. When you close the ski at the centre, check what happens to the running surfaces. They should still be in close contact with no visible gaps all the way from the tails to the shovel area where the tips squeeze away. A slight movement at the shovel area is all right. As you squeeze the centre the point of contact will move back almost immeasurably: certainly it should move back less than half an inch. And there must still be firm contact in the shovel area.

3. Now release the skis. They should spring sharply back to their original shape. They must be resilient.

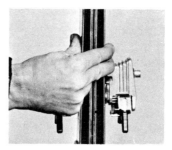 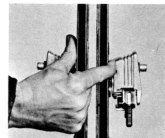

The flexibility of your skis is about right if you can close them together with two fingers (*left*) but not with one

4. Close the skis together again, but this time use only the thumb and *one* finger. If they are still very easy to close *tight* then we suspect that they might be too soft. We preferred it to be difficult or even impossible to close the skis with just one finger and thumb, although there is a drift towards using softer skis.

You can juggle a bit between length and flexibility. If you cannot get a ski short enough for you, then at least choose from among the more flexible ones which are easier to turn. When buying or renting skis, we expected informed advice based on personal experience of his stock from the salesman. This you may not always get. But there are certain giveaways that reveal the charlatan or total ignoramus.

He asked no questions about our experience, weight, whether we intended to ski on or off piste, or even how often we intended to ski. A failure to ask your age could be ascribed to misplaced delicacy. Your height should be self-evident. But if he does not ask the other questions *he cannot possibly know what skis are best suited to you.*

Whether you buy or rent skis, note the number that is usually stamped on them. This will enable you to identify them if you lose them, or if you are looking for them in a rack that contains other skis of the same make and size.

BINDINGS

Bindings are the safety release systems which hold boot to ski. This is where you should never economize. There are cheap bindings which are not safe enough. Modern ski-ing demands that the boot be rigidly bound to the ski. Without a good release mechanism, you risk injury every time you fall. The long ski, if it stays fixed to your legs, acts as a lever on the bone. Nasty.

On the face of it, you ask an impossible task of your bindings. There is constant transmission between boot and ski. The actions are strenuous, rapid and constant. In a sense you are asking your bindings to think for you: to stay on when you want them to stay on, and, in a bad movement, to stay on long enough for you to recover, but not to stay on beyond your point of recovery. Then you want to part company with the skis quickly.

In the first edition of this book we criticised at some length the shortcomings of binding design as we then saw it. Happily design has come a long way since then. We felt that skiers themselves were partly to blame, and while it is still true that many never pay enough attention to the design of their bindings, or to their adjustment, there has been enough consumer concern about safety, especially in the United States, to effect a small revolution. The most obvious result is a radical change in the nature of ski-ing injuries. Whereas once the classic ski casualty was a broken leg due to a binding failing to release, casualties are now fewer; they are more likely to be caused by collisions on today's busier slopes.

Skiers' lack of concern about their bindings, how they work and how they should be adjusted, is part laziness, part unwillingness to make a fuss, and part doltish imitation of racers. Racers prefer to ski on tightly adjusted bindings (this, as we shall explain, means they only release when considerable force is exerted upon them) because they rely on their skill and experience to get them out of trouble. The racers have done wonders for ski design, and they are obviously not totally indif-ferent to the finer points of binding safety. But to them a finely adjusted binding which will release at the first possibility of injury, or one which will release in several directions, is also a binding which will lose a race and perhaps create its own injury as the racer hits the snow at speed. Ski instructors and good recreational skiers also tend to share this philosophy, and the example has tended to percolate down to intermediates who hazard much by a delayed release.

Before explaining this in more detail it is necessary to understand how bindings work.

With a few exceptions (notably footplates, see below), most bindings hold the boot separately at toe and heel with a toe-piece and a heel-piece. You step in. You slot the toe of your boot under the lip of the toe-piece, and press down with the heel on to the heel-piece until it clamps shut. You remove your skis at the heel, too, either by pressing on the heel-piece with your ski pole, or by bending down and pulling a lever upwards. Different makes have different methods. Bindings which release with just a jab of the pole are the most convenient. Unfortunately one usually has to choose between this and another

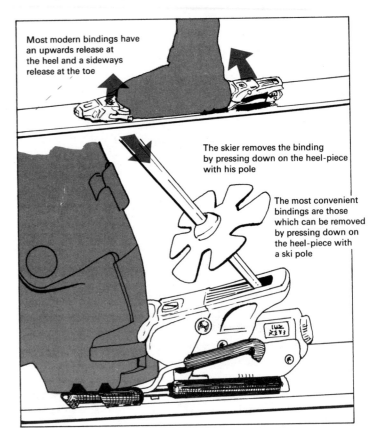

Most modern bindings have an upwards release at the heel and a sideways release at the toe

The skier removes the binding by pressing down on the heel-piece with his pole

The most convenient bindings are those which can be removed by pressing down on the heel-piece with a ski pole

desirable quality which is for you to be able to release the heel-piece with *hand* pressure only. Why bother with this? Wait until you have parted company with a ski in deep soft snow. You'll find that instead of it snapping shut, when you stand on it, the ski just sinks into the snow under your weight. Infuriating. A binding you can just reset your boot on with minimal pressure and then snap shut by hand solves this problem. Some bindings have to be re-set after release before you can step back in to them. This can be a minor irritant.

The traditional function of our ski bindings has been for the toe-piece to release the foot in a sideways twist. And for the heel-piece to come up and release you in the event of a forward fall. The trouble with this system, admirable on paper, is that falls are not usually a clean sideways twist or a direct forward plunge over the tips of your skis. They are mostly a combination of these forces.

As a result, the forces which open your heel bindings can actually prevent the toe-piece from twisting open. Both are set at a certain release pressure (see 'adjusting your bindings', p. 72. The heel bindings snap open once the heel exerts a given upwards pressure. The toe does the same when the front of the boot twists sideways with a given force.

But, if the heels are straining up, then you are inevitably pressing *down* on your toes. The result is increased friction between the toe of the boot and the ski. The toe is pressed hard onto the ski, and so grips it better. And the sideways twist necessary to open the toe binding is harder to initiate. Tests have shown that, in these circumstances, the force needed to open a toe-piece can increase by up to five times. It will, of course, still release when the force for which it has been set is applied to it. But it will take a twist of the boot by the ankle of five times this force to exert this pressure on the binding. Injury will probably result. No slide means no release.

Anti-friction devices

Once this problem was recognized, anti-friction devices were introduced. These do not prevent the build-up in pressure at the toe, but seek to minimize its consequences by eliminating the resultant friction.

Once this problem was recognised a variety of solutions were adopted. None prevents the build up of pressure at the toe. They seek to minimise its consequences either by reducing the resultant friction or by automatically lowering the pressure at which the toe-piece will release (this is known as its 'release load'.) The simplest of these devices is the third essential component of any binding, the Teflon anti-friction pad. It supports the front of the boot, and it is relatively slippery. The boot slides sideways more easily when it is under pressure. Teflon is white; pads of any other colour (you are likely to find them only on older or rental skis) are likely to be plastic, of minimal value, and should be avoided. The Teflon should be replaced when scratched or worn. This is easy to do. *It is an essential minimal safety device and you should not ski without one.* It has the added bonus of providing improved contact between the boot and ski. It also facilitates upward release at the heel in a forward fall. The pad acts as a pivot for the boot.

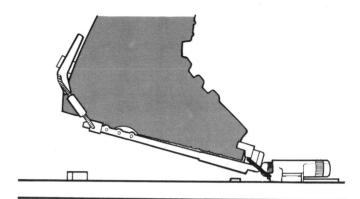

When a skier goes over a dip his bindings grip his boot harder.
Longitudinal elasticity in the bindings compensates.

Plate bindings were another anti-friction remedy. They combat friction by attaching the boot to a rigid, usually metal, plate. It is the plate, not the boot, which is then attached to the binding. The plate which comes away, with the boot, when the binding opens. The smooth plate creates less friction than a boot sole. It is also less likely to become worn or deformed or to get grit, snow, or ice beneath it, all of which can impair release with other types of bindings. Of course only fools ever ski with ice or snow under a boot. Anyone who succumbs to the temptation to force a boot into the bindings is ensuring inefficient ski-ing and almost certainly an awkward fall. Remove the snow, patiently and thoroughly, by banging the sole of the boot with a ski pole or jabbing and scraping the undersole. Expect to lose your balance and have to do it all over again. We all do. Don't scrape the snow away on the bindings—they're too precious to damage.

HOW THE BINDINGS WORK

Skis are marked showing either where the toe of the boot should rest when the bindings are accurately mounted, or where the mid-point of the sole should be. Accurate mounting is important and a job you should leave to professionals. It is usually included in the purchase price anyway.

The heels

These usually have two adjustments. One is a fine-adjust for the position of the heel-piece on the ski. It enables you to move it a small amount backwards or forwards. This is relevant if you buy or rent new boots or a friend borrows your skis. (You may even have to have the bindings re-mounted if the new boots have a sole length which is considerably different from the old). But it is not just a matter of fit. It is also one of safety.

One of the more desirable qualities in a binding is, as we shall see, elasticity. It means pretty much what you would expect it to mean: it is springy, it has bounce. The elasticity of the release mechanism is what concerns us the most, but a binding needs to have longitudinal elasticity also. This is because as a ski curves and flexes as we go over bumps and around corners, our boots are effectively pinched by the bindings at toe and heel. The ski flexes but the boot is rigid. This can affect the release load and so the heel-piece needs to 'give' a little, to move backwards and forwards, to compensate. The movement is minimal. In fact we have to admit that we had ski-ed for some time before we learned about it. The result is to keep the forward pressure of the boot against the toe-piece roughly constant.

When a skier goes over a dip his bindings grip his boot harder, If they are dependent on forward thrust this can increase the release load

But it must not just be constant. It must also be right. There is therefore a forward pressure indicator which tells us if it is. Types vary from make to make, and some are not as easy as they might be to read. But it is not something one has to do often, and the manufacturer's instructions should be specific. It is usually a matter of an arrow having to point somewhere between two spots (rather like the dip stick which measures the amount of oil in a car). It only works with the boot in the binding. If the fine adjust on the heel-piece position has got the forward pressure right, then the binding should release when it is meant to.

Just when this is will depend on the other adjustment which needs to be made. This sets the release load. Happily a lot of the

guesswork has gone out of this with the adoption of a DIN standard for all bindings and their settings. This rates from 1 to 13 (or sometimes 1 to 10 plus an 'R' for racers) the force which must be exerted on a binding before it will release. An indicator on the binding shows the DIN level of the release load for which it has been set. This can, of course, be changed.

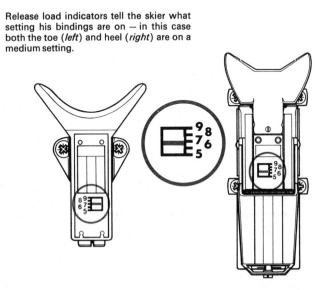

Release load indicators tell the skier what setting his bindings are on — in this case both the toe (*left*) and heel (*right*) are on a medium setting.

Unfortunately there is not total accord as to what DIN level we should set our bindings to. The most widely used method correlates a skier's weight, sex, fitness and ski-ing expertise to produce the appropriate DIN number, (we describe other criteria later). But different manufacturers recommend different settings for otherwise identical skiers, which is not quite as unreasonable as it may sound since different bindings have different characteristics. Our chart shows some of the most commonly recommended settings. Beginners, females and the unfit—no disrespect to any of them—should go down half a DIN or more, whereas aggressive males will want to go up the scale. *But do not accept this chart as a hard and fast rule.* There can be variations of one DIN or more between the recommendations of different manufacturers. It is an indication of the level of DIN setting you are likely to need. You need to know

Weight	kms.	20	30	40	50	60	70	80	90	100	110	115	120
of skier	lbs.	45	65	90	110	130	155	175	200	220	245	255	265
DIN setting		1	2	3	4	5	6	7	8	9	10	11	12

this before buying or renting since no one binding covers the full DIN range. Two to 6, 3 to 9, 5 to R are typical adjustment ranges. Always follow the manufacturer's own recommendations for the DIN setting of your bindings.

Bindings which can also be adjusted without the use of a special tool, other than a coin, are convenient. This means that if during a day's ski-ing we suffer what we consider to be too many premature releases, we can stop and adjust our bindings. Always find out how your bindings are adjusted, even when renting. We would not advise inexperienced skiers to tighten rented skis, however; only loosen them. If you suspect they need tightening you should consult your instructor or take the skis back to the store for adjustment. Better a few premature releases than an unwanted hold.

Toe-pieces

The heels are only half the story. The function of the toe-piece is to release the boot sideways. *Never* use toe- and heel-pieces which are not of the same make and model. It is dangerous.

There are two types of toe-piece. A single pivot toe-piece rotates as one piece to release the boot in a fall. The mechanism of a double-pivot one remains stationary but one of the two pivoted arms gripping the boot on either side swings open to release it. There is little to choose between the two systems. The mechanism of single-pivot systems is usually sealed and thus less prone to maintenance problems. But the distance between the two arms must be adjusted to accommodate the differing widths of boots (and it is important when doing so to adjust each side equally to ensure they are correctly centred—see p. 74) If they are closed too tight the boot can be forced back. The tip of the toe should remain in contact with the toe-piece, yet be firmly gripped.

Toe-pieces, too, must be adjusted to release at the proper release load. Their indicators have the same DIN numerals as the heel-pieces, but, at a given setting, will release at approximately one quarter of the force which would be needed to open the heels. This is because the knee—God's mistake, some skiers say—is the most intricate mechanism in our legs and easily damaged in a twisting fall. Manufacturers recommend that both heel and toe should be adjusted to the same setting. We have found no harm in slight variations. One of us, who has a cartilage problem, always skis with his toe-piece set half a DIN lighter than the heel and no ski mechanic has yet succeeded in convincing him that this is misguided.

The boot should always be held in position by forward pressure and the arms of the toe-piece, never by the downward pressure of the toe-piece. This can create friction at the toe and delay release. It is one good reason for never stepping into your

bindings with snow on your boot soles. All toe bindings have a height adjustment. This is almost always on the top of the toe-piece, whereas the release load adjuster is usually at the front. When the height is properly adjusted you should usually just be able to slip a thin piece of paper between the binding and the top of the boot sole. Some toe-pieces have vertical elasticity and move upwards with pressure from the boot. With these and those with 'toe compensators', the paper-thin gap is not always necessary. But make no assumptions. The manufacturer's instructions should be explicit about this.

There is one more potential friction problem at the toe. As the binding releases, the front of the boot sole slides across those surfaces of the toe-piece with which it is in contact. Friction must be minimised to make our exit a predictable and orderly affair (this is also the principal reason for those forward pressure adjustments at the heel.) Some manufacturers place small Teflon pads at the points of contact between sole and toe-piece. Others use a roller mechanism to reduce friction. The important thing when checking rental bindings, or one's own at the beginning of the day, is to ensure that the rollers roll freely or that the Teflon pads have not fallen off or are excessively scratched or worn (in which case they should be replaced.)

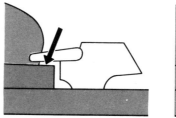 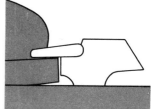

A correctly adjusted toe-piece *(left)* does not press down on the lip of the boot
If it does *(right)* friction delays release

Elasticity

This is an important criterion of binding performance. Modern bindings do not remain immobile until their full release load is attained and then suddenly snap open. They are elastic. They start to 'give' at something less than the full release load. It still takes the full release load to open them entirely. That is the point of no return. But if it is not reached, if the skier recovers, or the fall is not serious, then they will not release after all, but return to their normal position, gripping us as firmly as before. Building elasticity into a binding is an attempt to approximate to one that 'thinks' for us. The intention is that in a potential fall they should begin to release in good time but not do so

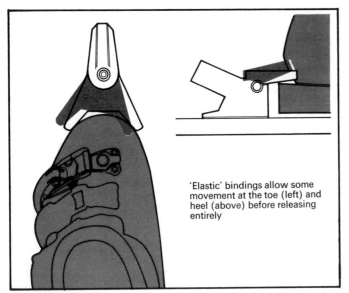

'Elastic' bindings allow some movement at the toe (left) and heel (above) before releasing entirely

entirely until the last possible moment. It is important that they should be able to 'change their mind' because premature release can be every bit as dangerous as no release, especially for fast skiers or on steep terrain. An elastic heel-piece has the added advantage that it will also tolerate a certain amount of snow under the boot without the release load being unduly affected. Elasticity is measured. A highly elastic heel-piece will allow as much as 35 mm of upward movement before releasing. An elastic toe-piece is likely to tolerate as much as 30 mm of lateral movement overall (i.e. 15 mm to either side.)

Elasticity used to generate some passion amongst skiers. Now most of us are agreed that it is a desirable quality in a binding, and that the more of it there is for the average recreational skier the better. Most of the arguing now is being done by the manufacturers. For instance those who make the most elastic bindings argue that they can be used on a lower DIN setting than their less elastic competitors, and our own experience inclines us to agree with this claim. But does that necessarily make them safer? Is that what really counts? Is it even the whole story? What about the 'return to centre time' (RCT), 'recentering force' (RCF), or even the 'displacement and return to centre time' (DART) of a binding? The RCF matters because if it is inadequate (and in the latest bindings it is unlikely to be) then the boot will not be returned to a dead-centre position on the ski if the toe-piece begins to, but in the end does not, release. (Always check that your boots are properly centred when stepping into bindings incidentally, since an off-centre boot can affect ski-ing and the release load of our bindings). Some manufacturers quote the RCT of their bindings

(the quicker the better, of course) as the measure of their excellence. Others contend that this is but half the story and that it is the DART which really counts. There is merit in all these arguments. Certainly the briefer the period the boot is away from its normal position on the skis the better.

Multi-directional release

We have already noted that falls are rarely those best suited to the upwards-at-the-heel, sideways-at-the-ankle, convention of most bindings. There is worse news. Every single piece of research we have ever seen on ski injuries concludes that it is precisely the combined forward (or backward) twisting fall which does the most damage, usually to the knee. In fact probably the single most useful release mode would be one in which the boot simply rolled sideways off our skis, like an edging motion in which the skis get left behind.

Manufacturers have responded to this by forays into multi-directional release; bindings which release in several different planes. Few have had any lasting success. All too often there have been problems with release load settings (when a binding has released satisfactorily in one direction there have been problems in another) and skiers have come to see multi-directional release as yet another direction in which to part company from their skis before they are ready to.

However the top bindings in most manufacturers' ranges now seek to combat the combined twisting fall by one or both of two devices. One is the only type of multi-directional binding which has had widespread acceptance: a heel-piece which releases sideways as well as upwards. This is sometimes referred to as 'diagonal' release. The other is a toe-piece mechanism capable of distinguishing whether the loads being exerted on it are the result of a simple twisting fall or of a combined one. In the latter case it automatically lowers the release load setting of the toe-piece in recognition of the fact that a combined fall can be dangerous while exerting lower lateral forces on the binding than those produced in a critical sideways fall.

Adjusting and checking bindings

However safe your bindings, their efficiency will be impaired if they are improperly adjusted. A basic principle is that bindings should release you before you get hurt. And clearly bindings that are set to release a big muscular man short of injury cannot be expected to do the same for a frailer person.

Many ski shops now have a machine for testing bindings. Once again Europe has lagged behind America, where no store without such a device can expect to survive. A chart which correlates leg bone thicknesses, weight, and the experience of the skier tells the assistant what the ideal release loads are for that person's bindings. The assistant then adjusts the bindings, and tests them in the machine to check that they will in fact release at this load—and not before.

These machines are a definite improvement on the hit-and-miss methods of the past. We recommend them. A number of experts, however, feel that neither the charts these machines use, nor the manufacturer's recommended settings, nor any of our past criteria of binding safety, take the possibility of muscular damage sufficiently into account. It is not enough that a binding should only save us from broken bones. Torn and strained ligaments can be just as painful and incapacitating, especially a torn Achilles tendon.

Generally, most holiday skiers ski with their bindings too tight. Simple ignorance is mostly to blame. We skied for a considerable period before it ever occurred to us to query or even test the setting of our bindings. Ski rental shops tend to over-tighten bindings, or, even worse, not to check them at all. They know that a skier whose bindings are too loose will be back to complain. We have also come across ski instructors, irritated by their pupils constantly parting company with their skis, who have tightened bindings too much. It is a wicked thing to do.

It is definitely better for beginners to err on the side of lightly adjusted rather than tightly adjusted bindings. Indeed, there is a strong case for the argument that the best way of testing bindings is to start off on the lightest possible setting and tighten them only if premature release results when ski-ing. Beginners do not move at speeds which make the possibility of inadvertent release a serious hazard. And their chances of recovering from an incipient fall (and hence their need to hang onto their skis until the last possible moment) are much less than those of an experienced skier. The lightest setting that will keep your skis on when on the move is the best criterion. Fortunately the new brand of elastic bindings have made it much easier to ski on a very light setting. They are less likely to release entirely in a false alarm.

Checking for forward release: this usually means the upward release of the heel-piece.

We repeat: a machine test is best. Otherwise, if you are not sufficiently knowledgeable to test and adjust your bindings from the lightest setting upward on the slopes, test the heel-piece like this.

Test one at a time. Step into the ski and fasten the binding. Have someone stand on the tail of the ski. Then bend your knees and flex the ankle forward against the tongue of the boot. This provides an upward lift at the heel. You should

be able to break the binding upward without undue strain. (A cruder test: see if the heel will release under the leverage of a screwdriver. It should). Start at the lightest setting and work up. When the binding can only be opened with extreme difficulty, loosen it one setting. We usually found that the assistants in rental shops check this manually, jerking the boot forward and up by hand. Whatever test they perform—and especially if none is made—always put the skis on and perform the test yourself. Hand tests have a certain validity, but only when performed by the user. The setting should never be too tight for the user to open it by hand. (Some plate bindings need a combination of a forward and upward thrust to release them at the heel, which is what happens when ski-ing. Remember this when testing them indoors.)

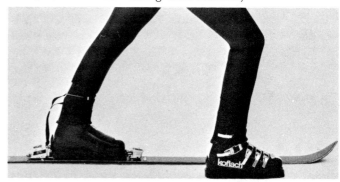

The DIN system may have taken some of the guesswork out of setting our bindings, but not all of it. And besides, with a rental binding especially, there is still no guarantee that the mechanism is working properly until it has been put to the test.

Checking for sideways release: This is, if anything, more important, and, alas, harder to do. Again a machine test or, failing that, testing and tightening as you go is best. We tend to use this rough and ready test before using a new binding for the first time: First we make quite sure that the toe-piece is not being pressed down by the height adjustment on the boot.

75

Then, wearing both boots, we test one ski at a time. Lean well forward, putting as much weight as possible on the toe of the boot that is in the ski. Then deliver a short sharp sideways tap to this boot with the other. You should be able to release it in this way. It should not need a goal-keeper's clearance kick either — the kind of kick you'd give a stone in the street should release it. The same test should be done a second time, but with the weight on the heel, for bindings with side releasing heel-pieces. Repeat with the other ski.

The only hesitation we have in recommending this test for a beginner is that we have to admit that an element of experience is involved. After a while you will develop a 'feel' for the right amount of force which should tap a toe-piece open.

Ski stoppers

What happens on a mountain when a boot comes out of a binding? The ski falls loose—but it is essential it does not run away from you. To walk with only one ski down a mountain in snow is a nightmare. And a loose ski heading down the mountain is a nightmare for somebody else. A maverick ski can kill.

Ski stoppers prevent this. They are an essential binding component and are usually integrated with the heel-piece. As you step in to the binding the pressure of your boot lifts them up and

they tuck away, rather like the undercarriage of an aircraft. When your binding releases, their arms spring down on either side of the ski and dig in to the snow to prevent it running away. Stoppers which point towards the rear of the ski, and which tuck away well above the upper surface of the ski (and preferably in from the edge as well) are a distinct safety advantage. They will need to be slightly hooked at the point of contact with the snow to stop the ski running away in the opposite direction to the one in which they point when lowered. There are two small snags with the safety stopper.

Ski stoppers in action: without the boot the spring snaps into the snow

If you lose a ski on a steep slope at speed you face a climb to retrieve it. Worse, in deep snow you can lose a ski and not find it again. This is still the argument for the retaining straps which fasten around the ankle at one end and are linked with the binding at the other, and thus prevent the ski being lost. Everyone used them before stoppers were invented. But stoppers are more convenient and safer. In long tumbling 'windmill' falls, skiers were often injured by colliding with their own skis when wearing retaining straps. You should *never* ski without either stoppers or retaining straps. In many places it is illegal.

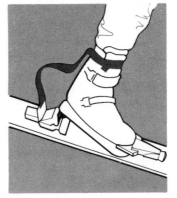 

Which bindings?

We repeat: never economise on bindings. Go for those which incorporate as many as possible of the safety features we have mentioned. Make sure that they are designed for a skier of your weight (i.e. that the release loads settings are for a comfortable range on either side of your own probable DIN rating). Go for a well-known manufacturer: Salomon, Look and Tyrolia have been the market leaders.

Binding maintenance

Your bindings should have a thorough check and lubrication at least once a year. There is a lot to be said for doing this at the end rather than the beginning of the season since the lubrication will prevent corrosion, ski shops are less busy then and will, perhaps, charge less too.

Ski poles

That leaves you with just your ski poles. The best are light as possible, and strong. But what matters most is their length.

Turn the pole upside down. Grip it immediately *below* the basket at the end. Keep your arm above the elbow tucked close into your body. Reach out with your forearm and place the pole on the ground. If the pole is the right length your forearm should be horizontal to the ground.

In snow, test poles by holding them in the normal way at the handle. The reason for turning them upside down in the shop is to compensate for the fact that, in the snow, the pole sinks in up to the basket.

If, in a rental shop, you cannot find an ideal pole, go elsewhere. If this is impossible, then err on the side of one too short if you are under 5 ft 10 in and one too long if you are taller.

A good ski pole will have a high centre of gravity, somewhere near the handle. This makes the pole easier to plant accurately. A light basket and a well-tapered pole lifts the centre of gravity. Try waving a pole around whilst wearing gloves, and see how accurately you can spear a given point on the shop floor. This is important for intermediate skiers and above.

There is no need to worry about the design of the basket, especially if you are a beginner, but check that the loops fit when you are wearing gloves or mittens. Adjustable straps are best.

The skipole test: instant way to determine the correct length for you

2
Lessons for beginners

4 THE FIRST DAY: Putting on skis. Walking. Star turn. Kick turn. The fall line. Edging. Walking uphill. Falling and getting up. 5 STRAIGHT RUNNING DOWNHILL. 6 STOPPING AND GOING SLOW: Snowplough stop. Snowplough glide. Half-plough. 7 GOING UP THE MOUNTAIN: How to ride the lifts. 8 THE TRAVERSE.

4   THE FIRST DAY

First day discovery; everybody falls. Even the experts, sometimes. But nobody cares. So forget your fears about falling. After all, what could be softer than snow?

the kick turn

straight running downhill

climbing on skis

falling — and getting up

carrying skis . . .

putting them on . . .

first steps . . .

When some of us learned to ski we had never so much as set our foot in a ski boot, let alone stood on a real ski slope. So we learned the hard way. There is no reason why you should do the same. The object of these first two teaching chapters is to help you avoid making the mistakes we made. It is easy. Nothing to fear. No steep slopes. As you can see above, everything you will learn here takes place first on the flat. Carrying skis, putting them on, taking your first steps. Then we'll teach you how to turn round, how to go up your first slope—and come gently down.

Left: Waiting for the lift. It all seems a bit formidable on the first day. But by the end of the week you will be joining the queue for the higher slopes

First climb your slope: a first day lesson at Klewenalp, Switzerland. Easy to see why this manoeuvre is called the 'Herringbone'

THE FIRST DAY

Our problems began the moment we staggered from the ski shop, clutching armfuls of skis and poles. The skis, which had looked so graceful and streamlined in their racks, suddenly became incredibly long and cumbersome. They had sharp metal edges. The bindings got in the way. How were we ever going to reach the nursery slopes?

Lesson one: skis are easy to handle if you hold them correctly. Set your poles aside for the moment. Spike them in the snow—they'll stand up quite happily on their own. Now place the skis upright together so that the running surfaces are face to face, then stand them on their tails.

A couple of cheap rubber ski straps make skis much easier to carry. They stop the skis scissoring apart. Clip one band at each end of your skis. Fit the claw end first, then hold it in place and pull the clip end round to connect. They are easier to manage if you stretch the rubber first.

At a pinch you can bind your skis together with the retaining straps that are joined to the safety binding. We generally preferred to carry our poles. You'll be a bit unsteady in your boots, especially on icy streets or nursery approaches. One ski pole (or both) makes a useful support.

If you've ever seen a window cleaner carrying a ladder you'll know the best way to carry your skis—over the shoulder. They balance easiest, and feel most comfortable, carried with tips in front and tails pointed up somewhat. Their centre of gravity—somewhere just behind the toe-binding—sits squarely on the shoulder. With your arm crooked over them and a hand to hold them steady, they can be carried a long way with ease. And your other arm is free to hold your poles.

A word of warning, though. Remember the window cleaner. If you turn round suddenly you can brain someone behind you or smash a shop window in the village street. Always look round before putting down your skis. Sometimes you'll find yourself in a place where you cannot carry your skis over the shoulder—in a crowded queue waiting to enter a cable car, or indoors. Grip the skis just above the toe-bindings and hold them in front of you with the tips uppermost.

Keep those tails up !
Skis are easy to carry when you know how

At a pinch you can bind skis together with the retaining straps

Always place your skis face to face

spike poles in snow

stand skis on their tails

Putting on skis on the flat

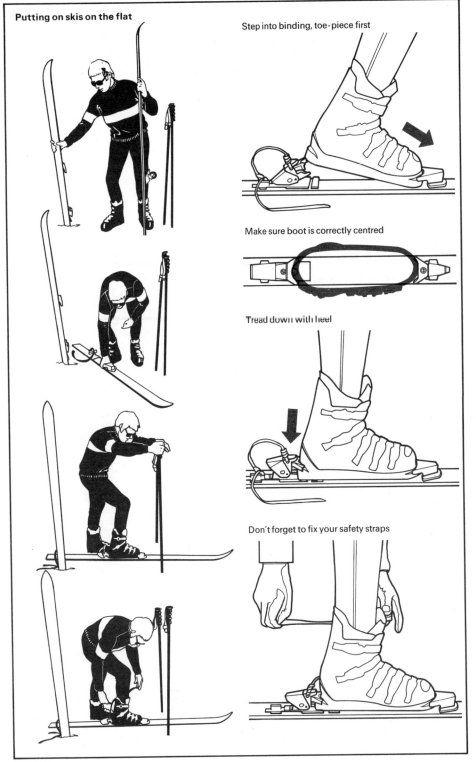

Step into binding, toe-piece first

Make sure boot is correctly centred

Tread down with heel

Don't forget to fix your safety straps

Putting on skis on the flat

This soon became an unconscious ritual once we had been shown what to do. Our preparatory routine on the flat went like this:

1. Stick poles in snow within easy reach.

2. Stand skis upright on tails. Remove rubber ski-straps. Check running surfaces. Any damaged edges? Patches of ice?

3. Check safety bindings. Open them so you can step into them in the next sequence.

4. Place ski on the snow.

5. Remove snow from underneath ski boot (see below).

6. Step into your bindings, toe-piece first, ensuring that boot is correctly centred. Then tread down smartly with heel so that you can hear the heel binding snap shut with a click. (Latch the heel unit if using 'latch-in' bindings. Or, if using cable bindings, make sure cable fits snugly in heel groove of boot.) Repeat with other ski.

7. Fix safety straps, so that if you fall and come out of bindings the ski will not run away.

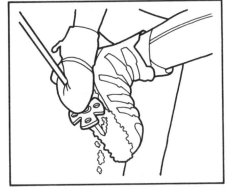

How to remove the snow from your boot soles

Dislodging the snow from the sole of your ski boot can be difficult. We found this the most awkward of all. The snow often adhered with limpet-like persistence. But it must be removed, for otherwise your bindings cannot work properly and your ski-ing can also be affected. It may even prove impossible to step into your bindings for the accumulation of snow. Some people scraped off the snow with the edge of a ski. We found it best to balance on one leg with the aid of one ski pole and use the other pole to prise off the snow, either with the point or by delivering a series of short sharp whacks with the shaft.

Putting on skis on a slope

stand at right angles to slope

stick both poles and one ski tail first in snow on your uphill side

always fit downhill ski first

press level ledges in snow so that skis will not slide away

Putting on skis on a slope

Stepping into skis on a slope was a little different. We always tried to avoid it, but sometimes found it unavoidable. We had to take precautions to ensure our skis would not slide away by themselves. So we learned the following additional rules:

1. Stand at right angles to the slope.
2. Stick poles in snow on your uphill side.
3. Stick one ski firmly in the snow, tail first.
4. Prepare to put on the ski on your downhill side. *Golden rule: always fit the downhill ski first when standing on a slope.*
5. When putting on your skis they must be placed across the slope at right angles to stop them—and you—zooming off downhill! At the same time they must be placed flat so they cannot slip sideways. Sometimes it is necessary to press out a level ledge of snow where it can rest without slipping.

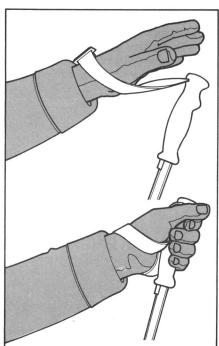

Get a grip of your poles

Here's how to hold your ski poles. Slip the hand into the leather strap so that the inside of the loop lies against the back of the wrist. Enfold both sides of the strap between thumb and forefinger. Close hand around strap and pole handle.

Stand easy

Ten o'clock on a Monday morning in the Alps. That's when the first ski school lesson of the week begins. For us the moment of truth has arrived, and it brings a momentary stab of panic. How on earth do we move around with what feels like a couple of awkward, wayward six-foot floorboards screwed to our boot soles?

But first things first. Before we could set off we had to learn to stand right. Stand easy should be the order of the day. This was one of the first tips we picked up in the absolute beginners' class. Standing rigidly to attention with feet close together looks fine on the parade ground, but has no place on the ski slopes. So relax. You are on holiday. No one is going to ask you to perform dare-devil acrobatics. You are simply going to learn how to stand up on skis. Elementary? Maybe. But the good stance habit, acquired early, will stay with you for the rest of your ski-ing days.

How to acquire the good stance habit

This is the head-to-toe rundown that helped lick us into shape:

Feet comfortably apart—say six inches—for good balance. Equal weight on both skis. Weight slightly forward on balls of feet.

GOOD STANCE

feel how much support your boots provide by rocking backwards and forwards

good stance

arms relaxed

knees flexed

weight comfortably balanced over balls of feet

Ankles bent forward until they press firmly against boot tongues.

Knees flexed so that they are almost over the toes. And the same distance apart as the feet.

Hips balanced squarely over the feet.

Upper body inclined slightly forward. But don't overdo it. Keep the center of gravity over the boots.

Head held with chin up and eyes looking straight in front. Try not to look down at your skis. This is a habit that is terribly hard to break.

Arms relaxed. Elbows slightly bent and a few inches away from the body. Hands held forward at around hip height.

BAD STANCE

And how not to do it

Feet too close together, reducing area of balance.

Ankles not bent forward.

Knees together. Knock-knee position tips weight onto inside edges, increases risk of catching an edge and tripping.

Legs straight. One of the easiest ways to spot an absolute beginner on the slopes.

Upper body bent too far forward. Bending from the waist and not the hips. Causes tension in back and makes bottom stick out. Another common fault.

Head held with chin on chest and gaze on ski tips.

Arms held too high. Bad for balance and feels uncomfortable.

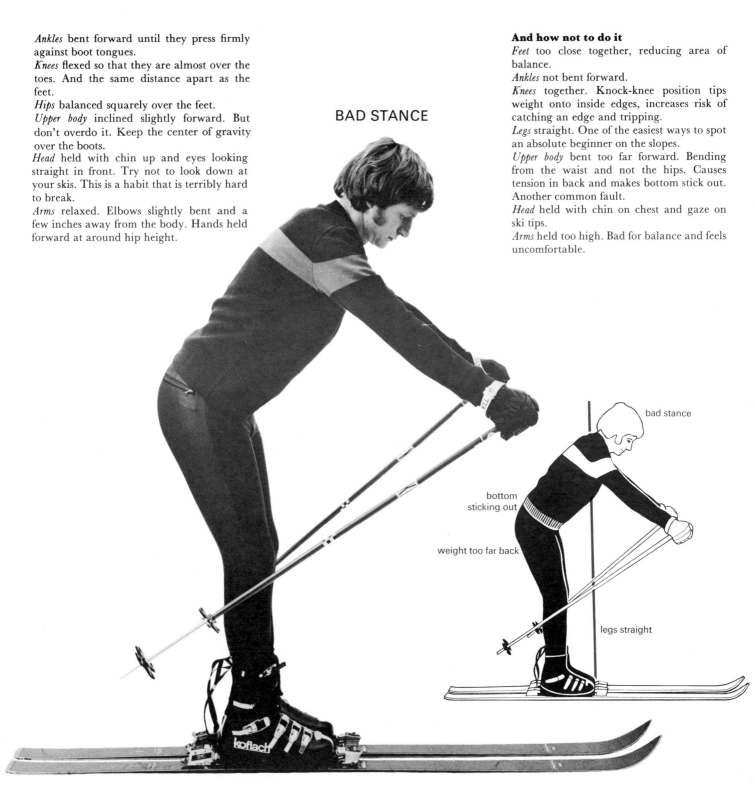

bad stance

bottom sticking out

weight too far back

legs straight

Feel the snow with your feet

A good skier 'feels' the snow through the soles of his feet. This is a fundamental fact of ski-ing. You ski with your feet. The quicker you develop 'foot sense' the sooner you will become a proficient skier. None of us appreciated this until we had been ski-ing several weeks or more. Rocking backwards and forwards on your feet is a good introduction. It also teaches you how much support your boots give you.

With knees flexed, lean forward until the weight of your body rests *inside your boots* on the balls of the feet. Feel how the front of your boots pressing on your shins is propping you up, preventing you from falling forward. It would be impossible to lean so far forward in ordinary shoes without falling. Now rock back until the weight is on your heels and your toes are pressing up against the top of your boots. Next, bend your knees as before and press them first to one side and then the other. The weight is then on the sides of your feet. All these movements have a vital part to play when you actually begin to ski.

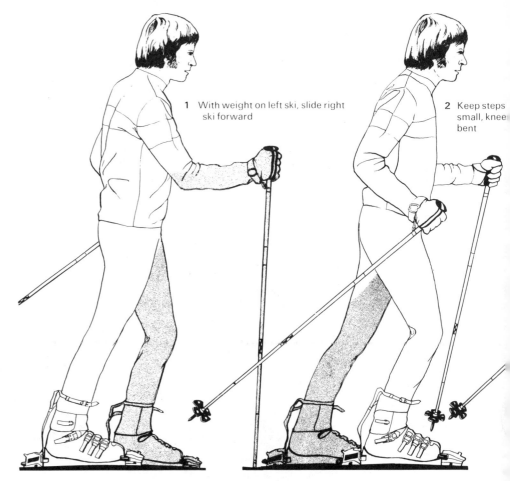

1 With weight on left ski, slide right ski forward

2 Keep steps small, knee bent

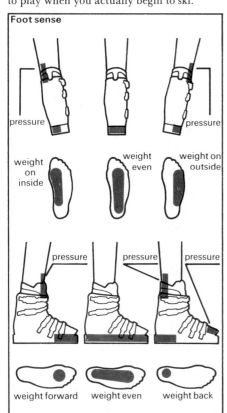

Foot sense

pressure   pressure

weight on inside   weight even   weight on outside

pressure   pressure   pressure

weight forward   weight even   weight back

Walking on skis—the first steps

Those modern, unbending ski boots had already taught us one lesson. Walking from the ski shop to the nursery slopes, we realized that our ankles had ceased to act as loose, highly flexible joints. In effect they were nothing more than stiff hinges between our legs and our boots. Putting on skis underlined this impression. The springy heel-and-toe, rise-and-fall progression of normal walking was impossible. The only way we could move was by bending our knees and taking short sliding steps which drove the skis forward without raising them from the snow. Dropping into a steady rhythm helped to maintain momentum. We discovered that walking on skis requires more effort than normal walking. But even this elementary exercise gave us enormous pleasure. We enjoyed the sensation of the skis sliding along underfoot. We had begun to ski.

Ski tips to remember

Use your poles to help you along. Let the arms swing back and forth naturally—as if you were walking down the street. At every step plant your pole to stop yourself sliding back as you launch forward. When you plant your poles, point them towards the rear of your skis to give yourself a better thrust.

Remain comfortable. Take easy strides. A couple of feet at a time is quite enough. Make sure you're the boss. Direct your skis firmly where you want them to go. Push forward steadily but purposefully.

Don't walk in a stiff, wooden-legged way— or your skis could cross.

Don't lift the whole ski clear of the snow. That's another way of getting them crossed. Don't hurry. And don't reach out too far with your poles.

3 Now transfer weight to right ski and . . .

4 Slide left ski forward

5 Use the poles to help
   you along

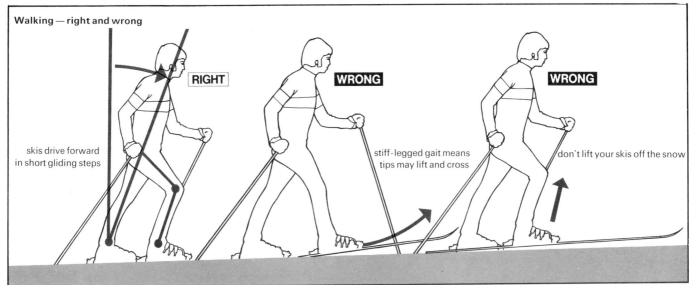

Walking — right and wrong

skis drive forward
in short gliding steps

RIGHT

WRONG

stiff-legged gait means
tips may lift and cross

WRONG

don't lift your skis off the snow

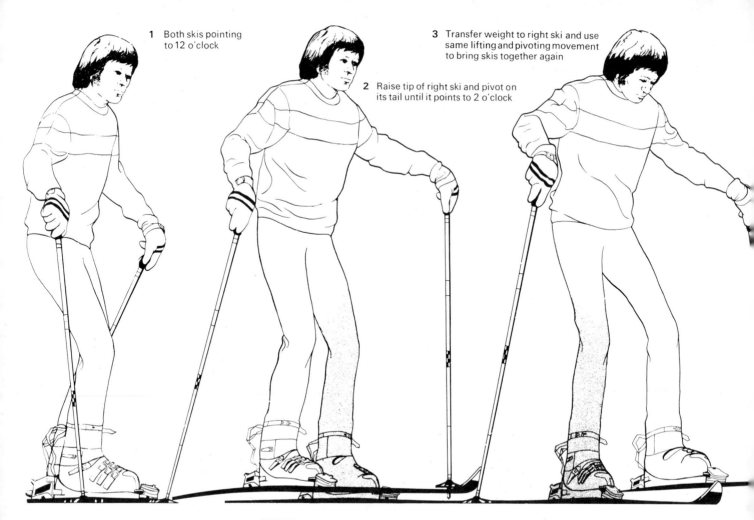

1 Both skis pointing to 12 o'clock

2 Raise tip of right ski and pivot on its tail until it points to 2 o'clock

3 Transfer weight to right ski and use same lifting and pivoting movement to bring skis together again

The star turn—how to turn around on the flat

This was the first way we learned to turn round. It is very easy. It is a series of steps in sequence without crossing the skis. Imagine your skis are the hands of a clock. Both skis are pointing to 12 o'clock. The tails are at the centre of the dial. You want to turn in the opposite direction? Right; here's what you do. With the weight on your left foot, bend your knee and lift the tip of your right ski three or four inches off the snow.

This is basically a toes-up, heel-down movement inside your boot. Now let the right ski pivot on its tail until the tip is pointing to 2 o'clock. Using the same lifting movement, bring the left ski alongside the other. Repeat the manoeuvre until both skis are pointing to 6 o'clock. Keep each step small. Don't lift the tips of your skis too high. You can also do the star turn with the tips at the centre of the clock, opening and lifting the tails instead.

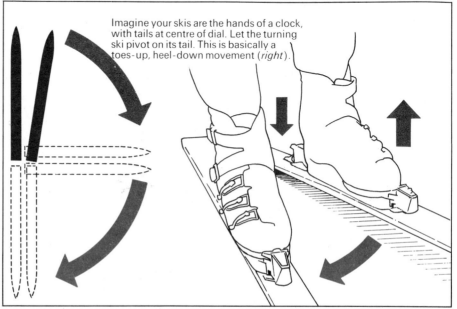

Imagine your skis are the hands of a clock, with tails at centre of dial. Let the turning ski pivot on its tail. This is basically a toes-up, heel-down movement (*right*).

4 Now transfer weight and step round again, using the same toes-up, heel-down movement of the foot

5 Use the poles to keep your balance - and don't lift the tips too high

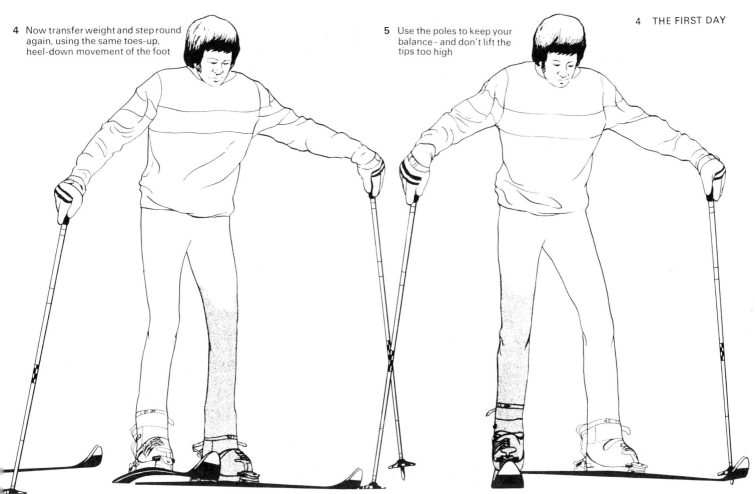

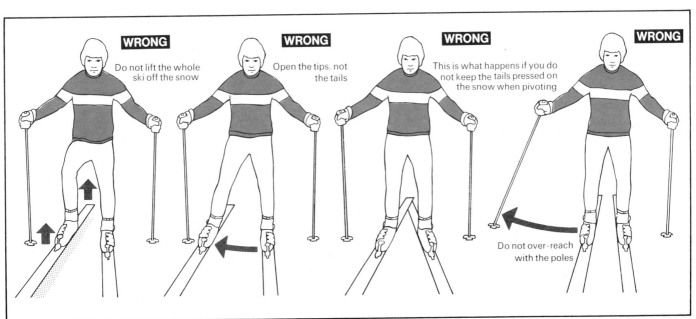

WRONG Do not lift the whole ski off the snow

WRONG Open the tips, not the tails

WRONG This is what happens if you do not keep the tails pressed on the snow when pivoting

WRONG Do not over-reach with the poles

Kick turn on the flat

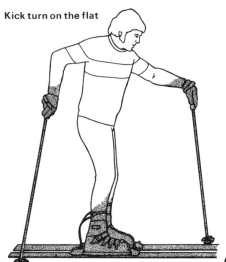

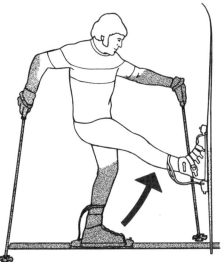

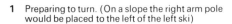

1 Preparing to turn. (On a slope the right arm pole would be placed to the left of the left ski)

2 Using poles for support, kick right ski vertical and rest it on its tail

3 Let ski pivot on its tail

The kick turn—helpful in a tight spot, but treat it with caution

The next turn we were shown was the kick turn. It was much harder to learn. We didn't like it then, and we still don't like it now. Nor do many of the instructors with whom we talked. They recommend that you should practise it on the flat or on very gentle slopes, and even then only after you have had at least one week on skis. We would add that elderly skiers or anyone with weak cartilages should avoid the kick turn like the plague.

Having said that, there's no doubt that the kick turn can be extremely useful. It certainly helped us out of a few tight spots when there was no other way we could turn around—such as when we'd skied to a precipice on a narrow trail and had muffed the turn at the last moment. A star turn was no good here. There was not enough firm, flat space. That is why we decided to introduce the kick turn at this point. Treat it with respect, and you'll come to no harm.

First, to state the obvious, you can't perform the kick turn on the move! But, unlike the star turn, you can perform the kick turn on a slope. Stand normally, skis parallel and two or three inches apart. (If you are standing on a slope the skis must be across the slope at right angles.)

Plant your poles firmly upright in the snow behind you. You will need their support. If you are turning to the right, set both poles to

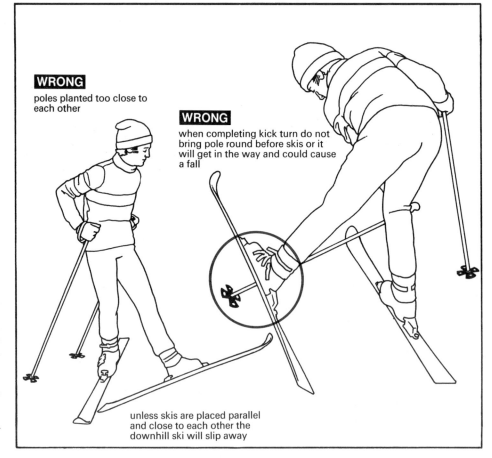

WRONG poles planted too close to each other

WRONG when completing kick turn do not bring pole round before skis or it will get in the way and could cause a fall

unless skis are placed parallel and close to each other the downhill ski will slip away

4 It looks impossible but it is quite easy, really

5 Now transfer your weight to the right ski and swing the other one round until . . . .

6 Both skis are together again, and the turn is completed by bringing the left shoulder round

the side of the left ski. Left pole towards the front and right pole to the rear.

Now kick the right ski into an upright position and rest it on its tail. The ski *must be vertical*. With the tail acting as a pivot, allow the tip to swing out until it is behind you.

Both skis are parallel again. But pointing in opposite directions . . .

It looks impossibly contorted. And indeed, some of us tried to stand in this splay-footed position without skis—and couldn't do it. With skis it is easy, and quite painless, provided you bend at the knees.

Here's the awkward bit. To complete the turn:

1. Transfer your weight to the right ski.

2. Raise your left ski level with the snow.

3. Swing it round like a propeller blade until both skis are together and pointing in the same direction.

4. As the un-weighted left ski swings round, 'follow through' with your left shoulder. This brings your left pole forward so that you finish the turn facing ahead in the normal standing position.

Ski tip to remember

Here's a little dodge we found helpful when doing the kick turn. Let the tail of your pivoting ski (right ski as described above) sink into the snow a fraction. Half-an-inch is enough. This will stop it skidding out of position as it swings round.

Kick turn on a slope. Note the difference between this and figure 4 *(above)*. When doing a kick turn on a slope both poles are placed behind the skier on his uphill side

91

How to cope on the slope

Having learned to move around with confidence on the flat, we set out to tackle our first slope. It was during this lesson that we were introduced to two of the most important terms in the entire glossary of ski jargon. 'Fall line' was one. 'Edging' was the other.

The fall line

This has nothing to do with falling. The fall line is simply the steepest line down any slope. If you were to go to the top of a slope and drop a tennis ball it would travel down the fall line. Gravity pulls it down the line of least resistance. Therefore the fastest way down a slope is to ski straight down the fall line.

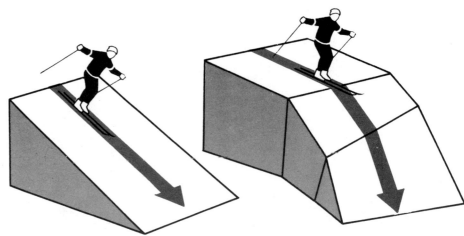

The fall line is the steepest way down a slope. The quickest way down any slope is to follow the fall line

Just where the fall line is depends on whereabouts on the slope you happen to be. Each of our five skiers has a different fall line, and it changes direction constantly as they ski down the slope

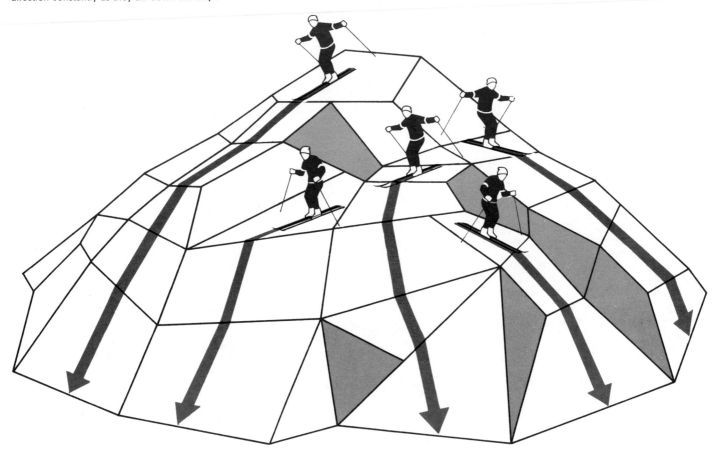

Edging

It was not until we stood on a slope for the first time that we realized why skis have sharp metal edges. They are there for a purpose: they are your brakes. If you don't want to slide down the slope there are two things you must do. First you must stand with both skis across the slope at right angles to the fall line. If your tips are down the slope you will slide forwards. If your tails are down the slope you will slide backwards. Even then, with skis at right angles to the fall line, you will slip sideways unless the edges of your skis 'bite' into the snow and form a little platform on which you can stand. This biting action is called 'edge-setting', or just 'edging' for short.

How to set your skis on edge

It is always the uphill edges of your skis which grip the snow. To set them press your knees forward along the line of the skis. Then push the knees—and your hips—sideways towards the uphill side of the slope. You should find all your weight is on your uphill edges.

Uphill—downhill

When standing on a slope across the fall line your body is divided into two halves, uphill and downhill. This is what is meant when your instructor talks about your uphill and downhill ski. Uphill refers to whichever side of you is nearest the slope above you. Downhill is the side nearest the valley below.

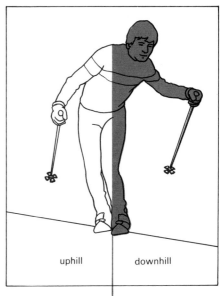

uphill   downhill

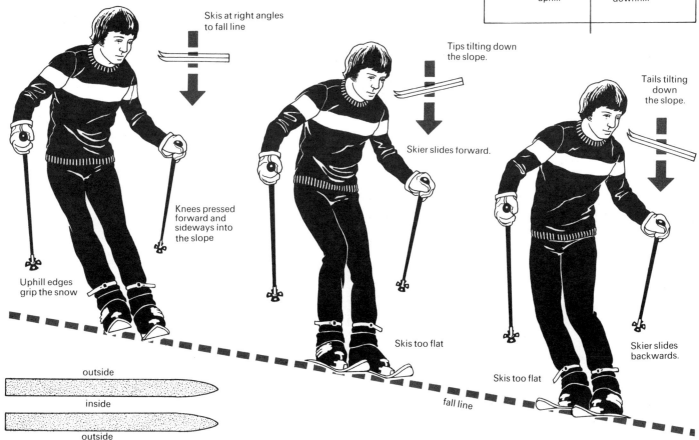

Skis at right angles to fall line

Knees pressed forward and sideways into the slope

Uphill edges grip the snow

Tips tilting down the slope.

Skier slides forward.

Skis too flat

fall line

Tails tilting down the slope.

Skier slides backwards.

Skis too flat

outside

inside

outside

Every ski has two edges, one inside facing the other ski's inside edge, and one outside facing the slope

How to walk uphill on skis

In spite of modern ski lifts and cable cars there are always times when the only way up a slope is on foot. We spent a lot of our first week doing the ski school shuffle—slogging up the same patch of nursery slope on skis. There are two ways of doing it. Both are exhausting. Both are good for your ski legs.

Side-stepping

This is the method we found easiest. We always used it when the going got steep. To side-step, the skier stands sideways to the slope. The knees are bent forward and pressed sideways towards the slope. So are the hips. This sets you on the uphill edges of your skis and stops them slipping.

Now plant one pole downhill. With your weight on the downhill ski push off from the pole and step sideways up the slope with the uphill ski. Don't try to step too far. Short steps of half a yard are better than over-stretching. Move the uphill pole at the same time. The next step is to transfer your weight to the uphill ski. Help yourself up on the uphill pole and bring your downhill ski alongside the other. To complete the movement bring your downhill pole up alongside the downhill ski.

Ski tips to remember

Always stand with skis parallel and at right angles to the fall line. Otherwise you will slide forwards or backwards.
Keep the weight on the uphill edges of your skis. Otherwise you will slip sideways.
Bend your knees when raising your skis. If you are stiff-legged your skis could cross through lack of control.
Keep your skis parallel to the snow when you lift them. The front of a ski is heavier than the back. So it will tend to see-saw down in front unless you counteract this tendency with a gentle heel-and-toe pressure inside the boot.
Don't overstretch. In our initial eagerness we sometimes tried to take too big steps. This prevented us from setting our uphill edges properly, and we kept slipping.

Diagonal side-stepping

This explains itself. We used it when we wanted to go forward and gain height at the same time. The movements are the same as before except that you lift your skis forward and upward at the same time.

The herringbone

This is the other way of climbing a slope on skis. The French call it *montée en canard*—the duck walk. We soon learned why. It's an ungainly, splay-footed waddle. It takes a lot of effort, but it is the fastest way up a moderate slope.

To start, face uphill directly up the fall line and make a wide 'V' with your skis. Bend your knees and turn them inwards to bring the weight onto your *inside edges*. Place your poles behind you ready for a good push uphill. This position requires a different grip. With equal weight on the inside edges of both skis and both poles for extra support, you are all set for your first step. So transfer your weight to the left ski. Lift the unweighted right ski uphill and set it down at an identical angle so that it forms one arm of the 'V'. Now transfer your weight to the right ski and advance the left ski in the same way to make the other arm of the 'V'. Push yourself forward each time from the inside edge of your ski. Use your poles to help you. They stay behind the skis all the time. As your right ski is advanced it is followed immediately by the right pole. The same happens with the left ski.

How to grip your poles for the herringbone

With the poles placed behind us it was impossible to hold them in the ordinary way and push hard without putting an intolerable strain on our wrists. The correct way for the herringbone gives you a much stronger grip. Reversing the handle and couching the butt of the handle in the palm creates an unbroken line of direct force from shoulder to pole tip.

We soon got the hang of the herringbone after a few false starts. It was nice to see the sharp 'V' patterns in the snow. Our worst tendency was not to open our skis wide enough. When this happened we slid backwards or our tails crossed.

Another fault we made was insufficient edging. This also caused us to slip. We soon learned to chop the edges into the snow, determined to leave our mark.

The herringbone and correct pole grip

raised ski will be set down on inside edge

ski on inside edge stops ski slipping backwards

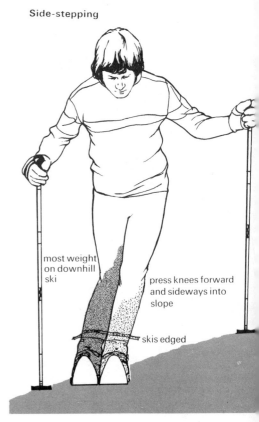

Side-stepping

most weight on downhill ski

press knees forward and sideways into slope

skis edged

Switch from herringbone to side-step when the slope steepens

weight on
uphill ski

step up

skis together again

weight on
downhill ski

step up

step up

setting skis on uphill edges carves
level platform, prevents side-slip

A good fall—knees and elbows safely out of the snow

Sit—but not backward on your tails. You will simply carry on sliding downhill—out of control on steep slopes

How to fall—and stay happy

Falling on the slopes is like breathing. Everybody does it. Even the experts. Beginners do it all the time. We fell a lot and made a pleasant discovery: it does not hurt! After all, there's nothing so soft as snow.

Once we realized there is no humiliation in taking a tumble, it didn't even hurt our pride. That doesn't mean to say we capitulated to the force of gravity every time we had that banana-skin feeling. We fought the fall. We widened our skis to give ourselves a broader base to balance on. We folded up like concertinas to lower our centre of gravity.

But when you have to fall, there's a right and a wrong way to do it. The right way is to fall —or sit—sideways. Into the slope. Your body will act as a brake and stop you sliding.

You aim to keep your knees out of the snow. The worst way to fall is forward. The next worst is to fall straight backwards and sit on the tails of your skis. That way you'll just carry on sliding.

Try not to fall on your hands. That's how sprained wrists happen. Besides, you're going to need both hands to help yourself up. Above all—*relax* when you fall. And remember: the steeper the slope, the more harmless the fall. How can that possibly be? The answer is that invariably you will fall backwards or sideways into the slope, and on a steep slope the snow is that much closer to you.

The skier above, on short skis, has tried to fight the fall and ended up falling on his hands. The result is likely to be a sprained wrist or damaged fingers. Relax when you fall and keep your hands in front of you. Keep hold of your sticks.

This is the worst way to fall (right). You should always keep your knees out of the snow. A blow on the knee is one of the commonest causes of ski injury. Also, if the knee digs into the slope, your upper body tends to overtake the skis and you may injure the lower leg as well. Remember: sit to the side of the skis.

This is the classic way to get up after a fall on the piste when both skis have stayed on (in deep snow you need more support, see page 235). Note the three movements, ABC, before the skier attempts to stand on the slope, on his uphill edges.

Facing page, at top: An alternative. Get your skis in position, then walk your hand — and with it your body — up the sticks.

How to get up after a fall

For the first 30 seconds after a fall—relax! Get your breath—the air is thin at these alpine heights, and you can easily wind yourself. Spend your time locating your skis, poles, sunglasses and hat. Check that you are still safely in your bindings. If 30 seconds is not up, admire the view. Then it's time to get up.

First of all, sit on your bottom and *turn your skis across the fall line.* Now bend your knees into a jack-knife position. This will bring your skis up as close to your bottom as possible. Finally, put both poles behind your uphill ski – either separately as left or together (above). And up you go. The vital thing when you get up is to *set your uphill edges.* Cut them into the hill-side. Otherwise your skis will slide from underneath you as you push yourself upright. Whenever we had difficulty after a fall it was nearly always due to three common faults, seen below.

1 Skis not at right angles to fall line.
2 Skis too far away from the body.
3 Poles set too far back. They did not give us enough leverage.

When your ski comes off

Often when you fall one ski boot will come out of the binding. The ski will hang on your boot by its retaining strap. Fine. That is what bindings and retaining straps are for. But take care—it is very easy to lose the ski. One of us has done it. He undid the strap with both hands so that he could get his boot into the binding. That left no hands to hold the ski, and the moment the strap was undone away went the ski down the piste and, like a bullet, straight over the mountain top. It could have maimed or killed anyone in its way. It certainly immobilized one skier for hours on a mountainside. The same thing can happen to you unless you treat the ski like slippery mercury. If you cannot undo the retaining strap with one hand, wedge the ski firmly under boot or bottom. Don't trust the apparent flatness of a bit of snow. The correct drill is to stand up with boots completely out of bindings and undo the retaining strap. Then, with the ski wedged, it is certainly easier this way to step back into the binding.

Getting up after a fall: three common faults

skis not at right angles to fall line

fall line

skis too far away from body

poles too far back

5 STRAIGHT RUNNING DOWNHILL

Straight running means exactly what it says: ski-ing in a straight line down the fall line from the top of a slope to the bottom. The popular ski-ing term for it is the 'schuss'. (Rhyme it with 'puss', as in 'pussy cat'). Before we took up ski-ing we thought it was all straight running. We did not realize that without turning frequently the skier would go downhill like a bullet.

After hours on the nursery slopes learning to turn we longed for the excitement of the schuss. Don't worry. You'll get plenty. When you move to intermediate or advanced ski-ing you will find most of the runs you do have a place or two where you can schuss with exhilarating speed and safety. Not one of us found it hard to schuss once we had got the idea. The braver would begin to schuss a little higher up a particular slope or come down without any braking, or schuss down a sharp slope, where others turned once or twice. But we all found this the easiest skier's movement, and it is the one ski-ing movement which is easier on long skis. If you can schuss easily on the small platform of the mini-ski (which is used in some ski-schools—see chapter 18), you'll be amazed at how much easier it is on the long ski.

You do not have to wait until you are up a mountain. You can learn the schuss on a gentle nursery slope—the skis go fast enough. It's a bit artificial, because here you set yourself up for the schuss in a special way. But you learn the essentials quicker.

Straight running downhill is the easiest ski-ing movement you will ever
learn. Most ski runs have one or two places where you can enjoy the
thrill of a good fast schuss down the fall line

Preparing for the schuss

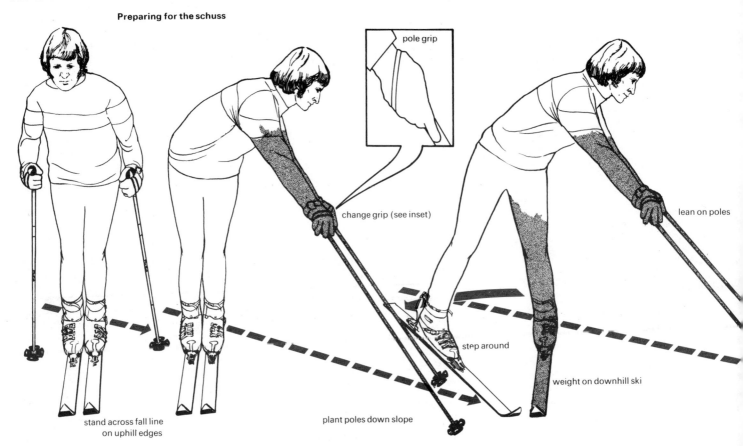

pole grip

change grip (see inset)

lean on poles

step around

weight on downhill ski

stand across fall line
on uphill edges

plant poles down slope

Find a gentle slope with a level run out at the bottom. This eliminates your main cause for concern—how to stop.

We'll assume you've side-stepped up the slope. Stop. Stand with skis across the fall line, right on the uphill edge, so you don't slip.

Now reach down the slope with arms almost straight and plant both poles in the snow. The tips of your poles should be three feet from your downhill ski. Keep the two pole tips shoulder-width apart. Skis, shoulders and the line between your two pole tips should all be parallel to each other.

Change the grip on your poles by couching

the butt of the handle in your palm. This will give you better support for the next movement. In this you move your skis round till they're facing downhill. You should do it this way. Transfer your weight to the downhill ski and open to form a narrow wedge. Proceed with small steps like this (as in the star turn) until you are facing down the fall line.

You are leaning on your poles to stop you sliding downhill. Your skis should be (**1**) parallel. Together, or almost. (**2**) Flat on the snow with no edging. (**3**) Pointing between

your poles. (**4**) Your weight should be equal on both skis.

Now get ready for take-off. Bend your knees. Lean forward until you feel your ankles pressing firmly against the tongues of your boots—and let yourself go by lifting the poles. As you pass between your poles revert to your normal grip. The poles should be carried with tips to the rear and not trailing on the snow. The arms are relaxed. The hands are slightly forward.

Most people—we did the same—fall the first time. They fall backwards a few seconds

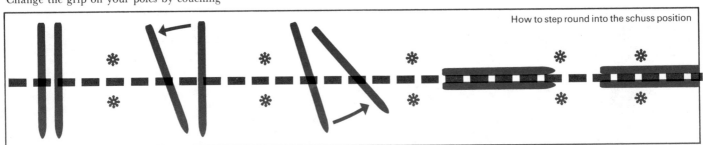

How to step round into the schuss position

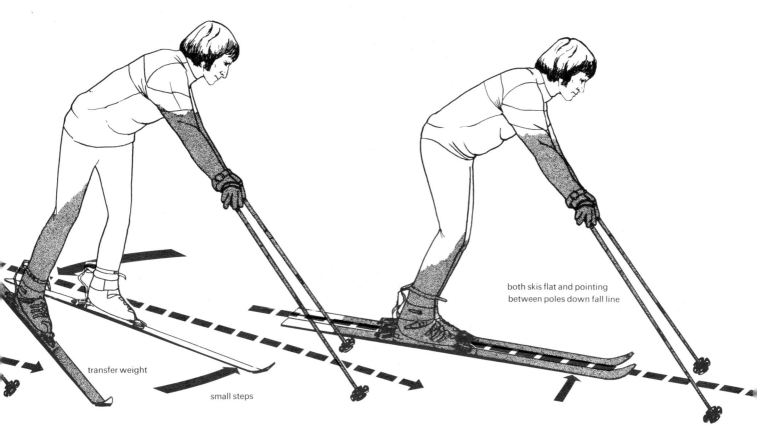

transfer weight

small steps

both skis flat and pointing
between poles down fall line

Learning the schuss calls for a gentle slope with a run out at the
bottom to slow you down

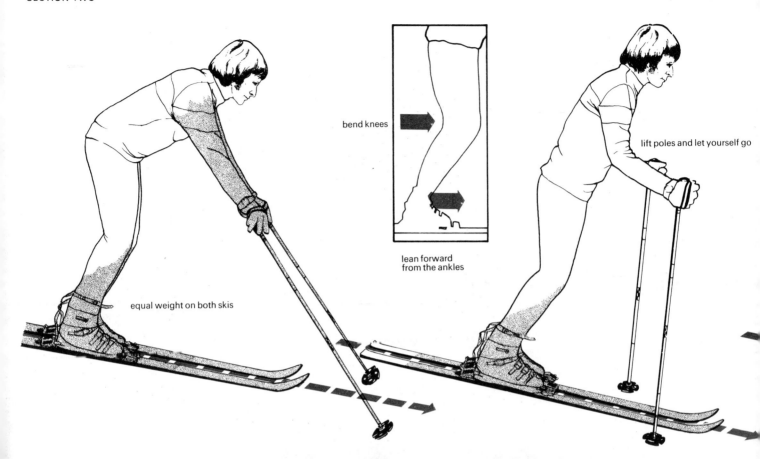

bend knees

lift poles and let yourself go

lean forward
from the ankles

equal weight on both skis

after letting themselves go. We asked ourselves why. And we had to admit fear was the cause. To keep leaning forward down the slope takes a conscious effort of will. Our natural reaction was to lean back.

We were afraid that if we leaned forward we would plunge headlong over our ski tips. Nearly every beginner has this feeling at first. Later, you realize that your knees-bend position won't let you fall forward. Your boots and skis prop you up almost as surely as if you were leaning on a five-bar gate. If you lean forward you keep up with your skis; if you lean back they go ahead of you. Basically, the theory is that whatever the angle of the slope your body line must always be at right angles to it. Imagine your skis are a sailing boat and your body is the mast. No matter how much the waves toss the boat up and down, the mast always remains at right angles to the deck.

This is what happens when you lean back. Your weight shifts to the tails of your skis. The tips, relieved of your weight, shoot

Leaning back in the schuss; fear is the cause

think of your skis as a sailing boat, your body as the mast

poles to the rear

arms relaxed, hands forward

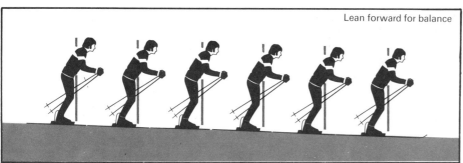

Lean forward for balance

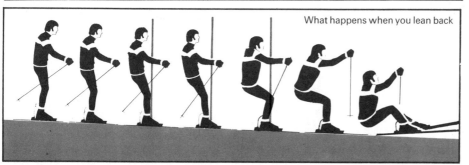

What happens when you lean back

forward at greater speed. The effect is like having a rug pulled from under your feet. Unless you can regain your fore-and-aft balance by throwing your weight forward you will sit down.

Tips to remember

Don't look down at your ski tips. A motorist does not look at the hood of his car when driving. Keep your chin up and eyes in front. Don't open your downhill ski first when manoeuvring into position for the start of your schuss. If you do your tails will cross. Don't plant your poles so close together you cannot pass between them.

Don't schuss with your poles held in front of you like a medieval jouster. The tips should point to the rear.

The best advice we can pass on is this: *if you lean forward from the ankles and keep your knees bent you will not fall.*

Keep saying to yourself: 'Well, I intended to slide down this slope, didn't I, so what am I sitting back for?'

Try wide stance for better balance

Watching the experts schussing effortlessly downhill we noticed how many of them were ski-ing with legs glued so tightly together you couldn't see daylight between them. It looked incredibly stylish. We wanted to emulate them. But the French have a theory about this which seems to work. They claim that by ski-ing with legs close together you become a one-legged creature balancing on a narrow base. With typical logic they argue that it is wrong and unnatural. Man is a biped, they say, who stands with feet braced apart when he wants to keep his balance. Therefore the same should .apply to a man standing on skis. Wide stance means more lateral stability. Certainly as beginners we found it much steadier when schussing with skis hip-width apart. Later, when we became more advanced, we tended to discard the wide stance but only because we wanted to look stylish.

Riding the bumps

Rare indeed is the piste without bumps. Even the most innocent looking nursery slopes usually have a few humps and dimples. Running into them unawares can come as quite a shock, especially when visibility is such that the bumps look flat and they're much more difficult if you ski on mini-skis.

There is a knack in running downhill over bumps. Soon it comes to feel quite natural. We would describe it as a kind of 50–50 movement. Half of it is performed by raising your knees as your feet ride over the bump. The other half is the bump itself actually pushing your knees up towards your chest. As you come over the bump, push down with your legs and straighten up again. In this way the dip is also absorbed, and the skis don't leave the snow. Notice how all the work is done by the legs. They are like con-

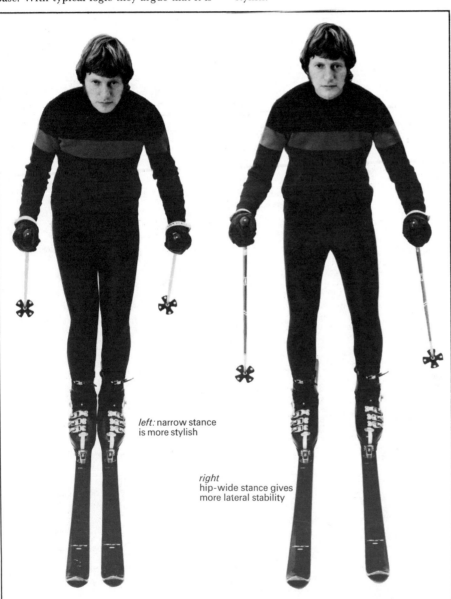

left: narrow stance is more stylish

right hip-wide stance gives more lateral stability

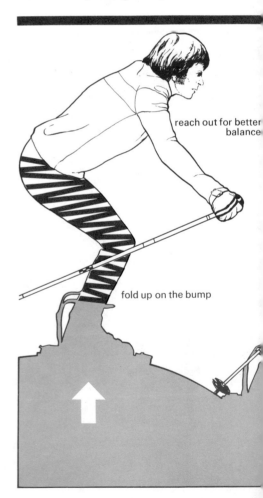

reach out for better balance

fold up on the bump

certinas, compressing on the bumps and extending down into the dips. The upper body is hardly disturbed at all.

Can you pass the ceiling test?
Look at the illustration below. You are ski-ing down a bumpy slope. Try to imagine a ceiling just above your head. Since you will want to avoid banging your head, when you are lifted by bumps you will have to bend. If you are ski-ing correctly you will keep your head clear of the ceiling and also be able to absorb the bumps.

Ski-ing over a bump will surely throw you off balance unless you absorb the shock by folding up (below)

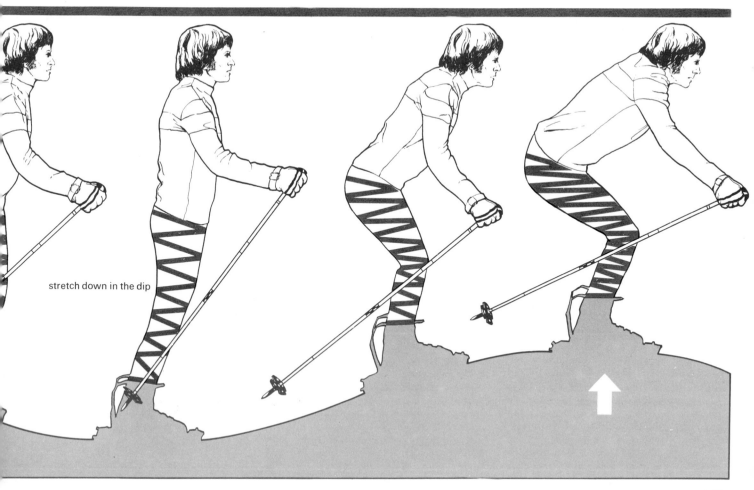

stretch down in the dip

if you find yourself airborne
after running over a bump . . .

lean forward from the hips

flex knees on landing

Leave deliberate jumping like this to the experts

The Egg

You will hardly believe it when you start out, but later you will want to increase the speed of your schuss. There are times when it saves you a boring slog of a walk. To go further and faster you get into the 'egg' position. You tuck the ski poles under your arms and almost sit on the tails of the skis so that the weight there makes them go faster. You look straight ahead. It's a bit tiring on the thigh muscles at first, but you soon get used to it. Even the best of us came to grief from time to time on a good fast

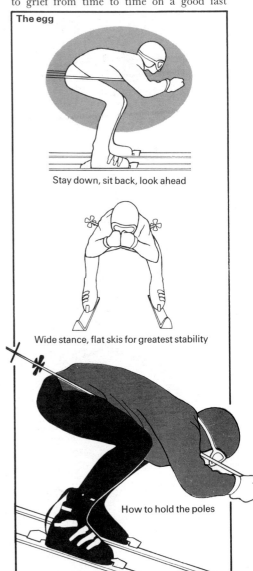

The egg

Stay down, sit back, look ahead

Wide stance, flat skis for greatest stability

How to hold the poles

What to do if you find yourself airborne

We don't recommend deliberate jumping. The whole object of absorbing those bumps when you ski over them is to stay in contact with the snow. But sometimes, after making a run downhill, a hillock will creep up under your skis unawares. Before you know it, you are already on the crest without having had time to bend your knees to swallow the bump. It is at times like this that you are liable to find yourself airborne. You will feel as if you have reached the stratosphere, even though you are maybe only a few inches off the ground. All of us collapsed in heaps on crests like this, because we were not ready for the surprise and the very idea of coming off the ground put us into a panic. If this happens to you there is only one way to bail out of trouble. If you reach the crest without having absorbed the sudden rise it is too late to do anything except lean forwards from the hips—as near as you can to imitating those marvellous birdmen who take off from the ski jump platforms. Flex your knees as you touch down to absorb the shock of landing. If you are still leaning well forward the renewed friction of the snow under your skis will tend to push your body back into a more upright and normal downhill schuss position again.

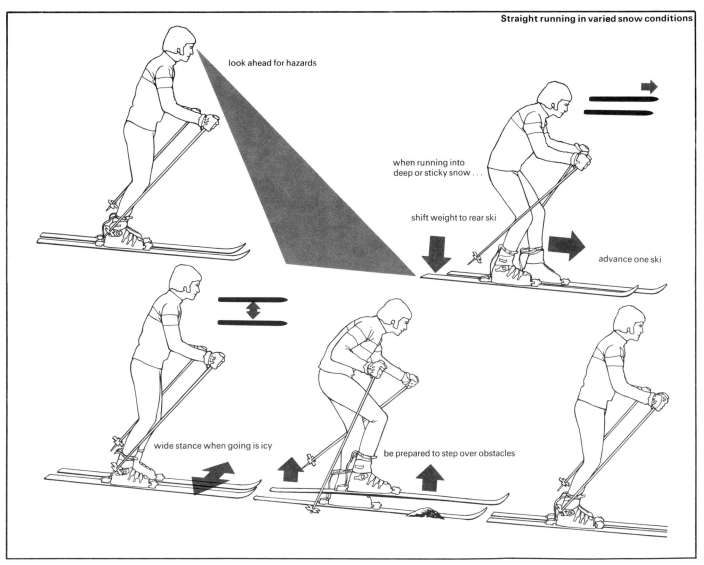

schuss. Sometimes it was the visibility, which did not let us prepare for the bump. Sometimes it was the manoeuvring to avoid other people ahead—who have the right of way. One should, anyway, never schuss out of control.

After these fairly obvious difficulties we found the worst thing then was the condition of the snow changing, especially when the track had become rutted. We found there were some days when we could relax almost completely on a schuss, but on others we had to watch all the time that our skis were flat and that we were not catching an edge on some snow rut or hill. When snow is thin you will also have to cast your eyes ahead for the small discolourations, which may indicate a root or rock.

Straight running in varied snow conditions

Question: What happens if I ski from firm, smooth-packed snow into deep untracked snow or sticky snow?

Answer: The sudden increase in surface friction will tend to throw you forward. To avoid potential disaster you should advance one ski and transfer your weight to the rear ski. This way you are braced for the shock. Also, by advancing one ski you have created a longer fore-and-aft platform on which to balance.

Question: What do I do when the piste is icy?

Answer: A wide stance (hip-width) is advisable for straight running on ice.

Question: How do I cope with slush, rocks, roots, rutted snow and ice?

Answer: Be prepared to 'step' from one ski to another in order to lift your ski over the obstruction.

6 STOPPING - AND GOING SLOW

The aptly-named snowplough stop. Pushing the skis into a broad wedge has brought the skier safely to a halt. This is sometimes called a wedge stop.

So far our ski-ing experience could be likened to riding downhill on a bike with no brakes. In fact we had brakes—our inside edges—but we did not know how to use them. It is one of the frightening things for beginners that they seem to be ski-ing out of control. We therefore break with tradition here by telling you how to stop.

The second after anybody has moved on skis he has an immediate question: how do I stop? The ski schools we went to as beginners did not tell us in our early days. One of our party in a mini-ski class was not told, and he was our first casualty in the field work for this book. He had great difficulty, he found, in keeping both legs going at about the same speed. One leg fell behind the other, so much so that he was doing a ski-ing version of Groucho Marx's famous comic walk. He made a sudden effort from the knee of the trailing leg to get both legs together and put himself out of ski-ing for the rest of the week with a wrenched knee. Only later did we diagnose that because of a foot injury as a boy one of his legs is weaker than the other. This leg imposed less weight on the ski, and so it fell behind. We should have realized his problem sooner and worked out some special exercises to compensate.

This sort of thing should never happen. We dissent from the ski schools, whoever and wherever they are, who do not teach stopping right at the beginning. By that we mean *stopping*, and not stopping as part of a turn. Of course there are stops and stops. There is the 'christie stop' of the expert, which is a devastating deadstop from speed with a spray of snow. That will come. Most of us soon learn a very effective stop of this kind on our stronger leg. But for the moment, on the first day or so you will be glad of something practical which is not the last word in elegance. The knowledge that you can stop or slow down when you wish to will increase your confidence ten-fold. You will gain your first taste of the freedom of the slopes.

Do sit down if you get in difficulties. It is much better than trying to stop by using kneebones and ligaments, and much better than jabbing your poles in front of you. That way invites a nasty jab in the face or stomach or a sprained wrist. It is also the irredeemable mark of the beginner.

It is no disgrace to stop by sitting down if you get in difficulties. But remember — sit sideways into the slope

The irredeemable mark of the beginner is trying to stop by jabbing the poles in the snow. Don't do it — you may hurt yourself

The Snowplough Stop

This is what is generally taught. The mini-ski schools shun it. They do not like anything which opens the skis. We understand that, but we think they exaggerate. Most of us learned to open our skis, but the better of us have also learned to close them again. The mini-ski schools also say that the open ski is defensive. Well, so it is, but there are times on the slopes when you will want to be defensive! So do not listen to modern sceptics who will tell you that the snowplough is for maiden aunts. Those who scoff at the snowplough should explain how they think a beginner is supposed to survive on a mountain path without a snowplough. It's absurd to expect even a mini-trained skier to 'wedel' down in the first few weeks. We have tried all the methods, and we are still glad we learnt the snowplough. It is also the only way to ski side-by-side with a child.

The snowplough stop is not an emergency stop. But it will give you perfect control over your speed on a gentle slope, and that is its beauty. Moreover there are times—such as on narrow woodland paths—when the snowplough is the best thing you can do.

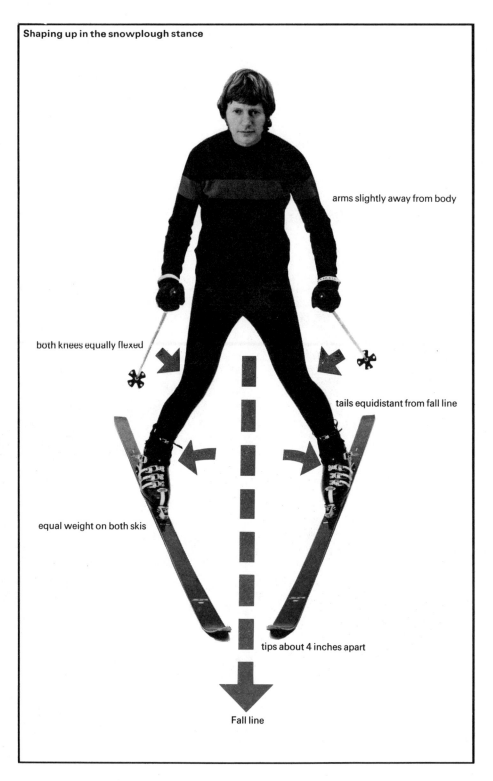

Shaping up in the snowplough stance

arms slightly away from body

both knees equally flexed

tails equidistant from fall line

equal weight on both skis

tips about 4 inches apart

Fall line

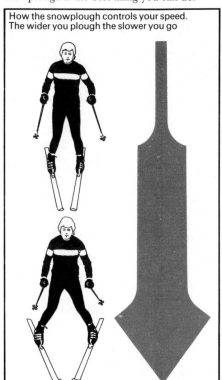

How the snowplough controls your speed. The wider you plough the slower you go

112

The basic stance

In the basic snowplough stance the skier faces straight down the fall line. Poles point to the rear. The hands are held slightly forward at hip height or thereabouts. Arms are relaxed, while elbows are gently crooked and held slightly away from the body for better balance. Ski tips remain about four inches apart, but the tails are thrust out an equal distance on either side of the fall line. In this way the two skis are made to form a broad wedge. Hence the name—snowplough.

How to shape up

Use your poles to step around into position as if for a straight schuss downhill. Once you are moving downhill, push out with your heels. The tails of your skis should be equally displaced either side of the fall line *as far as is physically comfortable.*

Bend the knees well forward. There is a temptation to press them together. Resist it. This will only lock you in a cramped position. Instead *push them forward along the line of the skis.*

Make sure each leg is equally flexed. This will keep your body where it should be—between the skis. In the snowplough it is important that the left half of your body is the mirror image of your right. Your weight must be equally distributed on both skis. Otherwise you will find yourself veering off course and away from the fall line.

How not to do it; unequal flexing of the legs has shifted the body out of its central position between the skis

Snowplough stance —side view

Arms relaxed, hands forward and down

Push knees forward along line of skis

Fall line

Point poles to the rear

Bend knees

Fall line

Push out with heels as far as physically comfortable

Ploughing to a stop

The combined effect of having the knees bent forward and heels thrust wide apart sets your skis on their inside edges. The wider you make your snowplough the more you will set your skis on edge, the sooner you will stop. Use a little muscle. Dig your heels in. On good snow you will stop effectively.

Where we came unstuck

It's not easy, especially for men, to splay their hips and edge properly. You may never, as a beginner, feel you have perfected the snowplough. Never mind. Move on to a glide (p. 116) which is more fun. But here are the main snowplough faults:

1. Ski tips too wide apart.
Our snowplough had a hole in the middle. It let the snow through and did not allow the edges to grip.

2. Unequal weight on both skis.
Excessive weight on one ski caused it to edge more than the other. The result was that we veered off to the side. We found this our worst fault, and most of us in fact have one leg stronger than another. Time and practice solved our trouble.

3. Forgetting to bend the knees.
Our skis stayed flat on the snow. We began to pick up speed, and tried to stop by jamming our poles in the snow. Catastrophe!

4. Snowplough not wide enough.
Our legs were too straight. And worst of all, we leaned forward from the hips with our bottoms sticking out. Later we learned to open our skis more, flex our legs more, and to sit back on our heels, relaxed and comfortable.

For the maximum braking effect make your snowplough as wide as is physically comfortable

How not to stop; jamming the poles in the snow is ineffective and potentially dangerous

114

How not to snowplough
Above: stiff legs, bottom sticking out, arms thrust forward giving false sense of security; typical faults of the timid beginner.
Below: ski tips too far apart to enable edges to brake effectively

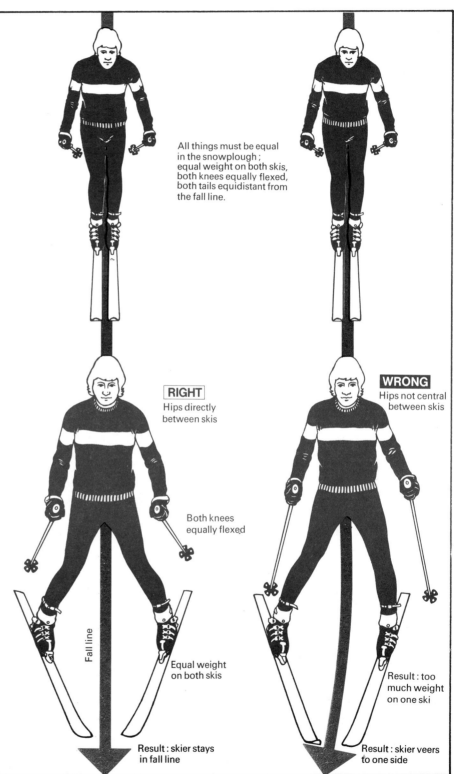

All things must be equal in the snowplough; equal weight on both skis, both knees equally flexed, both tails equidistant from the fall line.

RIGHT
Hips directly between skis

WRONG
Hips not central between skis

Both knees equally flexed

Fall line

Equal weight on both skis

Result: skier stays in fall line

Result: too much weight on one ski

Result: skier veers to one side

The snowplough glide

This is a narrow version of the snowplough, in which edging is reduced to a minimum. It's a compromise between a straight schuss downhill and the basic snowplough. The skier stands in a more upright position. The tails of his skis are not so wide apart. The skis are *almost* flat on the snow. The result is a smooth, controlled glide down the fall line. Not as fast as the schuss. Not as slow as the full-braking snowplough. Once again it is essential to keep your weight evenly divided between the two skis.

How to perfect your snowplough

Here's an exercise we liked. It helped us to get used to the idea of using the snowplough to regulate our speed. Start off in the snowplough glide (narrow 'V'). Now, with a 'down' motion of the body, drop into the basic snowplough position (wide 'V'). As you thrust your heels wider your inside edges brush over the snow and cause you to brake. When your tails are as wide apart as you can push them, straighten up into the snowplough glide until you pick up speed again. This means narrowing the 'V' made by your two skis. Repeat several times with a regular down-and-up motion of the body so that the skis open and close like a pair of scissors. With every outward push of the heels as you open your snowplough you will feel yourself slowing down. As you bring your tails closer together into the narrow snowplough glide you will feel your speed increasing again. The more rhythmic your movements, the easier the exercise becomes.

In the snowplough glide (*left*), the skis are *almost* flat on the snow. In the full snowplough (*right*), they are strongly edged

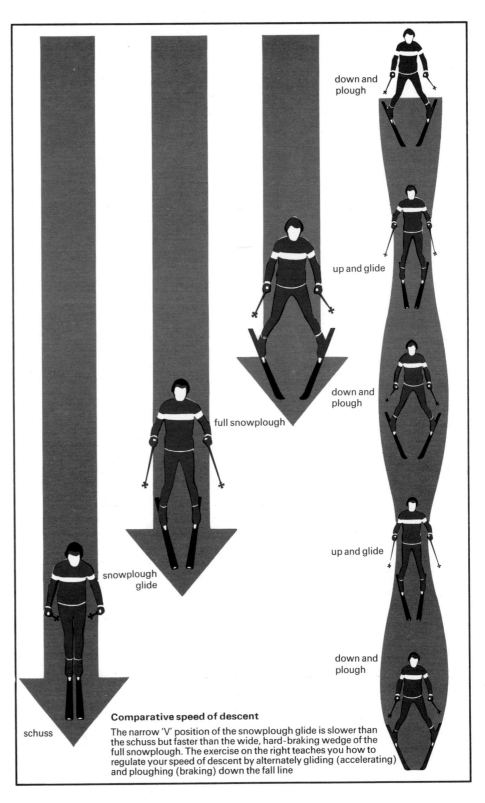

down and plough

up and glide

full snowplough

down and plough

snowplough glide

up and glide

down and plough

schuss

Comparative speed of descent

The narrow 'V' position of the snowplough glide is slower than the schuss but faster than the wide, hard-braking wedge of the full snowplough. The exercise on the right teaches you how to regulate your speed of descent by alternately gliding (accelerating) and ploughing (braking) down the fall line

116

The half-plough

A good exercise for beginners. It comes in useful on narrow woodpaths where there may not be room for a wide basic snowplough. Start as for a straight schuss. Now lean on your left ski. This must remain in the fall line and stay absolutely flat. The left knee is bent well forward to hold you on course. Now open the tail of your right ski. Slide it out with your heel until your right leg is almost straight. The right ski is set on its inside edge and forms a half-plough which acts as a brake. In other words, one ski is going forward while you brake with the other.

Ski tips to remember

Stay as relaxed as you can. Snowploughing is tough on the thigh muscles.

Keep your ski tips in the correct position. If they are too far apart your snowplough won't slow you down properly. If they are too close they may cross and give you an awkward fall.

Don't try to stop by jamming your poles into the snow in front of you. The result could be a nasty jab in the face or stomach.

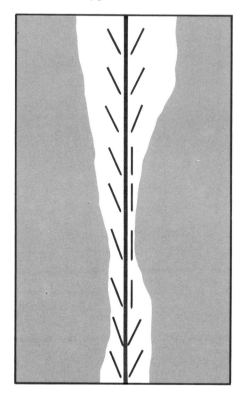

Above: the half-plough
Left: the half-plough comes into its own on narrow woodpaths where the trail may not be wide enough for a full snowplough

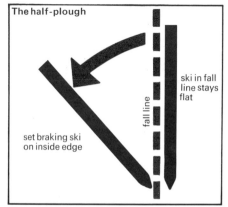

The half-plough

fall line

ski in fall line stays flat

set braking ski on inside edge

7 GOING UP THE MOUNTAIN

mountain railway

T-bar tow

poma-lift

chairlift

gondola

cable car

Going up the mountain

In earlier days, if a skier wanted a good run for his money, there was only one way of getting to the top of the mountain—leg muscle power. Today's generation of piste-bred skiers are a pampered lot by comparison.

Gone are the hours of foot-slogging up interminable slopes for one all-too-brief downhill run. Instead we are lifted swiftly and with little effort to the topmost summits, from which we can enjoy maybe a dozen or more downhill runs in a day.

We very quickly got to know the main kinds of mechanized uphill transport on which modern skiers depend—and learned that not all of them are as easy to cope with as they look in the holiday brochures.

Getting off a chairlift.
It's not too tricky if you
remember these points:
1 Watch for the end of the
lift: a sign will tell you
when to raise the safety bar.
Do it as soon as you see
the sign ahead.
2 Make sure you and your
partners' skis are separated.
3 Keep the tips up as you
reach the hillock of snow
where you get off.
4 Agree how you will split
when you get off, easing
yourself forward on the seat.
5 Brake and get out of the
way of the next pair.

The T-bar

One of our most jittery moments came when we were confronted with a ski-tow for the first time. Subsequent *après-ski* conversations with other holiday skiers established that this fear was virtually universal. It was not the danger that worried us; that is almost non-existent. It was the indignity of falling off in full view of the lift queue. And you have only to stand by any lift on the nursery slopes to see how many beginners tumble.

The most common type of ski-tow is the T-bar tow—better known as the 'meat-hook'. As our pictures show, it's an inverted wooden T attached to a spring-loaded wire which runs up the slope in a kind of endless conveyor belt of strong cables supported on metal pylons. Normally you ride the T-bar in tandem, but you can also ride it solo. Ride it with someone else when you can; it's easier.

The T-bar; easier to ride when there are two of you. The man is wearing 'snow cuffs' around the top of his boots. These keep the snow out when ski-ing off piste or in a deep fall of fresh snow.

Engelberg, Switzerland

Inevitably there will be a queue of shuffling skiers. Inevitably there will be a queue sneak. Some nationalities (chauvinist thought) are worse than others. The usual technique is for the sneak to creep past you on the side of the line, especially when you have been a bit slow sliding forwards. Close up the gaps —but try not to put your tips on top of the ski tails of the skier in front. Some people don't like their paint being scraped off; your weight obstructs their movement; and it is bad manners. Feel free to grimace if it happens to you.

Use the time in the ski queue to think of what you have to do next. For instance, have the correct money ready for your lift ticket. If you have a ticket already, keep it handy to show the lift man. As you approach the take-off position, take your hands out of the loops of your poles and hold the poles freely in one hand. You will need the other for the lift. Take this opportunity to watch how others do it.

When it is your turn, move into position promptly but not at breakneck speed; if you rush you may trip over your skis. If you are right-handed you will probably feel more at home on the left-hand arm of the T-bar.

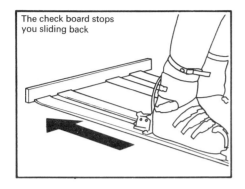

The check board stops
you sliding back

The vital point in getting into position is to locate the check board. This is a piece of wood sticking up across the end of the track and an inch or two above the snow. Push the tails of your skis parallel. Have them a couple of inches apart, as if you were about to schuss (you *are* about to schuss—but *up-hill*). Do this expeditiously, but again do not be bullied into rushing by the thought of people waiting. It is much worse to get into a stew and have a tangled take-off which delays them longer—and upsets you.

The T-bar will, of course, approach you from behind. So you should be looking back over your shoulder, ready to take the bar from the lift man who guides it to you. Pull the bar down so that the arm of the 'T' lodges comfortably under your bottom. *Do not sit down on it.* (If you do, the spring-loaded wire will just stretch and you will fall backwards.) Having lodged the bar comfortably under your bottom there will be a momentary pause as the wire takes up the slack. Then —a sudden jerk—and off you go. Be prepared for the initial jerk by keeping your knees slightly flexed.

Be ready to grab the bar
as it approaches,

but do not sit down on it
or you will fall

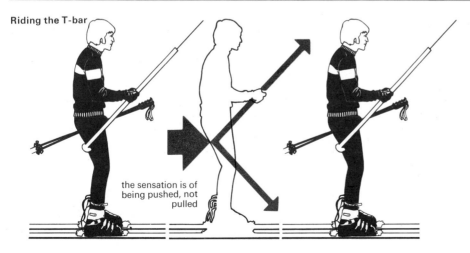

Riding the T-bar

the sensation is of
being pushed, not
pulled

We came across some ski lifts that jerked so fiercely we were literally swept off our feet for a second. But nursery slope tows are designed generally to produce no more than a gentle tug. From then on it should be easy sliding. If you do fall going up, slither quickly out of the way of the lift-riders behind you. Although we were being *pulled* uphill, the sensation was more as if someone was pushing us from behind. Once we were able to survive that initial take-off, we all of us quickly learned the knack of riding the tow. It is really a question of balancing the *push* of your legs (knees constantly flexed) keeping your skis on the snow—and the *pull* of your arm holding onto the bar. (keep your poles in one hand).

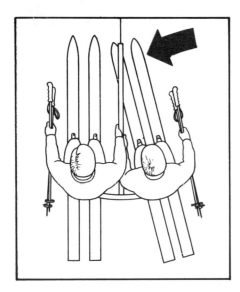

You can relax, but not daydream. When you are riding tandem you have to watch that your skis do not drift across the track to cross with your partner's. Quite a lot of holiday romances are jolted this way.

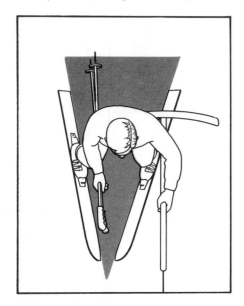

There are some lifts which, disconcertingly, go downhill for stretches on the way to the top. It can be alarming because your skis go ahead and you are still trying to hold the bar. You have to slow the skis down, and usually the best way is to edge them in a small snowplough.

Most of the time our skis ran along quite happily in the ruts worn by previous passengers. But occasionally we would come to a spot where they tended to wander off and we had to make a conscious effort to stay in the right tracks. At the same time our flexed knees were constantly busy, absorbing the gentle bumps and dips along the track. As we rode over a bump we folded our knees more to absorb the shock. As we crossed gentle dips we extended our legs downwards. Meanwhile our arms were doing exactly the same kind of job by absorbing or compensating for any sudden increase or decrease of tension in the wire.

Sometimes you will come across an exposed rock or very deep rut in the track. You can lift the tip of the ski a few inches.

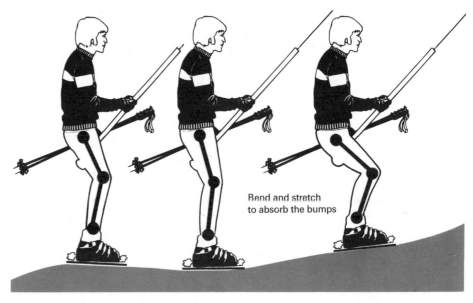

Bend and stretch to absorb the bumps

Sometimes the tow may slow down or even stop altogether when you are still only half-way up the slope. When this happens, just let yourself slide back gently, still holding the bar, until the tension is taken up and you come to a stop. The sound of the overhead cables starting to move will tell you when you are about to start moving again. You should be prepared for the same kind of jerky take-off that you experienced at the start.

Let yourself slide back gently if the tow stops

When you reach the crest of the slope, but not before, be prepared to release the tow and move off to one side. There is usually a flattish, easy run-off onto which you can escape without trouble. Decide with your partner before you reach the top which of you is going to get off first.

Ski tips to remember

If you are first off, all you have to do is let go and move out of the way to make room for the skiers coming up behind you on the next bar. If you are last, let go the bar gently so that it does not spring wildly into the air. Above all, keep an eye open for the empty tows turning round and coming back down the slope. They give you a crack on the head you won't forget if you don't move smartly off the track. The commonest mistake is to release yourself from the lift a fraction early while you are still coming up the hill. You then slide back, creating havoc.

Getting off at the top

let go gently— but not too soon

move off to the side

Left: Poma-lift; ride it the same way as the T-bar tow. *Above:* Poles under arm leaves both hands free

The poma-lift

The poma-lift is the other main type of ski-tow. It works on exactly the same principle as the T-bar, but is for only one skier at a time. It consists of a metal pole with a rubber disc the size of a tea plate at the end. The skier places the pole between his legs so that he is standing astride it with the disc wedged under his bottom. The technique for riding the poma-lift is the same as for the T-bar, except that when you arrive at the top you may need to pull down the pole a little in order to release the disc from between your legs. Also, by tucking your poles under your armpit, you can grasp the pole with both hands.

Chairlift

Chairlifts are used on longer, steeper slopes. In our experience, swinging silently and restfully up over the frosted forest tops is one of the great joys of a ski holiday. But on a cold day a long lift ride can be purgatory unless you are well wrapped up. This is one good reason why it's always best to wear too many clothes rather than too few. At some resorts a rug or canvas cover is provided in bad weather to keep you dry in a heavy snowfall.

Chairlifts are invariably two-seaters, and you can usually wear your skis or carry them, as you wish. The skiers stand side by side on a wooden ramp or platform. They look over their shoulders to see the lift man guiding the chair towards them. As the edge of the seat knocks them behind the knees they sit down. If they are wearing their skis they keep the tips up to avoid any possible obstruction.

As soon as they are airborne they pull down a metal 'gate' from behind their heads. This acts as a safety bar and prevents them from falling forwards out of the chair. Usually the bar has a metal foot rest attached to it on which you can rest your skis.

The last pylon before the top of the lift usually carries a warning sign which tells you to raise the safety 'gate' and push it back over your head. Once again, keep your ski tips up as you reach the top so that you don't catch them on the edge of the ramp. Arrival is usually slow and gentle. As the lift man grabs your chair you stand up and move away off the ramp.

Riding a chairlift; one of the joys of a ski holiday — provided you are well wrapped up

The mountain railway; slow but sure and warm inside

A two-seater telecabine

The telecabine

Telecabine, gondola, bucket lift—they all amount to the same thing, a sophisticated, weatherproof version of the chairlift. Obviously you can't wear your skis. They are carried in a rack on the outside. Your poles you take inside with you. For the romantically inclined a long ride in a two-seater telecabine can be a delicious experience. For the rest of us they are cramped and somewhat claustrophobic.

The mountain railway

Slow but sure. The somewhat old-fashioned mountain railways beloved of resorts like Zermatt and Wengen take a long time to crawl up those unbelievably steep gradients. Marginally more comfortable than cable cars—and more time to admire the view. Skis are carried in a separate truck at the back.

The cable car

For the longest, steepest high-rise of all, the cable car can whisk 40 or more skiers at a time from 5,000 to 10,000 ft in a matter of minutes. As with the telecabine, there is no special knack to learn before you can come aboard. Just hang on to your skis and your stomach, cram in with your fellow skiers, and away you go.

Six-passenger gondola car at Vail, Colorado

8 THE TRAVERSE

Traversing is when you ski across a slope instead of going straight downhill. Note in both photographs how the skier stands on the uphill edges of his skis to stop him slipping sideways down the slope

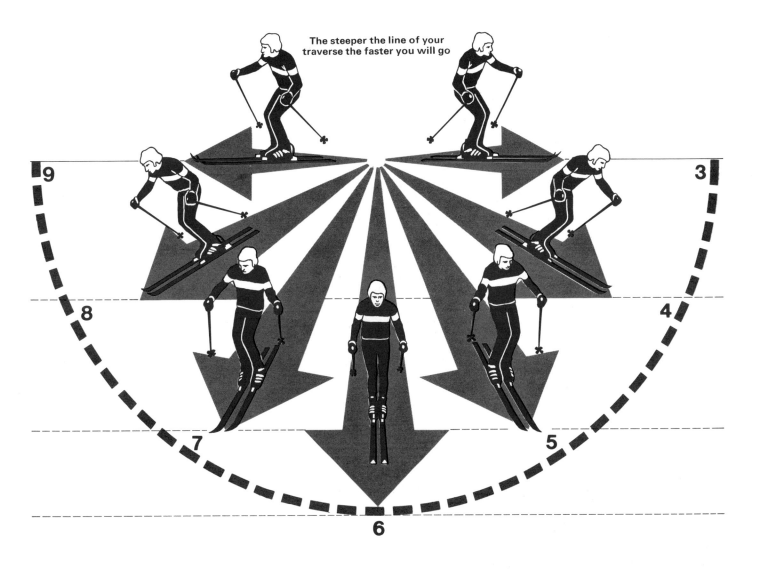

The steeper the line of your traverse the faster you will go

Let's learn the traverse

You will enjoy the traverse. All of us soon felt relaxed and safe doing it. More time is spent in the traverse position than in any other. Everybody, short of a downhill racer, comes down the mountain by doing a lot of traversing. And nine out of every ten turns begin from the traverse position.

So what is this delightful ski movement? It is when you ski *across* a slope instead of going straight downhill. Theoretically you make a traverse every time you ski in any straight line other than the fall line. As the fastest way down is to take the fall line, a traverse is obviously slower. But the speed of the traverse can vary, and depends on what line you take across the slope.

If you ski across the slope with the skis at right angles to the fall line you will hardly move, even on a steep slope. This is called the 'dead traverse'. Think of it as 'three o'clock'. Your skis are pointing at three; if your skis were pointing down the fall line they would be at six o'clock, and you would be doing a schuss.

When your skis point to seven o'clock you are in a traverse—but one so steep there is little difference from a straight downhill run.

Mostly we found we pointed our skis at about four o'clock.

Of course four o'clock on one slope is faster than four o'clock on another, but if it is too steep and fast you simply go back nearer three o'clock. The joy of the traverse is that it is up to you. Set your skis at the 'time' you want, and set your speed to suit yourself.

We start with the dead traverse. Master this position and the rest will follow. It is not really difficult, once you have got used to the idea that you must do something that will at first feel unnatural. But first the part that is natural.

How to traverse

Stand across a modest slope with both skis parallel and at right angles to the fall line. Put somewhat more weight on the downhill ski—the steeper the slope the more weight on the downhill ski. Allow your stance to be as natural and relaxed as you can. At this stage there is no need to press knees and skis close together to look stylish. If the skis are more than hip-width apart and it feels good —do it. We found a wide stance was more comfortable and gave us better balance. (If you are in a school where the instructor is cross unless you attempt the full stylish position with skis tight together from the word 'go', try to please him. You may be able to do it easily. Some can, but do not worry if you cannot.)

So far so good. But if the slope is anything at all, you may find yourself slipping sideways down it. That is not the idea at all— that is 'sideslipping', which we go on to explain in Chapter 13. Your intention is to ski across the slope, not slide down it, and to ski across a slope of any steepness you have to use your edges.

Push your knees and hips into the slope and the edges will bite into the snow. That will hold you. But it will introduce a new problem —stability.

If you simply push inwards with your knees and hips, you may fall into the slope. To counterbalance the inward thrust of knees and hips, you must lean out into the valley with your head and shoulders. Lean *out*?

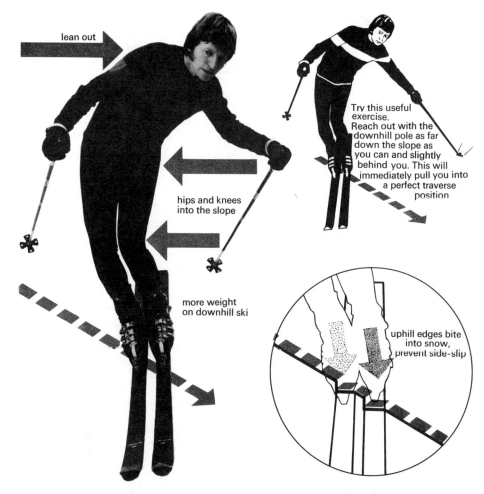

lean out

hips and knees into the slope

more weight on downhill ski

Try this useful exercise. Reach out with the downhill pole as far down the slope as you can and slightly behind you. This will immediately pull you into a perfect traverse position

uphill edges bite into snow, prevent side-slip

Left: The gravity test (see page facing) will help you understand about leaning out. *Above:* Both skis on uphill edges

Into the far away valley? Here is the essential point of the traverse which bothers most beginners and intermediates. It bothered all of us. Every instinct told us to hug the slope for dear life instead of leaning away from it. Instinct is wrong. Here is a simple demonstration to convince you. It convinced us. Stand with your skis across the fall line. Ask a friend to grab your ski pole and pull you down the slope. Your body will react naturally by settling into a perfect traverse position. Why? Because the person trying to drag you down the slope is giving a perfect imitation of the force of gravity. And to resist the force of gravity you move your own centre of gravity (the hips) in the opposite direction.

You have now assumed a famous position. The Americans call it the 'comma position'. The French dub it 'angulation'. Call it what you will, we rate this as the most important body position to be learned in ski-ing. Knees and hips into the slope. Head and shoulders into the valley. Force yourself into it. Find a steepish slope and see what instinct does for you. Lean into the slope and see what a tangle you get into. A few falls in this position may be worth any amount of theory.

It is all a question of balance. The steeper the slope the more you must edge your skis and weight the lower ski to stop yourself slipping downhill. The more you push your knees and hips into the slope, the more you must lean out with head and shoulders to compensate for the change in weight distribution over your skis, and the greater your degree of 'angulation' becomes.

Lean out into the valley

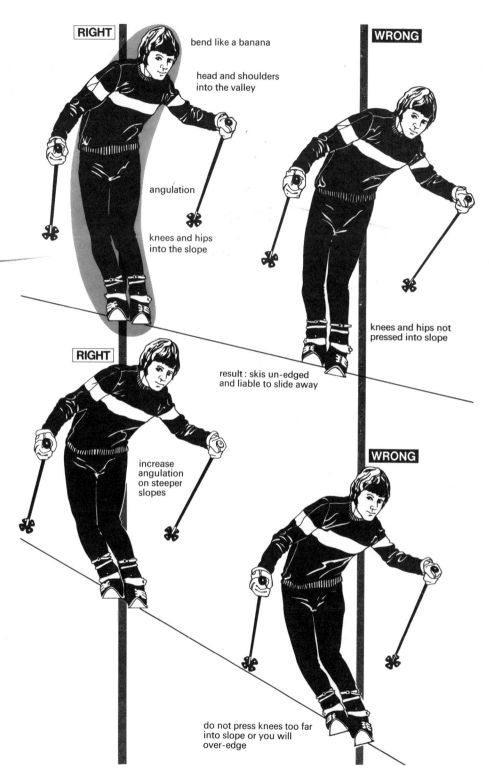

RIGHT

bend like a banana

head and shoulders into the valley

angulation

knees and hips into the slope

WRONG

knees and hips not pressed into slope

result : skis un-edged and liable to slide away

RIGHT

increase angulation on steeper slopes

WRONG

do not press knees too far into slope or you will over-edge

However, if your body is facing squarely forward in the direction of your ski tips you will find it almost impossible to push your knees and hips into the slope—unless you unlock your body line. To do this simply lean forward, bend your knees forward over your toe-bindings, and advance your uphill ski by about half a boot's length. Immediately you will feel freer, less rigid, more supple and able to bend.

This distance (half a boot length) should be reflected all the way up your body, so that your uphill knee, hip, arm and shoulder are all 'leading'. In other words your body assumes a stance very much like a boxer. Advancing the uphill ski turns the body away from the slope so that you lean naturally with head and shoulders in the correct position—into the valley. Enjoy the view. We found it helped a lot to keep telling ourselves this as we assumed each new traverse position after a turn. Look into the valley, enjoy the view. If you find yourself looking uphill, you are making a mess of it. And remember: *In the traverse position the uphill ski and uphill hip always lead.*

stance like a boxer

uphill hip ahead

lean forward

advanced uphill ski prevents ski tips crossing

Advance uphill ski half a boot length

Quite apart from setting your body in the right position, leading with the uphill ski performs another useful task. It prevents your ski tips crossing. Whenever you are traversing a slope there is a tendency for the uphill ski tip to wander downhill across the path of the lower one. By keeping the uphill ski advanced the tips cannot cross. If the uphill should slide down, it will merely come to a stop against the side of the lower ski's upcurving tip.

Your poles will give you additional balance in the traverse. Hold them with hands slightly forward and down, elbows a few inches away from the body, and both baskets to the rear and to the uphill side of the skis.

Above: Wrong ! Leaning into the slope instead of the valley.
Result : un-edged skis slide away and cross

Exercises

If you still feel awkward in the traverse here are two exercises which helped to loosen us.

1. Choose a gentle traverse line (say 3.30 on our clock system) and ski across a slope with knees flexed, moving gently up and down with a light, bouncing motion.

2. Choose a steeper slope and traverse across with the weight on the downhill ski and then lift the uphill ski a few times. You should, after a bit, still be able to keep your balance and it will remind you how little you need the uphill ski if you are in the right position.

Exercise 1   up   down   up   Exercise 2   lift uphill ski

WRONG   1   The skier leans into the slope

2   His feet start to slide away . . .

3   He falls into the slope

Falling foul of the 'fear factor'

Here is a classic demonstration of the 'fear factor' at work. This may sound like something from some Len Deighton spy thriller, but it is in fact a recognized term in ski-ing. What it boils down to is fear of the fall line. The beginner knows he is supposed to lean out into the valley. But instinct, especially the fear of falling downhill on a steepish slope, creates a mental block. He forgets what he has been taught. Fear of falling downhill causes him to lean inwards towards the false security of the slope. The result? He transfers most of his weight to the uphill ski. His centre of gravity is destroyed. His

balance is gone. His uphill ski slips because of the uneven weight distribution, and he falls into the slope.

Is your traverse a travesty?

Well, is it? If so, it could be due to any one or more of a number of bad habits. Before you begin your next traverse, flip through this mental check-list to make sure you are on the right track. For a steep slope:

Skis comfortably together. Uphill ski leading. More weight on lower ski.

Knees bent forward and rolled sideways into slope. Uphill knee leading.

Hips pressed into slope. Uphill hip leading.

Get hips right and body position will tend to follow naturally.

Body turned away from slope so that head and shoulders lean into valley, creating 'angulation'. Upper shoulder leading.

Hands held slightly forward and down. Uphill hand leads.

Arms held comfortably with elbows slightly away from body.

Poles pointing behind body and to uphill side of skis.

Eyes looking ahead; not fixed on what ski tips are doing.

3 The first turns

9 WHAT THE SKI WILL DO FOR YOU: Theory of the turning ski explained. Skidding and carving turns. 10 THE SNOWPLOUGH OR WEDGE TURN 11 THE STEM TURN. 12 THE BASIC SWING

9   WHAT THE SKI WILL DO FOR YOU

The art of ski-ing is turning. You turn to control your rate of descent. Of course you also turn if you want to avoid a hazard, or navigate a corner, but that is not the main function of turning on skis. The expert snaking quickly down the slope and the beginner making a series of long, slow turns have the same tactic: they are turning to control their rate of descent. If you go straight down the slope, you would go so fast you would not be able to stop or choose your direction. This is the single most astonishing discovery for people learning to ski—how quickly speed builds up on skis. In five or six seconds, no more, a beginner can feel quite out of control. You may drive a car at 60 miles an hour with relaxation; even 10 mph on skis seems supersonic.

The modern ski is a marvellous tool. It is specially built so that you can more easily turn and control speed and line of descent. Yet amazingly few skiers know *why* a ski turns. We certainly did not until we started writing this book. Ski lessons usually consist of being told to bend the knees, change the weight, plant the poles, and so on. Not one of us has ever had a lesson in any school which tells the skier why these movements help the skis to turn. You will find injunctions about knees and ankles and weight in the following chapters on turning, but we think it essential to relate all this to what it is supposed to do to the ski in the snow. We found that even expert skiers could not give us a reasonable answer to this basic question, and in the end we visited the research laboratories of a ski manufacturer (Rossignol) in search of a definitive explanation.

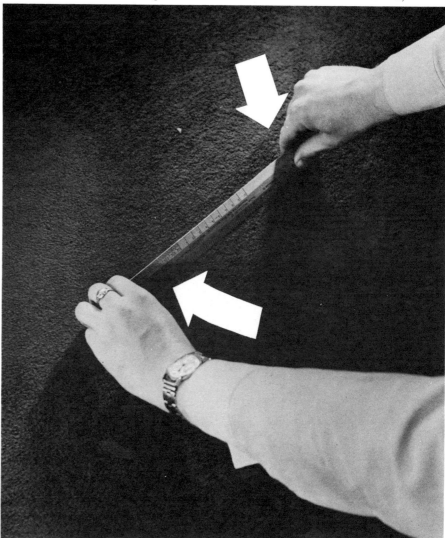

The answer turned out to be so helpful that we cannot understand why it is not explained to all skiers in their first lessons. It has helped our ski-ing even at this stage, and we are sure it will help you, whatever your standard.

The secret of the turning ski is in the 'sidecut' of the ski. Skis do not have parallel sides. They are 'waisted' near the bindings. A typical 205 cm (6 ft 8·7 ins) 'combi' ski has the following profile: maximum width at the front (the shovel area) 89 mm (3·5 inches); minimum width at the waist 69 mm (2·7 inches); maximum width at the rear 78 mm (3·1 inches). Note that it is wider at the shovel area than it is at the rear tail (as the diagram above shows). This is vital.

To understand how the sidecut turns our skis, we need to take a brief look at the most important ski-ing manoeuvre. It is called 'edging'. We say a ski is 'edged' when it is not entirely flat on the snow. Skiers do all that knee waggling and bending to edge the skis in some degree or other. Most of your ski-ing will be done on edged skis. If you could not edge the ski, you would never be able to turn or brake; all you would be able to do is ski down a mountain in a straight line. Edging is therefore the basic movement of ski-ing (though some ski schools place more emphasis on edging than others), and we will be returning to it in greater detail.

Whatever technical ski-ing movement you use to turn or brake, as beginner or expert, you edge your skis. This produces either a controlled skid or a 'carved' turn—about which more later. For the moment it is important to understand what the sidecut of a ski does when an edged ski is placed at an angle. Take a ruler and try the following experiment on a carpet of moderate pile. If you put the ruler flat on your carpet you can push it forward easily; sideways slightly less easily. Now place the ruler on its side. It can still be pushed forward quite easily, but it is harder to push sideways or in a diagonal line. A ski acts in the same way in snow—but with one vital difference. The ruler is not waisted; the ski is. Because of this sidecut, when a ski is edged and placed at an angle to the line of travel the side of the ski bites deeper into the snow at the front than it does at the rear. (It

is broader at the front.) It therefore exerts fiercer braking action at the front than the rear. So what happens? The ski pivots at the front. In other words, it turns. You can get the same effect with the ruler if you use weight as a substitute for sidecut to provide extra bite at one end. Edge the ruler and, holding it at each end push it diagonally across the carpet. Now, press down harder with the front hand while maintaining the same

amount of diagonal push at each end (see photo below). The ruler pivots around the end on which you are pressing the hardest. It is 'biting' the carpet harder at one end due to the extra weight, just as an edged ski bites the snow hardest at the shovel area. The result is identical. (In fact you can transfer your weight fore and aft on your skis in precisely the same way either to increase or minimize the effect of the sidecut.)

Stemmed turns

To see how you would exploit this in practice we need to take a look at 'stemming'. A skier who is going downhill with both skis parallel and who then places one ski at an angle to the other is said to be stemming. He is forming one half of a letter 'V', the apex of which is at the tips of his skis. The stemmed ski is at an angle across his line of descent. If he edges that ski on the *inside*, it will behave in precisely the same way as the ruler did when you tried to push it diagonally and on edge across the carpet. Because the edged ski is wider at the shovel than at the rear, it bites the snow better and brakes more fiercely at the front. The rear of the ski starts to catch up with the front, pivoting in precisely the same way as the ruler. What happens to the other ski? That, of course, is still flat on the ground. And, like the ruler when it was flat on the carpet, it has less resistance to being pushed sideways than if it were on edge. The pivoting force of the stemmed ski is greater than the flat ski's resistance to pivoting. The skis change direction, and the skier with them.

Stem turn: edged ski (right) is braking at the front and skidding so that skier turns

The tracks left by the stem turn above. Note skidded area (right)

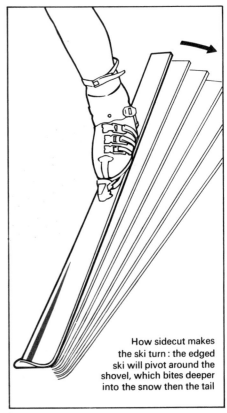

How sidecut makes the ski turn: the edged ski will pivot around the shovel, which bites deeper into the snow then the tail

We have made no mention so far of what the skier does with his weight. This is because a stemmed ski, thanks to the sidecut, will turn the skier, even if his weight is evenly distributed on both skis. You do not *have* to move your weight around, but you will turn much better if you do. And, in practice, 'weighting' is just as vital a part of turning as edging. You can vary your weight distribution, putting more weight on one ski than on the other, or shifting your weight towards the front of the skis, or towards the rear. If you bring your weight forward on a stemmed ski —by pushing your ankle down against the tongue of your boot—you will increase the braking action of the shovel area, just as you did by pressing on the ruler. Your turn will be correspondingly sharper.

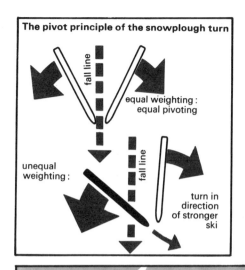

The pivot principle of the snowplough turn

equal weighting: equal pivoting

unequal weighting:

turn in direction of stronger ski

fall line

Plough turn

The first turn you will learn will most probably be the plough (unless you are using the short ski method, see pp. 184). Although most people find the plough easier to perform than the stem, its mechanics are a trifle more complex. Your experiments with the ruler will help you to understand exactly why the plough turn works. They will also enable you to grasp something which baffles every beginner: why it is that, when they put weight on one ski in the plough, they turn in the *other* direction.

Let us just take a quick look at the theory of the plough. It involves stemming *both* skis so that you are ski-ing down the slope in a full 'V' configuration with both skis edged. What happens if your weight is evenly distributed on both skis? Each ski is braking more fiercely at the front than at the rear. Each one is trying to pivot; but they are trying to pivot in *opposite* directions. The result is that both forces cancel each other out. You keep going straight on, but with a loss of impetus, or you even stop due to the skis expending their energy in vainly trying to turn. If you could arrange matters so that the pivoting action of one ski was far stronger than that of the other, then that ski would take over. Both skis would then pivot in the direction of the stronger ski. You can achieve this effect by transferring most of your weight to one of the skis. The shovel area of the weighted ski will then bite harder into the snow than that of the unweighted ski. This, as we have already seen, will increase the pivoting effect of the weighted ski, and decrease that of the unweighted one. And—presto!—you turn.

Carving

The theory of the turning ski so far explains how beginners' turns work in stem and plough. They are mostly 'skidded' turns—braking at the front, with a sideways skid of the tails.

The parallel turn as taught in most ski schools works in much the same way. The difference is that the skis are kept parallel throughout the turn. It is triggered by a series of body movements which enable the skier to place *both* skis at an angle to the direction in which he is travelling. This in itself has a certain pivoting effect. But, when the skier then edges his skis, the mechanics we saw in the plough and the stem take over and complete the turn. This type of parallel turn is faster and more efficient than either the plough or the stem, but it is still a skidded turn.

But ski-ing is faster and more sensuously enjoyable when there is no sharp braking at the front, no sideways skidding of the tails—when turns are carved in a smooth arc. Illustrated left is the difference between the two turns: trail A is a more jerky, skidded turn. Between the skidded turns the skier goes straight across the slope. Trail B is carved in a series of complete linked turns. This skier, as Warren Witherell puts it, has learned 'to use his skis as tools to carve an arc through the snow rather than as boards on which to ski sideways. . . . In a carved turn the entire edge of the ski passes through a single groove in the snow—as though it was on a rail.'

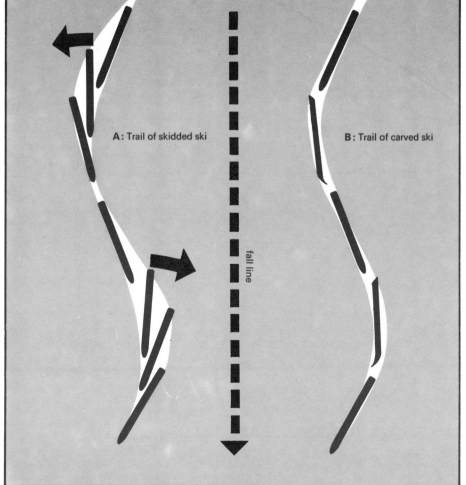

A: Trail of skidded ski

B: Trail of carved ski

fall line

To understand how you carve a turn you need to take another look at the shape of your skis.

The skis are waisted, as we have noted, but they are also cambered. The camber ensures that when you stand on your skis there is plenty of weight on the tips and tails. But the bulk of your weight still reaches the snow at the centre of the skis.

You get 'reverse camber' when weight is applied to the middle of the ski. Suspend a ski between chairs and press in the middle. The camber of the running surface is no longer concave but convex. When you are ski-ing, and edge a ski at speed, and so put it into reverse camber by the weight you apply, something very remarkable happens. The ski

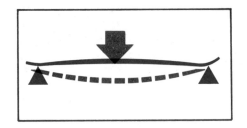

carves a turn. An edged and weighted ski pushed from the top of a slope would describe an arc as illustrated below right.

To understand how this is possible, take up the ruler again. This time place it flat on the carpet. Simulate reverse camber by pressing it down at the middle with your thumb whilst

lifting it up each end. Now, edge the flexed ruler as you might edge a ski. Roll it on to its side at an angle of up to 45 degrees to the carpet. Something is wrong. The last time you edged the ruler it maintained contact with the floor along its entire edge. Now you have bent it, it is making contact only at the middle (see photo below). Each end of the ruler is in the air. If a ski behaved like the ruler, it would be uncontrollable. We shall be dealing with the circumstances in which a ski will be both edged and in reverse camber. This is yet another reason for the sidecut. It ensures that the entire edge of the ski is kept in contact with the snow even when it is edged and thrown into reverse camber. This enables us to carve a turn.

How the flexibility and camber of a ski combine to distribute the skier's weight on the snow

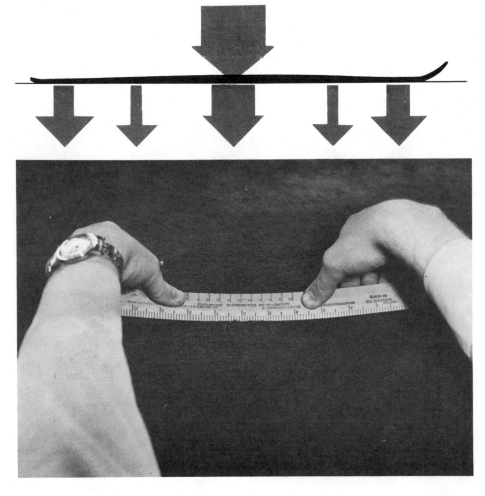

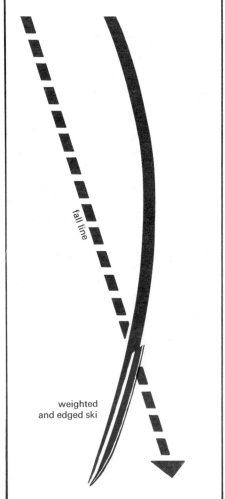

fall line

weighted
and edged ski

A further experiment will show you how this works. Take a thick piece of paper with a straight edge. Cut a shallow arc along the length of this edge. Now, flex the paper in the centre to simulate reverse camber, and 'edge' it on the carpet. Because you are not a ski designer it is improbable that the fit will be exact first time, but it will be abundantly clear that this is the way to keep the entire edge of the paper on the carpet when it is edged and flexed.

There are special ways of applying weight to force a ski into reverse camber: this is what the turning chapters are about. Once the turn has begun, centrifugal force—your speed—keeps the skis in reverse camber throughout the carving of the turn. It is up to you to balance yourself so that you stay clearly on the edges.

Three factors affect the radius of the carved turn: **1.** The sidecut of the skis. **2.** The amount of edging. **3.** The amount of pressure or impetus applied. The more the ski is edged and the more pronounced its sidecut, the greater the reverse camber that can be induced, provided the skier has enough impetus. And the greater the reverse camber, the tighter the turn. Watch the racers carve sharp, linked turns without skidding. Look at this picture—he is angled because he is edging his ski and keeping his balance. He has provided great reverse camber and is going at great speed. He can therefore carve a very sharp turn indeed. You will not ski as fast as that at first, but you will use similar forces to exploit the same superb qualities of the modern ski.

Reverse camber in action: a young competitor in the British championship slalom at Flaine, France

10   THE SNOWPLOUGH OR WEDGE TURN

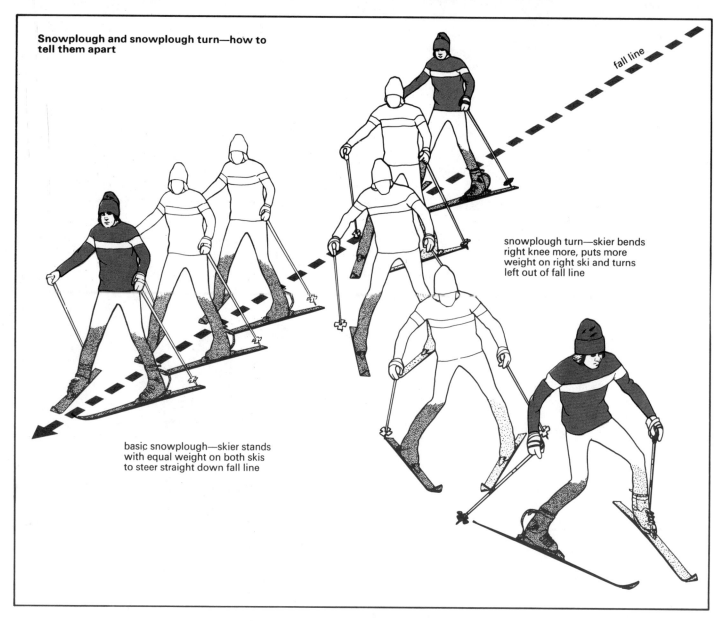

Snowplough and snowplough turn—how to tell them apart

fall line

snowplough turn—skier bends right knee more, puts more weight on right ski and turns left out of fall line

basic snowplough—skier stands with equal weight on both skis to steer straight down fall line

This is the turn people scoff at. They should not be so superior. A great deal can be learned from doing snowplough turns. Warren Witherell, the Director of the Burke Mountain Alpine Training Centre, makes potential racers do snowplough turns to get the feel of what the skis will do—how they will carve the turn for you if you get the edging and pressure right. The snowplough is so simple there is time to think and study what is happening.

You will not do snowplough turns in *ski évolutif*, which aims to discourage opening the skis. All of us, however, are glad we learned the snowplough turn.

Basically, the snowplough turn is a continuation of the straight snowplough. Then, you remember, we had to stand with equal weight on both skis to steer an even course down the fall line.

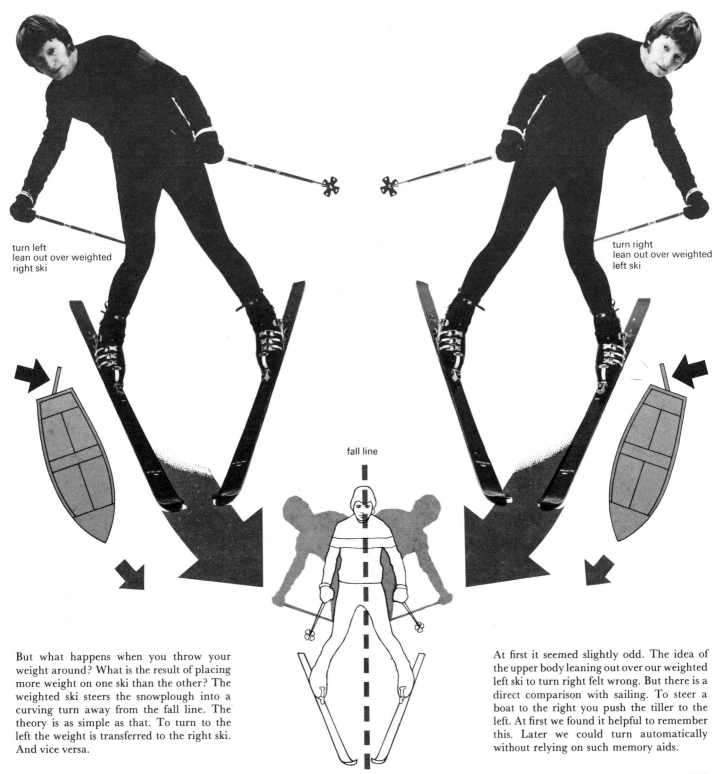

turn left
lean out over weighted
right ski

turn right
lean out over weighted
left ski

fall line

But what happens when you throw your weight around? What is the result of placing more weight on one ski than the other? The weighted ski steers the snowplough into a curving turn away from the fall line. The theory is as simple as that. To turn to the left the weight is transferred to the right ski. And vice versa.

At first it seemed slightly odd. The idea of the upper body leaning out over our weighted left ski to turn right felt wrong. But there is a direct comparison with sailing. To steer a boat to the right you push the tiller to the left. At first we found it helpful to remember this. Later we could turn automatically without relying on such memory aids.

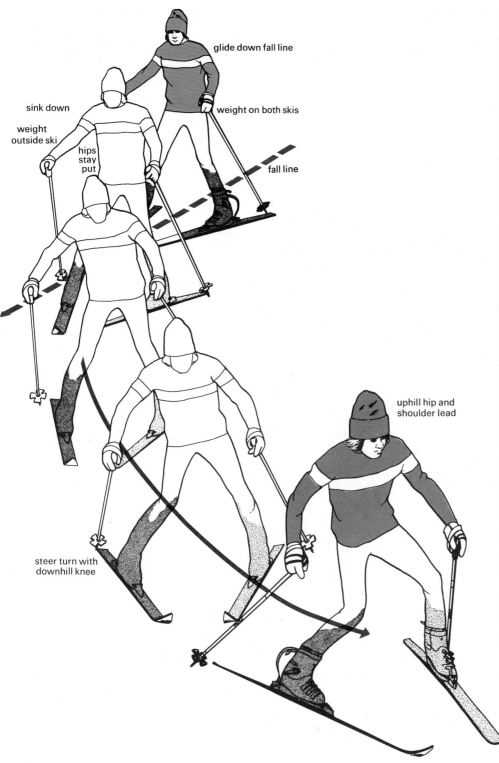

glide down fall line

weight on both skis

sink down

weight outside ski

hips stay put

fall line

uphill hip and shoulder lead

steer turn with downhill knee

How to turn out of the fall line

1. The skier starts with a straight snow-plough glide down the fall line. His weight is evenly balanced on both skis.

2. He sinks down. Both knees bend. But the right knee bends more as he transfers as much of his weight as he can to the right ski. Note the position of his hips, which stay exactly over the middle of his snowplough.

3. The 'V' of the snowplough position is unchanged. The tails of the skis are still the same width apart, but the right ski is doing all the work. It is now the downhill ski. It has also become the steering ski. Steering pressure is applied by a combination of two forces. **(a)** The skier's weight. **(b)** By the skier bending his right knee further forward in the direction of the turn, ie towards his ski tip and also slightly sideways towards the slope. The stronger the initial 'down' movement and knee-steering, the tighter the turn will become.

4. If the knees are bent correctly the upper body will lean out naturally over the downhill ski. (Some instructors emphasize this movement. They like it to be a positive, deliberate action—but more about that later.)

See how leaning out sideways from the waist has brought forward the left shoulder. As the skier turns this will become his uphill shoulder. This fits the basic rule: *uphill shoulder always leads*.

What happens to your edges

When both skis are equally weighted in the snowplough glide they are almost flat. There is just enough weight towards the inside edges to prevent you catching an outside edge.

When you turn, the amount of inside edge on the downhill ski should be slightly increased as you place your weight upon it (but don't overdo it). At the same time the ski on the inside of the turn should be kept fairly flat on the snow.

The additional amount of edge-set on the downhill ski should be enough to stop it brushing over the snow. You should feel it begin to bite gently and then start to track as your knee guides it into the turn.

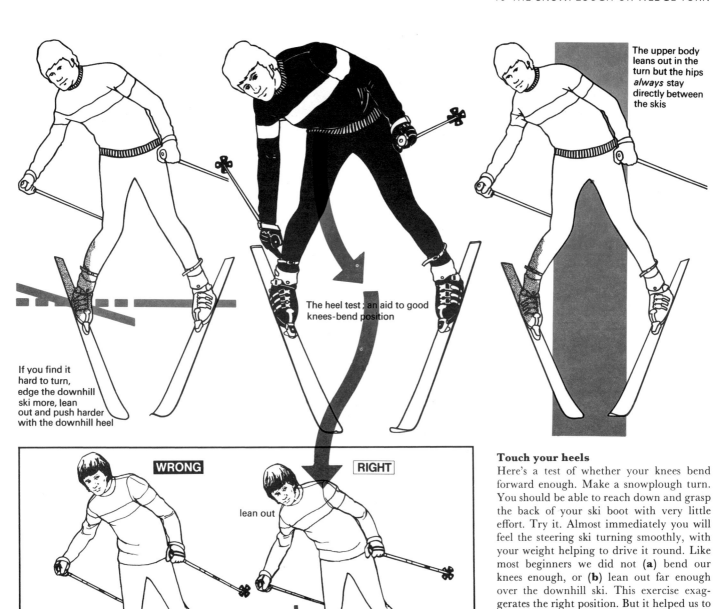

If you find it hard to turn, edge the downhill ski more, lean out and push harder with the downhill heel

The heel test: an aid to good knees-bend position

The upper body leans out in the turn but the hips *always* stay directly between the skis

WRONG

RIGHT

lean out

ski too flat

press harder with heel

edged ski begins to turn

Touch your heels

Here's a test of whether your knees bend forward enough. Make a snowplough turn. You should be able to reach down and grasp the back of your ski boot with very little effort. Try it. Almost immediately you will feel the steering ski turning smoothly, with your weight helping to drive it round. Like most beginners we did not (**a**) bend our knees enough, or (**b**) lean out far enough over the downhill ski. This exercise exaggerates the right position. But it helped us to feel what we ought to be doing.

How to cure the slide-away fault

Far left is one of our first attempts at the snowplough turn. It did not work very well, because our downhill ski kept slipping. Consequently we stopped turning. The cure is simple. First, slightly increase the set of the inside edge of the downhill ski. Probably the ski is too flat. If you are still not turning, try pressing down harder with your downhill heel and leaning out more. This should do the trick.

141

We tried to acquire a rhythm when practising linked snowplough turns. You should aim for a regular 'down'-'up' motion. Down as you leave the fall line, up as you return towards it.

If your skis cross or you fail to maintain the plough position, check what you are doing with your upper body. It is no use trying to twist the skis around. The edged and weighted ski will do the turning. And keep your hip still, too. Your hips should not stray out of their central position between the skis.

Doing the splits. You may find the skis going further away from you. You are almost certainly putting weight on the *outside* edge of the skis. This is dangerous. It is the inside edge that you weight.

Above: If you fail to maintain the plough position it is often the wrongly positioned upper body that is the cause. In this case the skier is trying to twist the skis around with his shoulders
Below: In a correct snowplough turn the hips never leave their central position between the skis

How to link your snowplough turns

glide down fall line

to turn into fall line:
stand up tall in gliding plough

fall line

to turn out of fall line: sink down, lean out, weight on downhill ski

end of first turn becomes beginning of the next

fall line

hen turning remember:
end downhill knee more
ep hips between skis

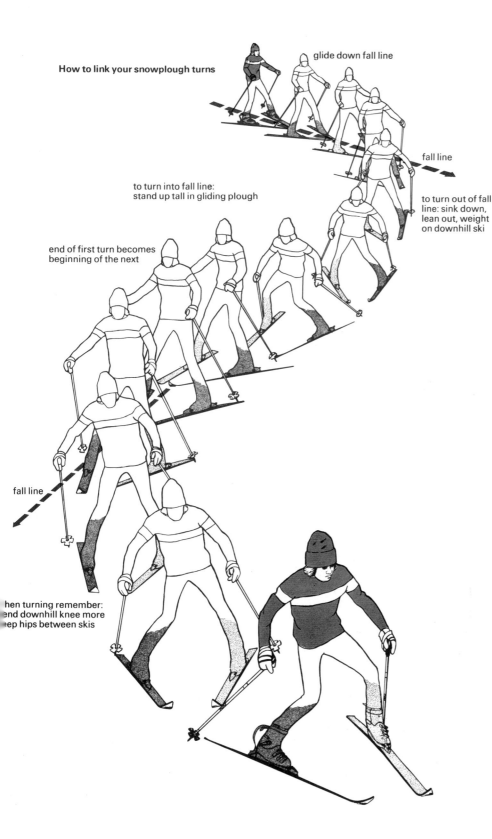

To return to the fall line release turning pressure by rising into a high gliding plough with legs almost straight

Link those turns

By stitching together a series of alternate right and left turns on a gentle slope we were able to build up confidence to ski almost any slope, provided it was wide enough.

To begin each turn *out of* the fall line we used the 'down' movement. We sank into a kind of semi-crouch. This helped us to apply turning pressure on the downhill or steering ski.

To turn back *into* the fall line, this is what we did. We used an 'up' movement, and released the turning pressure by rising into a high gliding plough position. Notice how our legs are *almost* straight.

At the same time we twisted our body slightly from the hips to face down the fall line.

Provided that the 'V' of the snowplough is maintained the skis will then run to the fall line.

When we returned to the fall line we resumed the basic snowplough glide position (both skis almost flat, and equally weighted).

From this position we were now ready to turn away again from the fall line in the opposite direction.

At first it is a good idea not to turn too far out of the fall line when trying a series of linked turns. The farther away you go the harder it is to turn back.

143

11 THE STEM TURN

Stem turn and snowplough turn—how to tell them apart

stem—skis open in mid-turn, but turn starts and finishes with skis together in traverse position

snowplough—skis remain open in broad wedge throughout turn

fall line

fall line

The stem was the first form of turn we had learned which enables us to link two opposite traverses without stopping. In a sense it is only a transitional turn, another step along the road from snowplough turn to the perfect 'stem christie', which was our constant goal. Yet we found it extremely stylish and satisfying. It's a useful turn to know in heavy or newly fallen snow. And, as one instructor pointed out to us: 'Many holiday skiers never progress beyond the stem-based stan-dard.' That is why getting it right is so important. *The stem turn may well form the basis of your ski holiday enjoyment.*

Snowplough and stem —how to tell them apart

Some beginners we spoke to found these two turns confusingly similar. To avoid confusion in your own mind, here's how to tell them apart.

In the snowplough turn we thrust the tails of both skis apart. Our skis remained in a 'V' throughout the turn.

In the stem turn the skier begins and ends his turn in a traverse position with skis together. Only in the middle of the turn—when he is turning from one traverse through the fall line into another—do the tails fan out. And even then it is only the uphill tail that is brushed out into a narrow half-plough shape. That is the difference.

1 From a moving traverse the skier opens a tail of the uphill ski. A *slight* up movement helps.

2 The uphill ski carries most of the weight. The ski stays flat on the snow.

3 Slowly, wait for it, the pressure on the top flat ski brings the skier round *across* the fall line.

4 The ski uphill in (1) is now becoming the downhill ski.

5 Weight stays on the downhill ski.

6 The lightly weighted uphill ski slides into the traverse position.

SPLIT THE TURN TO LEARN

Some people panic with the stem, impatient for the skis to turn them away from the speed-inducing fall line. This tends to produce jerky upper body movements to swing the skis around. Don't do that. You can think of the turn in two sections (see page 146). But note how little difference there is in both sections in upper body movements and ski pole position. The upper body stays quiet.

145

Split the turn

In most schools you learn the turn as one movement. We think you will learn it more quickly by splitting it in half. First practise turning from a traverse into a snowplough glide down the fall line. Then start on the second part—turning from a snowplough glide down the fall line into a traverse. Only then should you join the two halves together to make a complete stem turn. By this method of tackling the turn in two easy stages we found most of us made quicker progress. But it is essential, as in all new movements, to begin the practice on a gentle slope that does not frighten you.

Stem out

How to turn from a traverse into a snowplough glide down the fall line.

1. Move off in a traverse. Skis parallel. Uphill ski leading.

2. You will want to turn into the fall line. So open the tail of your uphill ski into a narrow half-plough shape. This tail-opening movement is known as 'stemming'—hence the name of the turn.

Some instructors teach the stemming movement with a slight 'up' motion of the body.

Some schools teach you to lift the uphill ski off the snow for the stem. That certainly gets you to realize that it should carry none of your body weight. It is worth doing the movement that way once or twice, and you may have to do it in some conditions where the ski edges might catch on ice or rock. Normally we found it best to learn to slide the ski into the stem and to slide it back.

3. At the same time as you stem out pull back your uphill ski. This will bring the ski tips alongside each other in readiness for the turn.

4. Until this moment your weight will have been carried on your downhill ski. Now—*gradually* is the key word—transfer your weight to the inside edge of your uphill ski.

5. As your weight increases on the inside edge of the stemmed uphill ski it will begin to turn of its own accord.

6. Keep turning until you face directly down the fall line. At this point your weight will be divided evenly between both skis. Retain this position and snowplough glide down the fall line.

7. Brake to a standstill by broadening your skis into a full plough.

weight on downhill ski
uphill ski ahead

Stemming out; practice by opening and closing the uphill ski during a gentle traverse

traverse

come up and stem out

traverse

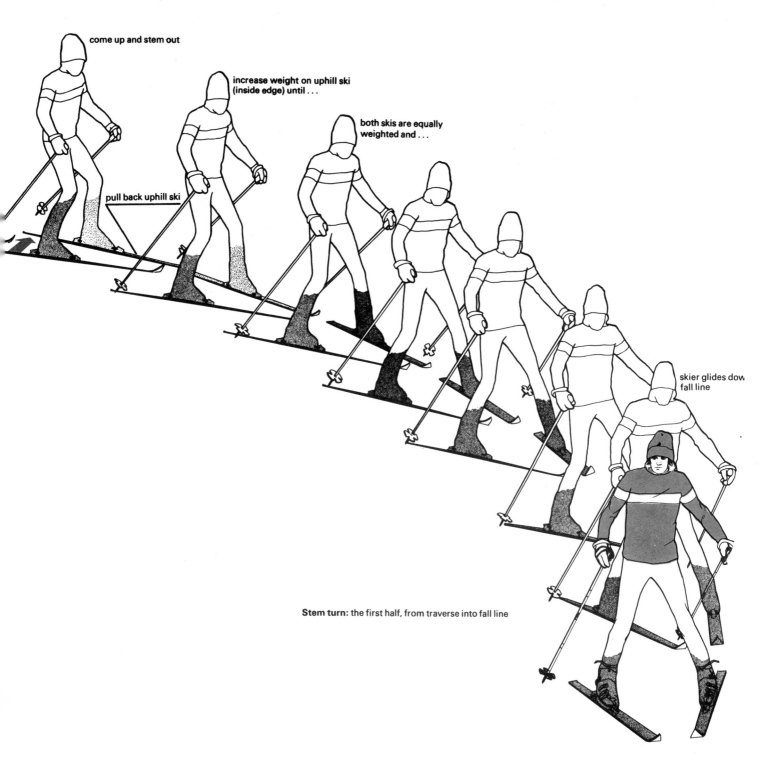

come up and stem out

increase weight on uphill ski
(inside edge) until . . .

both skis are equally
weighted and . . .

pull back uphill ski

skier glides dow
fall line

Stem turn: the first half, from traverse into fall line

Closing the stem

The second part of the turn—snowplough glide into a traverse.

1. Begin with a snowplough glide down the fall line. Equal weight on both skis.

2. To turn to the right, bend your left knee. Relieve most of the weight on your right ski, and transfer it to the left ski. This you do by angulation (leaning out from the waist over the weighted left ski with your upper body). Notice how your weight should be on the inside edge of the ski.

3. As you shift your weight to one side you will begin to turn. The outside of the turn is now the downhill ski of a new traverse. Your weight will already be placed correctly over it. Your uphill hip and shoulder are already leading, as they should be for a traverse. All that remains to be done is to bring the skis together.

4. Straighten up a little and allow the skis to run together.

5. You will now have completed the turn and will be traversing. Both skis are together.

Putting it together

Now you can do both halves of the stem. The next stage is to fit them happily together. Could we do it and make one complete turn? Suddenly there seemed to be a lot to remember. In the end we coped surprisingly well. The reason for this was the way we learned to link the two halves.

For our first attempts at a complete stem turn our instructors advised us to prolong our snowplough glide down the fall line. This proved to be a boon. It means we could concentrate on doing the first half of the turn properly. Then, snowplough gliding down the fall line, we had time to collect our thoughts before beginning the second part of the turn. The snowplough glide acted as a much-needed mental breathing-space in the middle of the turn.

As we improved we were able to shorten the time spent gliding down the fall line. After a while we did not use it at all. It took us a few days to the next step—a series of linked stem turns. When we had mastered the turn we were glad enough to do one, then stop, and prepare for the next. But soon enough we were trying two turns, then three, and then we tried to do the nursery slope without stopping at all. That is another great moment in ski-ing.

Smarten your stem

Balance is the secret of a good stem turn. It is balance that will enable you to take all the weight on one leg as you stem out with your uphill ski. Here are a couple of simple ski school exercises that will improve your balance and give you a smarter stemming action.

1. Ski in a traverse across the slope. With your weight on the downhill ski, raise the tail of your uphill ski. Repeat half a dozen times without letting your downhill ski slide away.

Say to yourself

Stem out. Lean out. Smoothly does it.

straighten up
let skis run together

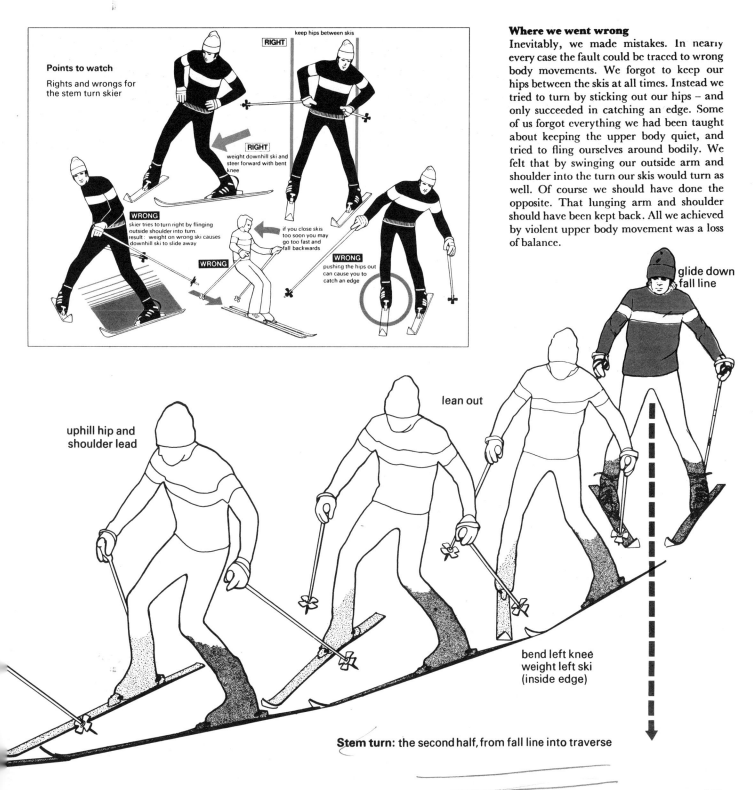

Where we went wrong

Inevitably, we made mistakes. In nearly every case the fault could be traced to wrong body movements. We forgot to keep our hips between the skis at all times. Instead we tried to turn by sticking out our hips – and only succeeded in catching an edge. Some of us forgot everything we had been taught about keeping the upper body quiet, and tried to fling ourselves around bodily. We felt that by swinging our outside arm and shoulder into the turn our skis would turn as well. Of course we should have done the opposite. That lunging arm and shoulder should have been kept back. All we achieved by violent upper body movement was a loss of balance.

Stem turn: the second half, from fall line into traverse

12 THE BASIC SWING

This is a relatively new movement in ski teaching. It seems to be catching on and overtaking the traditional progression from snow plough to stem, stem christie and parallel. We deal with all those turns, which are still widely taught, but we strongly favour the basic swing as a route to parallel. It also enables you to turn safely at speed, something we all long to do after a season. We commend the basic swing even to the more practised skier as an exercise, especially to anyone whose parallel is erratic.

The reason for learning to basic swing is this. Ski instructors realised by watching children that their leg movements were virtually identical to those of top ski racers. They were turning by knee and foot movements and *not* strong body movements. Body positions are only reactions to what the legs have done.

The new programme for beginners, which builds on the basic swing teaches: schuss, snowplough, snow plough turn, traverse and elementary side-slipping and then skips the stem turns in favour of basic swing.

The radical difference is that the stem and the plough are slow turns *across* the fall line. This is what makes them slow.

In the basic swing you ride down the fall line for a second and then turn with a controlled skid.

The turn is made up of three movements: a traverse (page 126), a snow plough glide (116) and a sideslip (154). When a skier can do it smoothly, you will see the following movement: He begins in traverse. When he feels like it, he splits the skis with an 'up' movement into a narrow glide and goes down the fall line. But this is not a stem turn. He does not transfer weight. On rising he puts his weight evenly on both skis. When he is proficient he then, fairly soon, bends both knees and steers the skis strongly forward and sideways in a skid. During this pivoting and skidding stage the v-stem disappears and the skis form wide-track parallel. The turn is completed by the skier continuing to sink and steer with both knees.

Note that in this description there has been no mention of the poles or upper body. All the concentration is on the feet and legs. The upper body follows the movement of the legs. And the poles are just held loosely.

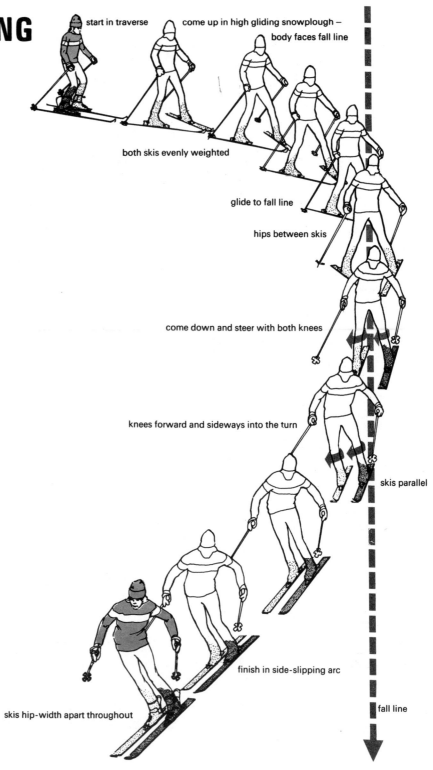

start in traverse

come up in high gliding snowplough –
body faces fall line

both skis evenly weighted

glide to fall line

hips between skis

come down and steer with both knees

knees forward and sideways into the turn

skis parallel

finish in side-slipping arc

skis hip-width apart throughout

fall line

Steps to the basic swing

Exercise 1: The traverse you know. Find a moderate slope and do a five o'clock traverse. Now with a 'down' movement roll your knees down the hill and relax your ankles. This will flatten the skis and you will slip.

As you do this, steer the skis with the knees and feet into a curve up the slope until you stop. This is called a side-slipping curve (see side-slipping, page 154).

Exercise 2: Practise this from the plough glide (or wedge) position (page 116). In this your skis are narrowly stemmed and you glide down the fall line. Do that for a few seconds and then turn out of the fall line by using a 'down' movement and push the skis round the corner in a pivoted skid. Push with your knees and drive the skis into hip-width parallel. You should resist the temptation to look down and see if the skis are parallel. If the movements are correct the skis will become parallel. These two exercises put together make the basic swing.

Let's try it. But it's essential to do it on a slope which gives some speed, yet has no fear for you. We have found that many people funk the turn when trying it on a stiffish slope. They stem and weight-transfer to turn across the slope instead of going down it. Here is the sequence:

1. Move off in a traverse with skis hip-width apart.

2. With an 'up' movement towards the fall line, open the skis into a narrow glide down the fall line, weight even on both skis.

3. Relax as you glide – remember you are not afraid of this slope. Take a moment or two to think about what you're going to do next on the turn.

4. Now sink and steer with both knees. Forget about your upper body.

5. If you have pivoted properly the skis will come into a wide track parallel in a new traverse position. Don't bring the skis together too soon. Let them glide into the fall line before you sink and steer.

6. Keep practising this on a moderate slope, doing one turn. Next try to shorten the time spent gliding down the fall line. You are aiming for a smooth continuous curving turn through the fall line.

Back to basics

At this stage it is important to revise side-slipping (page 154). This will improve your side-slipping curve at the end of the turn (actually no different from the uphill christie, (page 164).

From basic swing to parallel

Once you can turn as soon as you hit the fall line, you are ready for the achievement of a wide track parallel turn. You get there by making the stem or wedge narrower and narrower at each attempt.

Eventually you find yourself keeping the skis in hip-width parallel throughout – from the traverse into the fall line and through into the next traverse.

You will need good snow and a moderate slope to achieve this. It feels marvellous. It is not a full parallel – that needs more work – but if you can do this you are going to be able to ski anything.

More athletic skiers, especially children, may find they can link basic swings in the fall line without a traverse. The secret is to maintain a stable body position, facing down the fall line all the time. Combine that with a strong 'up-down' movement of the legs until the rhythm take over.

Where we went wrong

● Pivoting was difficult, and one reason at first was that we went too slowly. We made the stem too wide. It is easier if you have speed.

● If you have trouble getting the skis parallel – we did – it will be due to:
   (**a**) having too wide a plough; or
   (**b**) not steering with both knees at the same time. Result: you catch an inside edge and your hips swing out.
   (**c**) trying to bring the skis parallel too soon before you are actually in the fall line. You have to let the skis glide into the fall line before beginning the down movement.

● One of us fell a lot. He was trying too hard by using a violent upper body motion to get the skis round. Horrid – and inefficient, for violent movement like this from above will very likely make you catch an edge and will certainly tire you. The basic swing is a *knee* turn. Make the legs do the work. Keep the hips and bottom out of the act, firmly between the skis.

Say out aloud

Narrow the plough. Even weight. Stand tall in the fall line. Steer with both knees. Hips between the skis.

THE BASIC SWING: the three routes to parallel and beyond

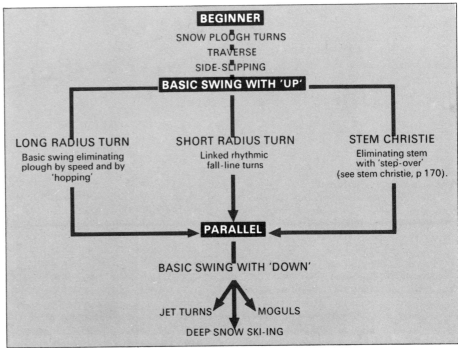

drop down and glide
to fall line

start in a traverse

The basic swing with 'down'

keep body
facing fall-line

rise up to normal height

steer with
both knees

skis parallel

Basic swing with 'down'

Once we had mastered the parallel we became aware that some good skiers appeared to be ski-ing very differently from us. We discovered that what they were doing was basically the same except for one vital difference: where we were stretching up to the fall line – as we have just described in the basic parallel – they were sinking down.

Which is right? Both. Our instructor reminded us how, as beginners, we learned to ride the bumps on a straight downhill run. We folded into a crouch to absorb the bump: failure to do this ensured an airbourne ride. That down movement also helps the skis to turn – for reasons we go into more fully on page 166. Turning with 'up' movements is fine for long turns on smooth moderate slopes. We found it easier to learn. But for short turns, steep slopes and bumps, a 'down' motion is best. Try it first on a smooth moderate slope, and imagine you are absorbing a bump (when you come to a real bump do the same thing – swallow it with a down motion).

Three exercises will give you the right idea for trying the down movement.

Exercise 1: Side-slipping with 'down' motion
Move off in a wide-stance traverse. Sink down into an exaggerated low position and release your edges with a pushing of the knees and feet away down the slope. This requires plenty of practice because the tendency at first is to fall into the slope.
Exercise 2: Uphill christie 'fan'
Start in a wide-stance 5 o'clock traverse. Sink down into the same exaggerated low

position and start to side-slip as before. But this time control the slide by steering uphill with the knees and feet and extending the legs. In other words, convert you slide into an uphill christie. Repeat from increasingly steeper angles until you are starting off directly down the fall line.

Exercise 3 : Plough swing

Move off down the fall line in a shallow gliding plough. Drop into the now familiar 'down' motion. Then start turning by extending both legs out of the fall line and steering with both knees.

Now for the real thing : the basic swing with 'down'. But before you set off, keep this vital ski tip in mind. Your body stays facing squarely down the fall line throughout the turn.

1. Sink into a low narrow gliding plough and go down the fall line.

2. Drive the skis out of the fall line, to the left, say, by extending the legs and steering right with knees and feet. As in the basic swing with 'up', this slowly converts the plough into a wide-track parallel.

3. To turn back into the fall line, sink down again into a low, narrow gliding plough and repeat as before, only this time turning left.

4. Repeat the last three movements so as to make a series of short linked turns down the fall line.

Say to yourself
Sink to the fall line, then stretch and turn.

Where we went wrong
Our main fault was allowing the upper body to rotate as we turned. The golden rule in fall line ski-ing is to stabilise the upper body and face downhill all the time. Face downhill! We would like that shout to you to penetrate to the ski slope wherever you are.

Ski-ing bumps
As we could ski parallel already, having learned our basic swing with 'up' motion, learning to parallel with 'down' gave us very little trouble.

The next logical step was to try out this newly acquired skill on a bumpy slope. We did it gradually, starting with gentle bumps and then moving on to bigger bumps and steeper slopes as our confidence grew. We had problems of course. Once again the upper body was not facing downhill. We found it helped to practice the following exercise :

● Move off across a bumpy slope in a traverse. Go down into a slide-slip over each bump, and stretch the legs into each hollow. Keep traversing and doing this with out turning, then turn on the last bump.

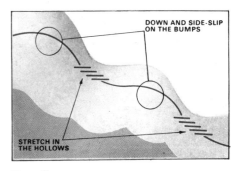

Deep Snow
● The same basic turning technique can be applied to deep snow ski-ing. What happens can best be explained in the diagram (below). As the skier comes to the fall line he goes down and the skis come up to the surface of the snow. As he turns up and out of the fall line the skis sink down again beneath the surface. In effect, the deep snow skier is ski-ing a trajectory with as many ups and downs as a mogul slope.

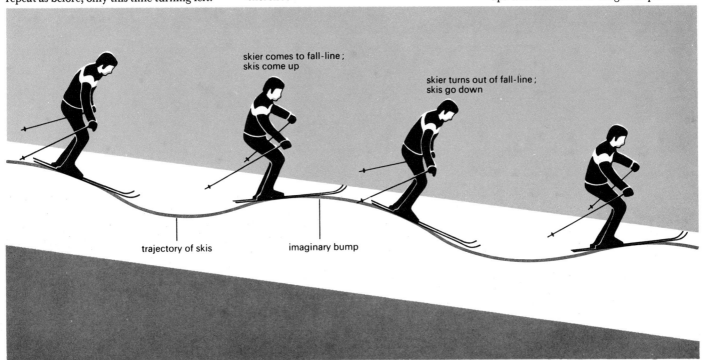

skier comes to fall-line ; skis come up

skier turns out of fall-line ; skis go down

trajectory of skis

imaginary bump

KNEES . . KNEES . .   KNEES . . KNEES . . KNEES . .

154

HAVING TROUBLE?
TRY THE KNEE-PUSH

If you have any difficulty with the basic swing – or whenever you feel things are not going right – try this knee-push exercise. We love it. Get yourself into the position of Alasdair Ross (left) on a tolerable slope, with one ski flat and the other edged in a small plough. Put your hands on your knees with the sticks just trailing. You are going to keep them there. Push off, in the nicest sense. As you move push both knees into the hillside, increasing the pressure. Make both bent knees angle into the hillside. Try and feel your hip going with the knees (this bit we found a little trickier). And forget about everything else – forget about upper body position, this shoulder or that. Later on you can remember to drop the downhill shoulder. Now you should just enjoy the ride round the corner. As you come round, bend forward more from the knees – and stay low. Whatever you do, make no heel-thrust movement, no jumping – nothing. You are ski-ing with your knees only.

Try to link turns just by rolling the knees – nothing else. As you go faster the skis will come together. But don't worry about that – it's called parallel ski-ing.

WRONG: Hip over ski, not into hillside.

PRACTISING THE BASIC SWING

1 Start with a small plough, upper ski on edge, knees bent forward, upper body quiet, poles behind.

2 As the ski turns you – and it is the ski doing the work – press the knee of the edged ski more into the hill. This edges it more. Upper body quiet.

3 Increase the pressure – knee into the hill and forward.

4 Knees into the hill and forward. The plough will tend to disappear so you end in a wide track parallel. Keep going, pressing down and forward with the knees.

POINTS TO REMEMBER

Small plough, edged ski.
Press, press into the hill with knees and hips. Push the knees forward and stay down and forward.

4

Lessons for intermediate skiers
13 SIDE-SLIPPING.   14 SIDE-SLIPPING ON THE MOVE.
15 THE UPHILL CHRISTIE: 'Up' and 'down' un-weighting. 16 THE STEM CHRISTIE.
17 THE PARALLEL CHRISTIE: Using the poles. Beating the fear factor.
How to turn with 'down' un-weighting.

13   SIDE-SLIPPING

Facing page: Side-slipping looks deceptively simple. Just release the uphill edges and away you go . . . But the delicate edge-control required needs much hard practice

Below: Learning the side-slip calls for a steeper slope than the one in the picture. But the skier's smooth track illustrates perfectly how you can lose height without having to turn or schuss downhill. (Here the skier has checked his side-slip by re-setting his uphill edges)

Side-slipping looked easy the way our instructors did it. 'Just release those uphill edges, and let your skis drift gently sideways down the slope.' When we tried it for ourselves we realized it was not so simple. There is a knack to side-slipping. Complete relaxation is a part of it. So is the ability we've mentioned already to 'feel' the snow with your feet. We did not master it straight away. We edged too much—due to our training. The mini-ski pupils found it easier, because edging is played down in their basic flat parallel turns on easy slopes. We persevered, and were glad of the extra time we spent trying to do it right. The gentle art of side-slipping is one of the most important basic skills of ski-ing.

Side-slipping enables you to lose height with control and comfort without having to turn or schuss downhill. Sometimes during a traverse we found ourselves crossing a steepish wall which inhibited us from turning towards the fall line. That is when we found the side-slip invaluable. We just slid down the wall until the gradient of the slope became manageable.

Learning the side-slip calls for a smooth, steep slope with a reassuring run-out at the bottom. This time it is no use trying to begin on a gentle incline. The steeper the slope the easier it is. And the less chance you will have of snagging your downhill edges.

How we learned to do the side-slip

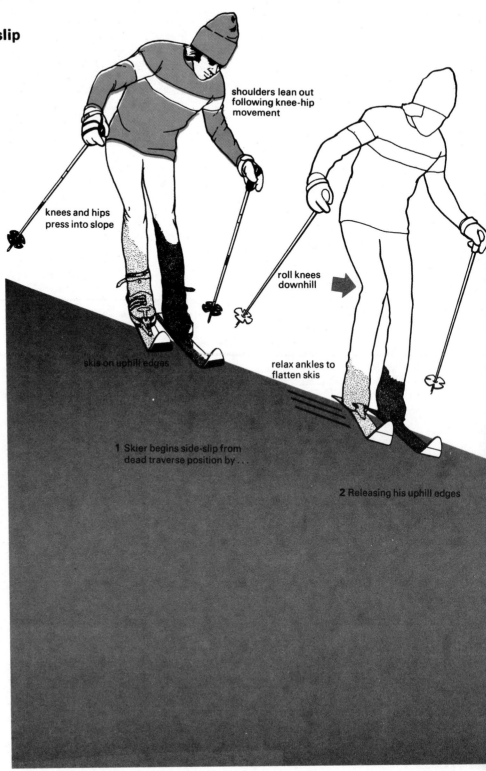

shoulders lean out following knee-hip movement

knees and hips press into slope

roll knees downhill

skis on uphill edges

relax ankles to flatten skis

1 Skier begins side-slip from dead traverse position by . . .

2 Releasing his uphill edges

Here we are standing across the slope in the dead traverse position, skis close together. Our weight is mainly on the upper edge of the downhill ski. The steeper the slope the more we edge the downhill ski. The uphill ski, hip and shoulder are leading. Knees and hips are pressed into the slope to hold us on our uphill edges. The upper body is leaning out to give a good angulation on the steep slope. The downhill pole is well clear of the snow so that it will not obstruct our movements.

Now all that is needed to begin to side-slip are two simple movements.

1. We relax our ankles.

2. We roll our knees away down the slope. This is enough to lower our skis until they are off their uphill edges and resting almost flat on the snow.

Immediately we begin to feel ourselves sliding sideways down the fall line.

What has happened? Having released our uphill edges (our brakes) there is nothing to hold us on the slope. The weight of our body pressing on the flattened skis is sufficient to set them moving. All this happens by knee and ankle movement—you do not relax edges by sticking your bottom down the hill. Keep the movement confined to the legs. Your hips should move as little as possible.

How to stop? Easy. To check your side-slip and come smartly to rest push your knees sideways into the slope. This sets you on your uphill edges again.

WRONG

Never try to flatten the skis by pushing your bottom out like a hula-hula dancer. You can easily catch your downhill edge and fall

3 and 4 He slides down fall line in controlled side-slip

knee action re-sets uphill edges, checks side-slip

push knees and hips sideways into slope to stop

fall line

5 Stops by smartly re-edging his skis

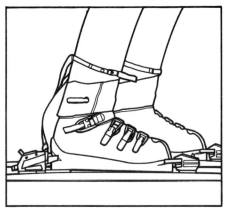

Uphill ski leads, as in the traverse

Where we went wrong

1. It is unnerving when you release your edges and the skis begin to slide. The common response is to put some weight back on the uphill ski to steady yourself. The result is that your skis come apart and you will fall. If you get a shock at the speed you go, simply put your knees into the hillside. The skis will edge and you will stop. If the slope is really steep, grind your heels into the snow.

2. The skis move apart and become more difficult to control. The usual problem is to stop the downhill ski from side-slipping faster than the uphill ski. We often got near to doing the splits.

There were two possible reasons for this.

- We had not leaned out far enough over the downhill ski—so there was too much weight on the uphill ski. Result: lower ski broke away through insufficient weight.
- We failed, perhaps, to roll the uphill knee sufficiently downhill when starting the side-slip. The uphill ski had too much edge and was slower.

Either of these faults will cause the uphill ski to drag more than the downhill one. It gets left behind. If, on the other hand, the uphill ski drags *less* than the downhill one, then that does not matter. It simply snuggles up alongside the other ski.

Skier unnerved by skis sliding away, puts weight back on uphill ski to recover balance

Skier has not rolled uphill knee sufficiently downhill to un-edge ski. Result: uphill ski has too much edge, causing skis to drag apart

If in trouble — stop! Simply push the knees sideways up the slope to re-set your edges

WRONG

WRONG

(a)

The diagonal side-slip; forward (*below*), and backwards (*above*)

(b)

Practice the zig-zag to improve your side-slip

3. First side-slips are rarely the neat sideways slide with skis always at right angles to the fall line. Sometimes the tips wander uphill. Sometimes they go downhill. Yet you must aim at getting tips and tails to go down at the same rate.

(**a**) Tips swinging up the slope . . . too much weight on the heels. We are leaning back.

(**b**) Tips swinging down the slope . . . too much weight on the front of the ski. We are leaning forward too much. Make a virtue of this correction exercise by practising the diagonal side-slip.

The diagonal side-slip

Once you are able to side-slip straight down the fall line you can put this simple technique of readjusting your fore-and-aft balance to work in a more positive way.

By bringing your weight forward onto your toes you will find you can side-slip diagonally forward. By transferring your weight to your heels and leaning back slightly you will be able to reverse your direction and side-slip diagonally backwards. Going backwards is harder.

An easy exercise to improve your side-slip

Zig-zag. Practice the diagonal side-slip by zig-zagging backwards and forwards down the slope. Use a friend's poles to mark out a makeshift slalom course to negotiate. Or use your own. You should be able to side-slip without your poles.

14 SIDE-SLIPPING ON THE MOVE

shallow traverse

bend knees
to lower the body

roll knees away
to flatten skis

ski tips
move up slope
as skier side-slips

rise up and
re-set uphill edges
to resume traverse

'You can get down any mountain with a side-slip,' we were told. We had not tried a whole mountain, but we had used the moving side-slip to get down sharp, narrow bits of mountain where, we suspected, we would still otherwise have been summoning up the nerve to try a turn. You do the moving side-slip from a traverse. Speed is easily controlled. It may be that you choose to side-slip slowly to a point where you can continue the traverse and turn normally, but even if the speed is slower the rate of *descent* need not be. You are taking a short cut, as the diagram suggests. Here are the movements:

1. Begin by ski-ing across a wide, steep slope in a shallow traverse. As before, when you want to introduce the side-slip you must flatten your skis. So roll your knees away from the slope to release your uphill edges.
2. But this time there is something else to learn. As your knees roll away, bend them. The movement comes almost automatically. You will have no trouble in doing it.
3. Bending the knees lowers the body into more of a sitting position. This has two advantages. It improves your balance by lowering your centre of gravity; and it makes it easier for you to push down with

your heels. Feel the snow crunching under the weight of your body concentrated on your heels.
4. As soon as your skis are flattened you will begin to side-slip. By maintaining the pressure on your heels your tails go down, and your tips will move up the slope by about a foot. But your momentum will keep you moving forward. You will continue to drift across the slope in a forward diagonal side-slip.

Make a conscious effort to remember that *most of your weight is on the downhill ski*. Otherwise you should be completely relaxed.

Rise and sink

We were taught to side-slip by introducing a 'down' movement (the knees bending as they roll away from the slope). Some ski schools teach an alternative method which starts with an 'up' movement. In this the skier extends his body upwards from the traverse position before sinking down. The effect is to create a stronger, more positive 'down' motion. There is probably little to choose between either method; try them both, and use the one you find suits you best.

Where we went wrong

1. We fell into the hillside. Basic fear usually lay behind this. We were frightened to turn and look into the valley as we should. We looked for comfort into the hillside. This brought the wrong shoulder round frequently with the result that we put a lot of weight on the uphill ski.

2. Once we had got the knack of riding on our downhill ski, we sometimes found ourselves in the odd position of one leg down the mountain and unweighted uphill ski still up the mountain. Very awkward. Very inelegant. We resolved: we would keep our skis together. We would nuzzle our kneecaps together, and produce that nice noise of ski edge against ski edge.

Ski tips to remember

When passing from a moving traverse into a side-slip the three main points to remember are:

(**a**) roll knees away from slope to flatten skis.

(**b**) flex knees slightly to bring weight more easily on to your heels.

(**c**) maintain a steady downward pressure with the heels.

The three movements happen almost simultaneously. The legs do all the work. The upper body remains undisturbed. This makes for better balance. Balance breeds relaxation. And you will never learn to side-slip properly *until you relax.*

How to stop: Once you have decided that you have side-slipped enough and want to begin a new traverse, do as follows:

1. Rise up from your slight sitting position.
2. Press knees into the slope again.
3. Uphill edges bite and the side-slip stops.
4. Press forward on your boots and start tracking forward in a traverse.

If you wish simply to slow your side-slip

leaning into slope brings wrong shoulder round, puts weight on uphill ski

WRONG

make conscious effort to keep knees and feet together to prevent skis sliding apart

WRONG

down, a 'touch of the edges' is not always enough, especially if the slope is steep or icy. Then you bring an additional braking force into action. You turn your skis at a greater angle to the direction in which you are travelling, twisting them across your line of movement by bringing the tips slightly uphill. This usually levels out your descent, so turn your shoulders to keep them at right angles to your new direction. We found that this dual braking action was usually essential if we wanted to stop on a sharp hill.

Error: We found ourselves jabbing at the downhill slope with the poles in an attempt to reduce our speed. Once the pole caught the downhill ski and we crashed. It is stupid to attempt to control speed by using the pole. It is better to sit down. It is easier to use the edges or turn the ski tips more uphill. Remember: the flatter the skis, the faster the side-slip. A *gentle* roll of the knees into the hill reduces speed.

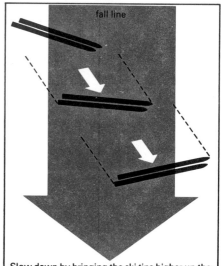

fall line

Slow down by bringing the ski tips higher up the slope until the skis are at a greater angle to the direction in which you are travelling

15 THE UPHILL CHRISTIE

Ever since we began ski-ing we had watched —and envied—the experts who could inscribe such fluid and graceful turns over the snow without ever opening their skis. Theirs is the art of parallel ski-ing, that ability to turn in a complete arc through the fall line with both skis seemingly glued together. Like all beginners we wanted desperately to do the same. We longed to ski parallel.

The uphill christie was our first introduction to parallel ski-ing. The turn takes its name from Christiania, the old name for Oslo, where this technique was first pioneered in the 1860s. The term 'uphill christie' itself had a formidable ring of professionalism and expertise about it. In fact we already knew the three basic elements as they are taught in Europe; traverse, side-slip, knee steering. It was only a question of linking them together to produce the skidded version of the uphill christie. As one instructor put it: 'It's nothing more than a curving side-slip.'

The uphill christie is the first turn to be taught in which the skis remain parallel from start to finish. It is a stopping turn used to bring the skier to a halt at the end of a traverse

Uphill christie with 'down'

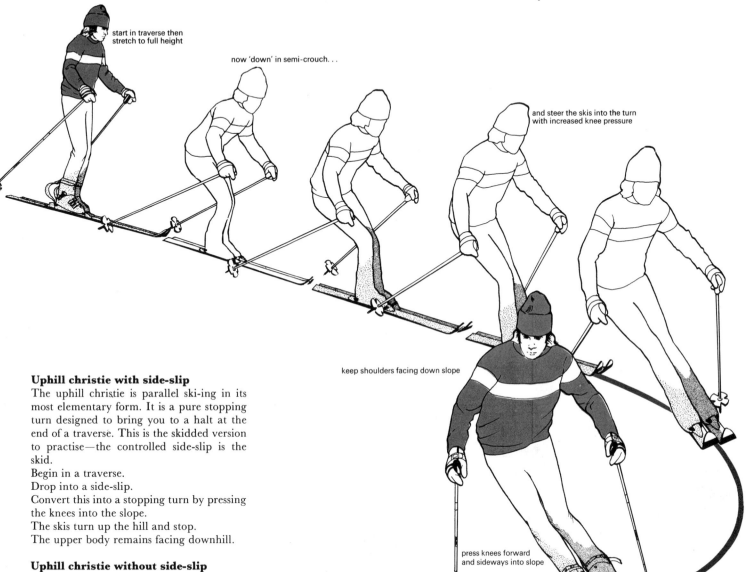

start in traverse then stretch to full height

now 'down' in semi-crouch. . .

and steer the skis into the turn with increased knee pressure

keep shoulders facing down slope

press knees forward and sideways into slope

Uphill christie with side-slip

The uphill christie is parallel ski-ing in its most elementary form. It is a pure stopping turn designed to bring you to a halt at the end of a traverse. This is the skidded version to practise—the controlled side-slip is the skid.

Begin in a traverse.

Drop into a side-slip.

Convert this into a stopping turn by pressing the knees into the slope.

The skis turn up the hill and stop.

The upper body remains facing downhill.

Uphill christie without side-slip

This is the carved version to practise.

Begin in a steepish traverse—say, 5 o'clock. Stand upright.

Now bend quickly at the knees and press your knees in to the slope. You will gradually turn up the hill, riding on the uphill edge of the downhill ski.

We go into the difference between skidded and carved turns later—and have mentioned them in the chapter on what the ski will do for you (Chapter 9). Try to do more and more uphill christies without side-slip.

The ups and downs of un-weighting

As with the direct side-slip from a moving traverse, we discovered there are two ways of doing the uphill christie. One uses an 'up' movement to trigger the initial turn. The other relies on a 'down' motion. Both methods produce the same result—it helps the skis to turn. We thought 'up' un-weighting was slightly easier.

The uphill christie is the first turn to introduce the technique known as 'un-weighting'. Briefly, un-weighting is an aid to easier turning.

Think about it. Why is it hard to make a ski turn?

Answer: because you are standing on it. The weight of your body is pressing it down hard on the snow. Therefore any force which is going to turn the ski must also be strong enough to turn you with it.

But what would happen if you were to remove your weight?

The ski would slide round with very little effort.

Obviously the skier cannot miraculously step on and off his skis at will. Instead he cheats. He uses a quick 'up' movement of his body. For the merest fraction of a second this takes his weight off the skis. A fraction of a second doesn't sound very long, but it is time enough for the skier to start his skis turning. Once they have begun to turn, other forces come into play; but parallel ski-ing as we know it would be impossible without the vital knack of un-weighting.

Try the bathroom scales test

If you think un-weighting is a myth, stand on the bathroom scales when you get home and see for yourself. Try 'up' and 'down' un-weighting. In each case you will see the needle flip back towards zero as you un-weight.

'Up' un-weighting

This is un-weighting with the help of an 'up' movement of the body. Stand on the flat with skis parallel. Flex your knees to give you more of a spring into the 'up' position. Now bounce erect, as if you were reaching up to your full height. Try to come forward slightly on your toes at the same time. But be sure your skis remain flat on the snow. The effect is to release your weight from the tails of your skis. In a turn this would enable them to start skidding round. Up un-weighting keeps the weight off the skis for a shade longer than down un-weighting.

'Down' un-weighting

The same result is achieved, but this time only a 'down' motion is used. Stand with skis together. Now suddenly bend your knees and drop into a crouch. Do it as fast as you can. You should be able to feel your feet almost coming off the ground for a split second.

Below left: 'up' un-weighting; rise up and slightly forward to your full height

Below right: 'down' un-weighting; bend the knees and drop into a crouch

Wrong! This skier tried to turn the skis with his upper body. Instead of facing down the slope he leaned into the slope which brought his weight onto the uphill ski. Result: the skis broke away from under him and he fell

Uphill christie with 'up' un-weighting

1. Start in a moderately steep traverse. Both skis on uphill edges. Uphill ski leading. Most weight on downhill ski.

2. Flex knees slightly in preparation for 'up' movement of the body.

3. Now rise up. Reach for the sky with your head as if bringing yourself to your full height.

4. Almost simultaneously flatten your skis slightly. The 'up' motion which straightens your legs automatically helps to pull your knees away from the slope. This in turn releases your uphill edges.

5. Gradually sink back into your original semi-crouch position. As you do so, drive your knees forward along the line of the skis and steer them into the turn. Remember that most of your weight must still be on the downhill ski.

6. Steer your skis into the uphill turn with your knees and push forward and sideways with the knees. You will begin to feel your edges biting. Keep both your shoulders facing down the slope as your skis come around. Eventually you will skid to a stop. Ideally, though you should, on a hill, cut down on the unstable skidding and stop by the fact that your edged skis are pointing uphill.

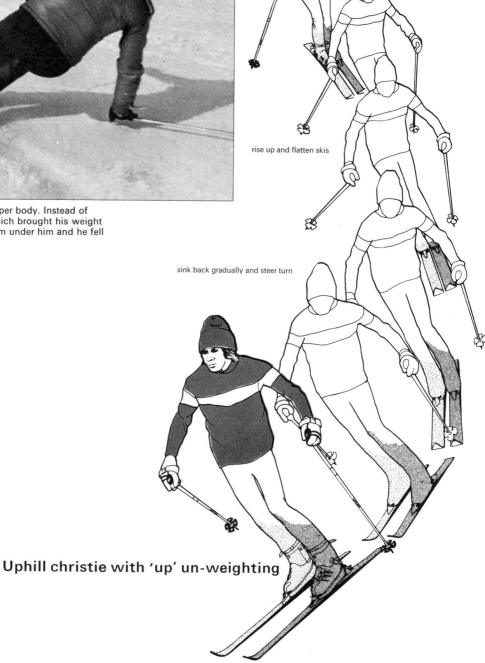

steep traverse

flex knees

rise up and flatten skis

sink back gradually and steer turn

Uphill christie with 'up' un-weighting

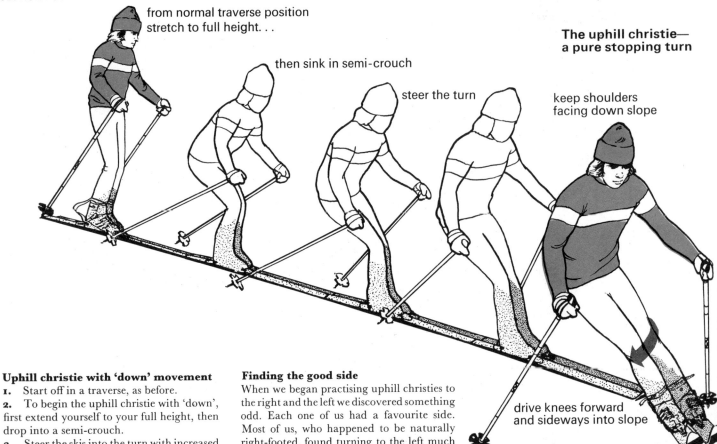

from normal traverse position stretch to full height. . .

then sink in semi-crouch

steer the turn

keep shoulders facing down slope

The uphill christie— a pure stopping turn

drive knees forward and sideways into slope

Below: uphill christie with 'down'. Increased knee pressure forward and sideways into the slope, together with angulation over the weighted downhill ski, steers the turn up the slope

Uphill christie with 'down' movement

1. Start off in a traverse, as before.
2. To begin the uphill christie with 'down', first extend yourself to your full height, then drop into a semi-crouch.
3. Steer the skis into the turn with increased knee pressure. The knees go forward and sideways into the slope until you can feel your edges biting. Remember to keep your shoulders facing down the slope as your ski tips turn uphill.

Finding the good side

When we began practising uphill christies to the right and the left we discovered something odd. Each one of us had a favourite side. Most of us, who happened to be naturally right-footed, found turning to the left much easier. Nearly all skiers have a good and bad side. We never lost our preference entirely. But extra practice on our bad side enabled us to turn right or left with much greater ease.

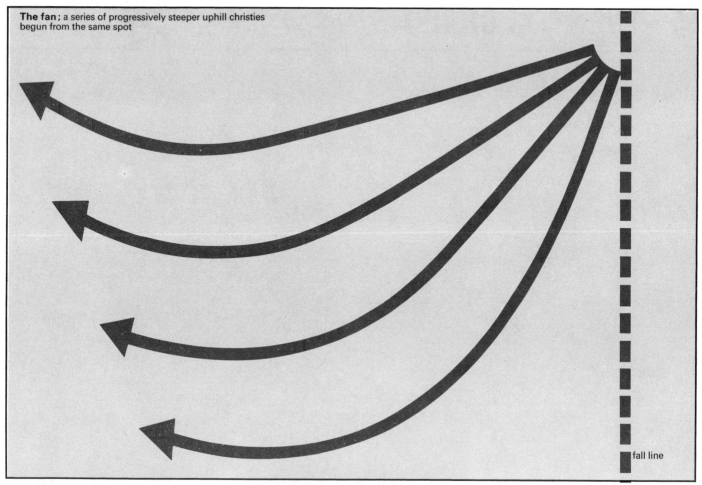

The fan; a series of progressively steeper uphill christies begun from the same spot

fall line

Fanning down the slope

Having worked hard at improving our 'bad' side, we began an exercise known as *the fan*. This was a series of uphill christies. Each one started from the same spot on the slope, but each time the line of descent became progressively steeper.

It was easy to see how this particular exercise got its name. Our ski tracks radiating from the single starting point resembled the ribs of a fan.

The idea was to teach us how to make longer, sweeping turns from increasingly steeper angles. In the end we were almost starting from the fall line. This, our instructor told us afterwards, is exactly how it feels when you complete the last half of the stem christie turn.

16 THE STEM CHRISTIE

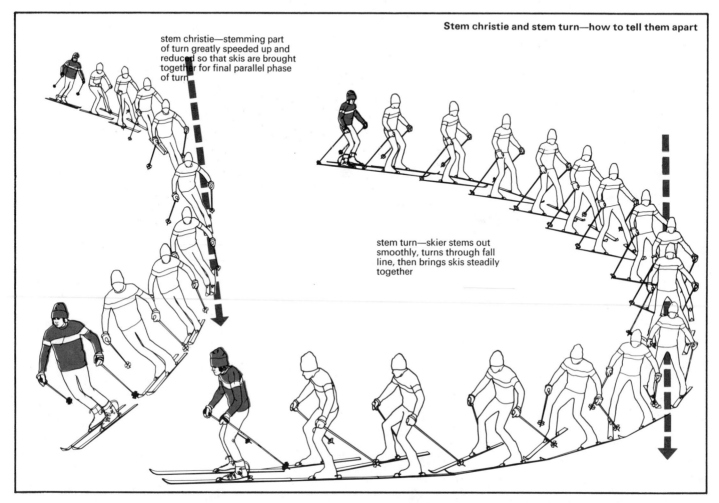

stem christie—stemming part of turn greatly speeded up and reduced so that skis are brought together for final parallel phase of turn

Stem christie and stem turn—how to tell them apart

stem turn—skier stems out smoothly, turns through fall line, then brings skis steadily together

We took a long time to master the stem christie. It is a faster turn than the stem turn, and more complex. There is more to remember and less time to remember it in, because everything happens more quickly. So it didn't surprise us when we were told that the stem christie is the peak of achievement for the majority of holiday skiers. It's the chief weapon in the intermediate skier's repertoire. It's a reliable turn too—a good all-rounder. Even experts sometimes rely on it in difficult conditions. And, most important for the ambitious skier, it can, in traditional teaching, lead directly to the pure parallel christie—of which more later.

In the stem turn we passed right through the fall line from one side to the other with our skis open in the stem position. The tails remained open until we reached our new line of traverse. Only then were they pulled steadily together. The essence of the stem turn was a smooth, steady opening and closing of the skis.

In the stem christie the stemming part of the turn is greatly speeded up and reduced. The tail of the uphill ski opens into a narrow stem position (no more than 18 inches). But this time the skier brings his skis smartly together as he reaches the fall line. The turn is finished with a 'down' motion that brings the skier sliding through the final phase of the turn in an uphill christie. *The skier there-fore has his skis parallel through the final phase of the turn.*

The stem christie as demonstrated by our instructors was beautiful—a perfect statement of balance and control. It seemed unlikely that we could ever emulate such skill and grace. Yet we already knew the three basic movements involved.

1. Stemming out from a traverse.
2. Transferring weight to the outside ski during the stem.
3. The uphill christie.

Therefore, we argued (whistling in the dark), if we could link these three separate actions and weld them into one fluid movement we could do the stem christie.

STEM CHRISTIE (vertical sequence, right)

1 Stem out with the uphill ski and pull back the uphill ski tip.
2 Spring up, bring skis smartly together and transfer weight to the outside ski of the turn.
3 Sink forward with a 'down' motion
4 Press knees forward and sideways into the slope to steer the turn — as in the uphill christie.

STEM CHRISTIE

A Stem out with the uphill ski and pull back the uphill ski tip. You gather speed as you move from the traverse to the fall line.

B Almost in the fall line, the skier comes up. Weight is transferred to the outside ski of the turn. (The uphill ski here.)

C Down, down, down. The skis are brought together, and the skier sinks forward with a down motion. Note the knees pressing forward and sideways into the slopes to steer the turn — as in the uphill christie. The hip, too, is pressed into the hillside.

How to do the stem christie

1. Set off in the traverse position, poles behind, skis parallel, weight mostly on downhill ski (uphill edge). Uphill ski should be leading, knees bent forward, good forward lean from ankles.

2. In the 'down' movement, exaggerating the traverse position, stem out the tail of the uphill ski. At the same time pull back the tip. Both tips are now in line.

3. With an 'up' movement bring the skis together. Immediately transfer most of your weight to the outside ski. It is a 'step across to one side' feeling. The outside ski is set on its inside edge, and the skier leans his weight against it.

4. As soon as the skis are together sink forward with a 'down' motion. This enables you to apply good turning pressure. See how the uphill shoulder comes into the lead. Notice also how you are angulating with your upper body to balance in a stable position on your downhill ski.

5. Knees press forward and sideways into the slope. As you increase the pressure on your uphill edges, the final phase of the turn becomes, in effect, an uphill christie. If you want you can finish the turn by increasing the knee pressure until you check to a full halt. Or you can rise up and resume a traverse position, ready to begin another stem christie in the opposite direction.

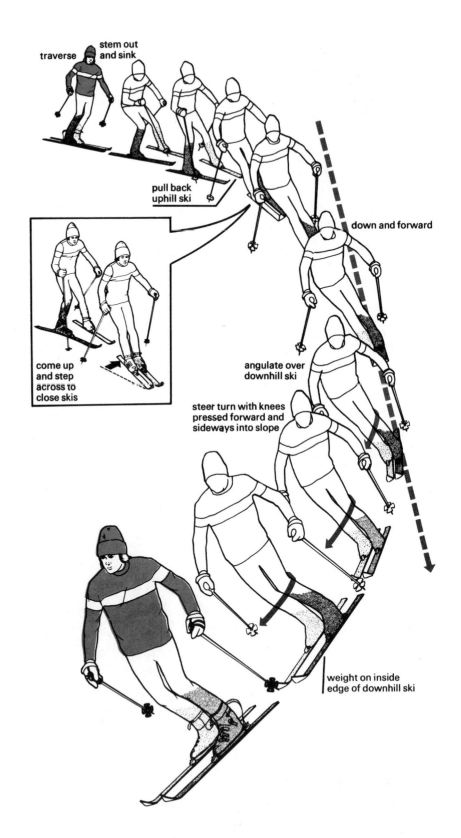

traverse

stem out and sink

pull back uphill ski

down and forward

angulate over downhill ski

steer turn with knees pressed forward and sideways into slope

weight on inside edge of downhill ski

come up and step across to close skis

The final phase of the turn is, in effect, an uphill christie

A useful exercise

When we first attempted the stem christie we did not have the confidence to bring our skis together before the fall line. So we used the following exercise to conquer our nerves.

1. Set off down the fall line in a shallow snowplough glide.

2. Sink down, and then spring up with a push off the inside ski. Bring the skis parallel.

3. Now transfer your weight and apply turning pressure to the outside ski of the turn. The weight should be on the ball of the foot, inside edge, the big toe. Say to yourself: 'I must keep my body facing squarely down the fall line.'

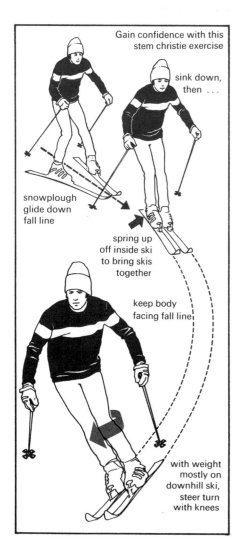

Gain confidence with this stem christie exercise

sink down, then . . .

snowplough glide down fall line

spring up off inside ski to bring skis together

keep body facing fall line

with weight mostly on downhill ski, steer turn with knees

Where we went wrong

1. 'Stem out, push up, sink down.' We shouted it out to ourselves. Fine: we managed that all right. Then we panicked. We hit the fall line and started to go fast. We forgot everything and fell. It may happen to you. We suggest—no, we insist—that you practise your stem christie on a gentle slope which holds no fears. On this kind of slope you can feel nonchalant as you stand up and the skis rush away.

2. The second failure is also due to fear and wrong choice of slope (many ski-schools teach the turn on slopes that are too steep for the nerves of the pupils). We managed to stem, push up, and survive the shock of the sudden rush down the fall line. All right. Now we had to sink down and lean out into the valley with the weight on the lower ski. . . . Lean out into the valley? At this speed? We muffed it. We kept our weight on our uphill ski. At worst, we leaned into the hill. The weighted uphill ski slid down the hill, and over we went.

Above: leaning into the slope is the single commonest fault
Left: skis in a tangle due to transferring weight to outside ski too soon
Above left: if you stem out too widely the tail of your downhill ski will slide away

This is the single commonest failure of the stem christie.

3. Our skis diverged and again we fell. This was due to transferring our weight to the outside ski *before* it had passed the fall line. The result was that the ski was on its inside edge (which is correct), but it was not pointing in the right direction. When we transferred our weight, the skis were bound to diverge and we could not go two ways at once.

4. When we stemmed out, the tail of the downhill ski slid away—because we had lost our traverse position. We were too widely stemmed and could not get round the corner.

5. A jerky short turn with awkward balance. Often this was due to excessive upper body movement. We would swing the outside shoulder forward in the turn so that we were facing uphill.

SAY IT ALOUD: Stem out and sink. Spring up to the fall line. Lean out.

17   THE PARALLEL CHRISTIE

The parallel christie, in which the skis are kept together throughout the turn.

There is nothing quite so beautiful to watch as an expert skier in full flight down the mountainside, carving a serpent trail in his wake, throwing up bow-waves of snow as he banks from one swooping turn to another. We wanted desperately to 'ski parallel'. To master this turn of turns was our greatest ambition. Its sheer elegance and economy of movement made it appear deceptively simple. We knew better. How, we wondered, having only just slogged through the complexities of the stem christie, was it possible to drift into the fall line without stemming. What was the trick, the knack, the hidden force that enables the parallel christie skier to keep his skis together throughout the entire turn?

The answer, as we discovered, is un-weighting. This enables the skier to make the changes of edges and weight that are enough to set the turn in motion. After that, speed, weight, and gravity do the rest, brought under control by the skier's legs and body position.

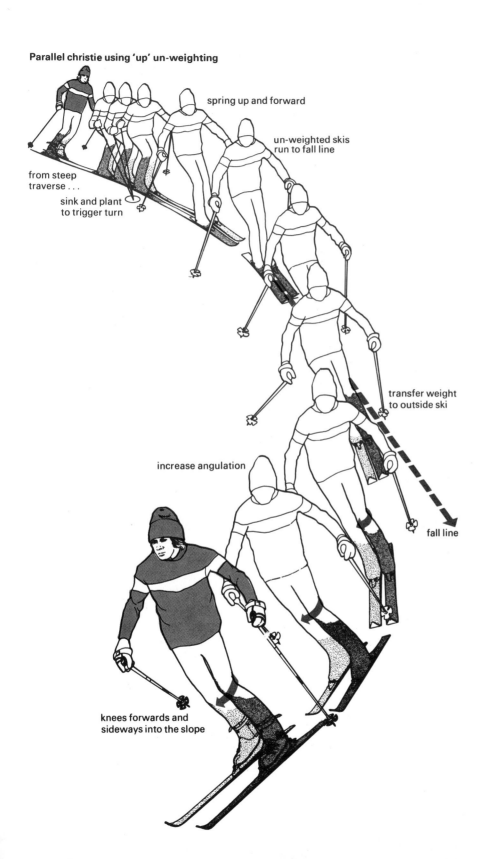

Parallel christie using 'up' un-weighting

spring up and forward

un-weighted skis
run to fall line

from steep
traverse . . .

sink and plant
to trigger turn

transfer weight
to outside ski

increase angulation

fall line

knees forwards and
sideways into the slope

The following sequence of illustrations shows what happens in the classic long radius parallel christie with 'up' un-weighting.

1. Set off on a fairly steep traverse.

2. Bend from the ankles, and sink with a slight 'down' motion into an exaggerated traverse position. As you sink plant the downhill pole. Your weight is still mostly on the downhill ski (uphill edge).

3. Planting the pole acts as a trigger for the next phase of the turn.

4. The instant you plant the pole you spring lightly forward and up. You are like a ball bouncing on the rebound. The forward-and-up movement brings your weight off the skis. The forward leverage created by the movement of the knees bending keeps the tips pressed to the snow and directs the skis towards the fall line.

5. For a brief fraction of a second there is no weight friction on the skis. You use the moment to transfer your weight to the outside ski. Now its edge is changed from the outside to the inside edge, as it becomes the outside ski of the turn. At the same time your inside ski should automatically come into the lead. (This is important. Whenever you are in a turn the inside ski leads.)

6. As you come out of the fall line you apply turning pressure. You carve the turn by pressing your knees forwards and sideways into the slope. The sideways pressure edges the skis. As you drift round you keep your body facing downhill and increase your angulation position. This helps to maintain a correct balance, with your weight mostly over the downhill ski.

7. Gradually you increase the bite of the uphill edges and turn your body into a normal traverse position.

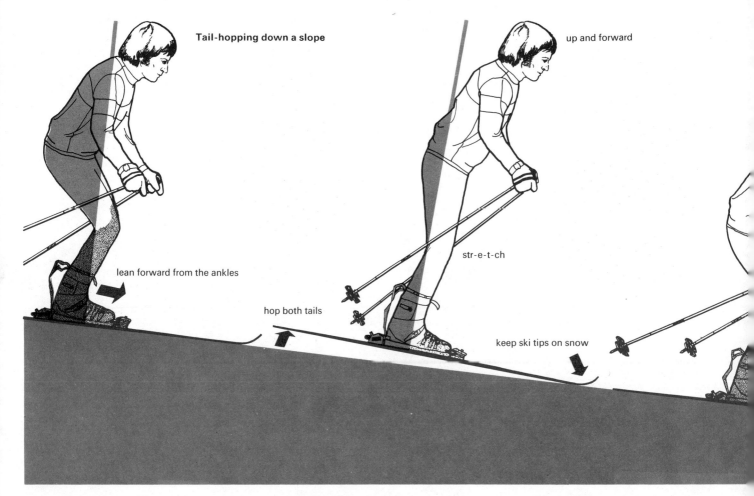

Tail-hopping down a slope

lean forward from the ankles

up and forward

str-e-t-ch

hop both tails

keep ski tips on snow

Five steps to the parallel

We did not attempt the parallel christie straight away. It is much too complicated a turn to attempt from scratch. Instead our instructors led us up to it in easy stages.

We found the following exercises extremely helpful. They taught us the importance of good forward leverage—ankle pressure on the tongue of the boot. And they introduced us to the hopping motion which un-weights the skis at the crucial moment the turn is begun.

Learning to hop the tails off the snow is alright to get the idea of unweighting. But there is no need normally to tail-hop. Provided you 'rebound' with a smooth forward and up motion you will feel your tails unweight even though they are still resting on the snow. Unnecessary tail-hopping during a run is needlessly tiring and risks catching an edge and tumbling.

Tail-hopping on the flat

Find a level patch of snow. Stand on it with the skis parallel. Lean forward from the ankles until your weight is on the balls of the feet. The idea is to hop with both feet to bring the tails of your skis off the snow. But don't let the tips of your skis move. They should remain pressed firmly on the snow. Hence the forward stance. It must be with a full extension of the legs.

Tail-hopping down a gentle slope

The same exercise as before, but this time in a shallow schuss straight down the fall line. Hop with your tails as you go. To keep your tips on the snow and maintain your balance you will really have to concentrate hard on leaning forward from the ankles. We needed a little courage to do this at first. We felt we were about to plunge over our ski tips at any moment. But remember: if the weight goes back the skis shoot forward and you will sit down. It is equally important to acquire a good rhythm as you hop down the slope. We found it helpful to count aloud to ourselves as we lifted out tails: 'One, two, three—*hop*! One, two, three—*hop*!

And we kept trying to think about the skis—not the body.

Tail-hopping in a traverse

This is slightly more difficult. A little closer to the real thing (or 'end-form', in ski-ing jargon. The word for a ski-ing movement in its final form).

Do the same hopping exercise ski-ing across the slope in an easy traverse. Hop your tails uphill slightly out of the traverse, then back again. Repeat as many times as you can.

176

Tail-hopping down a slope
Above: Flex knees and lean forward from the ankles
Below: Up-and-forward hop lifts tails, keeps tips on snow

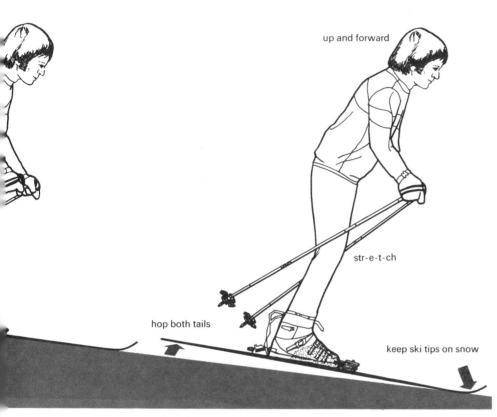

up and forward

str-e-t-ch

hop both tails

keep ski tips on snow

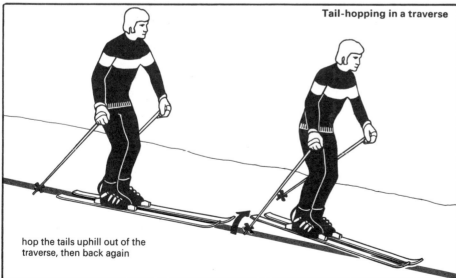

Tail-hopping in a traverse

hop the tails uphill out of the traverse, then back again

Above: Wrong! Do not lift the whole ski. Lean forward from the ankles when you hop to keep the ski tips on the snow

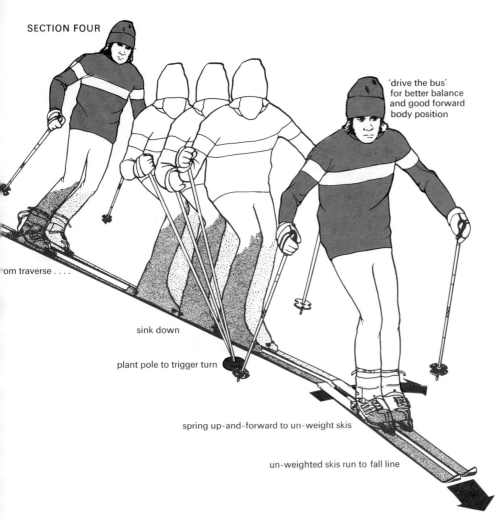

'drive the bus' for better balance and good forward body position

from traverse . . . .

sink down

plant pole to trigger turn

spring up-and-forward to un-weight skis

un-weighted skis run to fall line

Tail-hopping with poles

Planting the poles

Poles are essential for the parallel christie. The action of planting the downhill pole is the trigger which prompts the turn. All the other movements of the parallel christie follow in a chain reaction. Planting the pole also performs two other useful functions. It helps to remind us about bending the knees. And it acts as a stabilizer during the hop.

Where to plant the pole depends on a good arm position. Hold your hands forward. Hip level felt most comfortable for us. The arms should be relaxed and slightly crooked. Allow a little daylight between your elbows and your body, but don't hold your arms out like wings.

The important thing to remember is this: no matter how much your upper body rotates to one side or the other the distance between your two hands should stay more or less the same.

Our instructor asked us to imagine that we were driving a bus. It is a vivid and valuable comparison. You grip the big horizontal steering wheel with both hands. When you are in a traverse position (as at the start of a parallel christie), you turn the wheel 30 to 40 degrees downhill.

Keeping your hands on the wheel does three things for you.

- It helps to maintain a good forward body position.
- It settles your weight over the downhill ski.
- It keeps your upper body 'quiet'—that is, as settled as possible—and improves your balance.

In the normal running position the poles are held with the baskets to the rear. When the pole is planted it is swung forward from the wrist. Notice the wrist action. The pole is held with the wrist turned slightly down. When the pole is planted, bring it forward with a kind of 'thumbs up' movement of the wrist.

How far from the sides of your skis should you plant the pole? This was one of our first questions. The answer seemed to be: let the distance be governed by the steering wheel position.

Our next question was: how far forward? This can be determined by a simple rule. When the pole is planted try to keep the forearm more or less parallel to the snow. When we first attempted pole-planting we attacked the snow like a park-keeper stabbing at litter with a pointed stick. The correct method is much lighter, more deft. The point of the pole is not hammered in with a downward thrust of the forearm. Instead it is the body sinking in a 'down' motion that brings the pole point into the snow. A subtle difference, perhaps. But it greatly improved our effectiveness and style.

forearm parallel to snow

Planting the pole

Walking the poles

This is the exercise which introduced us to the correct pole action. We found a gentle slope. We skied straight down the fall line with skis parallel. As we descended we 'walked' the poles down the slope, planting the left and right pole alternatively. To try and acquire a steady rhythm we counted out loud the time to ourselves:
'*Plant*, two, three; *plant*, two, three.'

Hopping with the poles

Next we linked the two exercises together. We accompanied each tail-hop with an alternate pole-plant to right and left as we schussed down the fall line. This is how the two movements combined.

1. The skier is moving down the fall line. Both skis parallel and flat on the snow.
2. He sinks forward, bending from knees and ankles. At the same time he brings the pole forward.

3. His 'down' motion slots the point of the pole into the snow.
4. Almost instantaneously he 'rebounds' with an 'up-forward' motion that lifts (or un-weights) the skis.
5. As he lands he prepares to sink down again and bring forward the other pole.

Once again the key to success is *rhythm*. As soon as we hit a steady rhythm we found ourselves planting and un-weighting almost automatically.

We were also conscious of our tails moving very slightly out of the fall line every time we hopped. The angle of displacement was minimal, but it demonstrated to us how planting the pole helps to initiate the parallel turn.

Ski tip to remember

Don't deliberately lift the pole after you have planted it. Let it come with you as you carry on down the slope. It is then returned naturally to the rear.

179

How we conquered the fear factor

For the final exercise we moved to a steeper slope. By now we knew about un-weighting and pole-planting. Only one serious obstacle remained: the fear factor. As we explained in the chapter on traversing, the 'fear factor' is a fear of the fall line. Most skiers feel it at some time or other. We became nervous and tense. And tense limbs are a skier's worst enemy. Before we could attempt the parallel christie we had to release the butterflies in our stomach.

The remedy is a repetition of uphill christies begun from the fall line. This is the most extreme form of the uphill christie.

1. Begin with a straight schuss down the fall line.

2. Sink with a 'down' motion and plant the pole, (right pole when turning right, left when turning left).

3. 'Rebound' with an 'up-forward' motion that keeps the tips of the skis on the snow but un-weights the tails.

4. As you land, put your weight on the downhill ski. Set the uphill edges. Advance the uphill ski. Uphill hip and shoulder are leading. Angulate with the upper body to balance weight over the downhill ski.

5. Press forward at the ankles. Press hard with your knees forwards and sideways into the slope to steer the turn. You drift round and up the slope until you stop. Watch that you do not let your bottom stick out. Hips remain pressed to the inside of the turn.

After a series of uphill christies *from* the fall line we made our first attempt at a 'downhill christie'—that is, a parallel christie *through* the fall line. Because we took a very steep line the difference was barely noticeable. As we improved, of course, we started from progressively shallower traverse positions.

The mistakes we made

If anything was designed to sap the skier's morale it is the parallel turn. Let us be honest—we struggled. Some days we were pleased with ourselves, other days in despair. Lucky the skier who can consistently produce good parallel turns! A few of us felt we would never master it. The rest reckoned we would probably spend the rest of our ski-ing days getting it right. Our faults were legion. From a long list we chose these as the most persistent (p. 182).

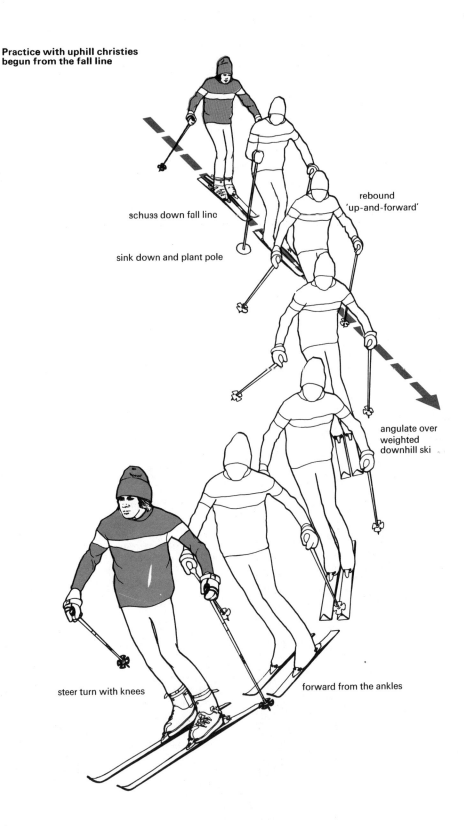

Practice with uphill christies begun from the fall line

schuss down fall line

sink down and plant pole

rebound 'up-and-forward'

angulate over weighted downhill ski

forward from the ankles

steer turn with knees

Parallel with 'up' un-weighting. Good pole-planting technique is the essential factor for smooth and fluid turns

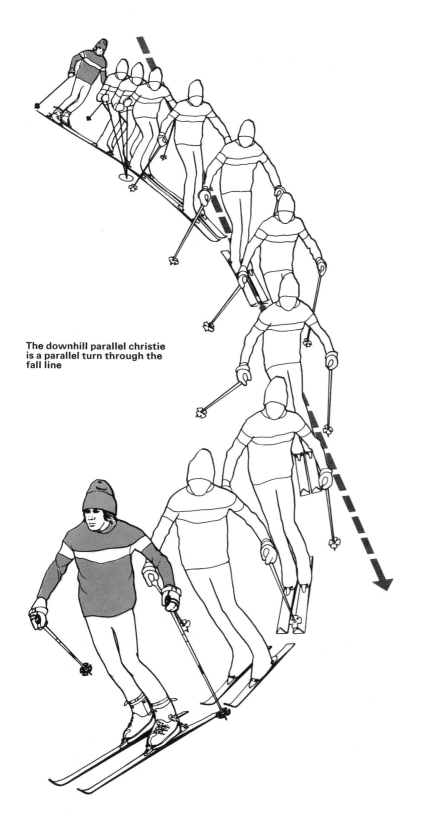

The downhill parallel christie is a parallel turn through the fall line

Where we went wrong

1. We failed to keep our skis parallel. They diverged, and so we fell. Often this was due to flinging that outside arm and shoulder ahead of us into the turn. Too much upper body movement induced the weight to go on the wrong (uphill) ski.

2. We found that just after the turn we were having a strenuous time with the downhill ski skidding on the snow. It was too hard to get everything right, and sometimes we over-compensated by bringing the downhill shoulder forward. The fault was again due to fear. We were trying to skid too hard to slow our speed. We were doing what our instructors called 'ski-ing with a wooden leg'. The outside leg was much too stiff and unbending, attempting to control our speed. We should, instead, have bent the knee and thrust forward with it, carving the turn and riding the edge. It is faster, yes, but controls your speed by choice of terrain.

3. An ugly, jerky turn with a short radius and edges catching, perhaps sending us sprawling. One cause was hopping too high and energetically. It was a dangerous reaction stimulated by fear of the fall line. We were hopping through the fall line too quickly.

4. Falling backwards as our skis seemed to accelerate like mad. This was another common fault from fear. We had 'rebounded' after planting the pole to begin the un-weighting of our tails. But it was only an 'up' motion. The fear factor, tugging at our shirt tails, pulled us back and prevented us from going into the correct 'up-forward' motion. Result: our weight came back on our heels. The fronts of our skis accelerated.

WRONG ! Outside arm and shoulder flung ahead into the turn causes weight to go on uphill ski. The skier is also at fault in looking down at his ski tips

WRONG ! 'Ski-ing with a wooden leg. Fear of falling has prevented the skier from angulating sufficiently over the downhill ski and from bending the downhill knee to carve the turn

WRONG ! Falling due to leaning back when 'up' un-weighting

The effect was like having a rug pulled from under our feet. We fell backwards. The remedy: think *forward*. Concentrate on pressing forward *at the ankles*, not just from the knees. This is particularly important at the end of each turn. Often we began with a good forward position, but by the time we had completed the turn we had settled back on our heels. So say to yourself every time: 'forward at the ankles'. It's a habit well worth acquiring as soon as you can. Feel the front of your ankle press into the boot.

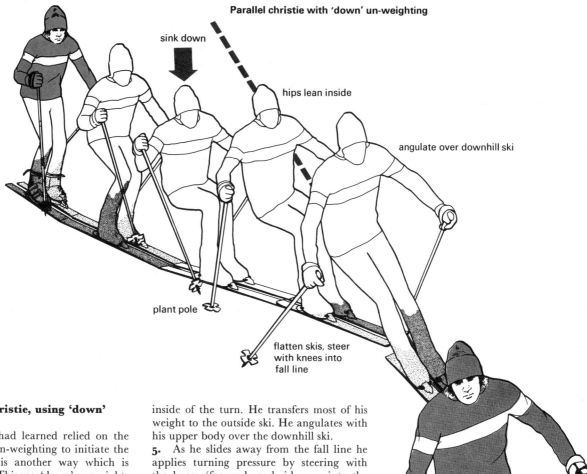

Parallel christie with 'down' un-weighting

sink down

hips lean inside

angulate over downhill ski

plant pole

flatten skis, steer
with knees into
fall line

stay down, steer
turn with knees

The parallel christie, using 'down' un-weighting

The christie we had learned relied on the tail-hop or 'up' un-weighting to initiate the turn. But there is another way which is equally effective. This uses 'down' un-weighting to begin the turn. Here one of our instructors demonstrates how it's done.

1. He starts from a traverse position. Weight mostly on the downhill ski. Uphill ski leading.

2. His downhill pole starts to come forward. His weight is still mostly on the downhill ski.

3. Almost instantaneously he un-weights, using a 'down' motion. The action is very fast. He suddenly bends his knees keeping his upper body erect. At this moment he plants his downhill pole, flattens his skis and steers them with his knees towards the fall line. Note how he is leaning forward from the ankles. See also how his forearm is parallel to the snow when the pole is planted.

4. This time he does not rise with an 'up' motion to transfer his weight. Instead he maintains his 'down' position. But as soon as his pole is planted his hips lean to the inside of the turn. He transfers most of his weight to the outside ski. He angulates with his upper body over the downhill ski.

5. As he slides away from the fall line he applies turning pressure by steering with the knees (forwards and sideways into the slope). The turn is completed when he resumes his new traverse position.

We felt that 'down' and 'up' un-weighting caused a certain amount of initial confusion. Especially when some fellow ski-school pupils, who had begun learning parallels the previous season with 'up' un-weighting, found themselves in a class where 'down' un-weighting was being taught. Although the 'down' un-weighting method is best for turning on bumps, since it lowers the skier's centre of gravity, most of us preferred to parallel with an 'up' motion wherever we could.

Somehow it seemed to have a more natural and logical rhythm. However, for anyone who wants to reach the advanced turns beyond the parallel christie, both methods of un-weighting are essential.

18 THE GRADUATED LENGTH METHOD

Short skis are fun: old timers may sneer at them, but beginners find them
easy to cope with and learn faster by the short ski method

There is another way of learning to ski: by graduating from short to long skis. It is called ski-évolutif by the French, who have pioneered the system in Europe, and the Graduated Length Method (GLM) in the United States. But a great deal of confusion in America exists over this because ski schools use the same term GLM to describe two very different systems:

Direct parallel GLM

This is variety in the methods but the essentials are
(a) that you begin on mini-skis of 100 cm (3 feet); (b) from the start you learn to turn the skis together side by side; and (c) when you have mastered the mini-ski, you move to slightly longer ones, and so on until you ski parallel on full-length skis. At the end of one week you may be on skis of 150 cm.
This is what the French call ski-évolutif: you evolve on different length skis.

Wedge type GLM

You begin on skis shorter than standard but nothing like the mini-skis of first day direct parallel GLM. The starting ski will not be less than 135 cm (4 feet 5 inches) and maybe 150 cm (5 feet). You graduate to slightly longer skis. The second big difference is that in this method you begin not with parallel turns but with stemmed turns—or the wedge turn as it is now generally called—in which you open one ski (Chapter 11). Some resorts move straight from this to wide track parallel. These are some resorts where direct parallel GLM is taught: Colorado—Aspen Highlands; Maine —Sugarloaf; Michigan — Boyne Country, Timberlee Hills; New Hampshire—Attitash, Waterville Valley; New Jersey — Great Gorge; New York — Gore Mountain, Greek Peak, Hunter Mountain, Snow Ridge; Vermont — Bromley, Glen Ellen, Killington, Stratton.
These are some wedge-type GLM resorts: California — Mammoth Mountain, Squaw Valley; Colorado—Aspen, Snowmass, Vail; Idaho — Sun Valley; New Hampshire — Cannon Mountain; New Mexico — Taos; Utah — Alta, Snowbird; Vermont Mount Snow, Sugarbush.
Beginners should realise that 'GLM' means very different things. Horst Abraham at Vail, who is chairman of the technical co-ordinating committee of the USA Professional Ski Instructors Association (PSIA), advocates calling wedge-type GLM systems by the name

The battle is already half won when pupils are enjoying themselves. And because beginners feel confident on short skis, many teachers turn lessons into games.

American Teaching Method, or ATM. It can also mean Accelerated Teaching Method. This would certainly help. The term GLM can then be kept for direct parallel schools. Our references to GLM or mini-skis will be to direct parallel methods. There are therefore three broad methods of teaching:
- Traditional—learning on standard skis, as tall or taller than yourself, and going from the snowplough, stem and stem christie to the parallel. This was for many years the commonest method in Europe. It is the one we favour least, because we are against beginning on standard skis. If you learn this way, insist on compacts.

- GLM—direct parallel turns
- ATM—wedge turns first

GLM in America and ski-évolutif in France are not ways of ski-ing; they are teaching methods. They have precisely the same aim as traditional methods — to teach us to do safe parallel turns on full-length skis and on all terrains. They simply take a different route. In the traditional method the equipment (i.e. the skis) remains constant and the technique varies. In the direct parallel GLM it is the technique that remains constant and the equipment that varies. The pupil learning the traditional way starts on full-length skis and builds up his turning technique through the plough and the stem and then the parallel. But the mini-ski pupil hardly changes his technique after his first day on skis. He changes

his skis instead. We will deal with the ideological schism between GLM and ATM shortly, but let us first discard the traditional method that still puts beginners on skis as tall or taller than himself. There are reasons for standard long skis—but they do not apply to beginners and intermediates who need something much shorter.
- Long skis are fast. (The beginner does not *want* fast skis — nothing terrifies him more. Studies of beginners on full-length skis have shown that they spend most of their energy keeping their speed *down* to less than 8 mph.)
- Long skis give better support on soft snow. (Today's beginner does not ski on soft snow, but on a firm piste.)
- Long skis provide a better bite on steep terrain. (The beginner does not ski on steep terrain.)

On the other hand:
- Short skis are far easier to turn. (Turning a 2-metre pair can take four times more effort than a 1-metre pair.)
- Short skis are less likely to cause leg injury. (Most ski-ing injuries are the result of skis acting as a lever on limbs. The shorter a lever, the less force it can exert.)

It is now accepted in the U.S. (and belatedly in Europe) that putting a beginner on full-length skis is about as logical as putting a learner driver in a high-power sports car. But what length of short ski—and what method of turning? Clif Taylor and Karl Pfeiffer in the U.S. and the late Robert Blanc in France have all been advocates of roughly the same method: mini-skis and the direct parallel. They all abominate the stem turn taught in ATM and traditional schools. Pfeiffer says: 'It doesn't make sense to teach the stem when everyone's goal is parallel ski-ing . . . . If I start with a 3-foot ski I can lead the pupil directly towards the parallel because I can teach him movements I can't teach him on the 5-foot ski.' Robert Blanc said the stem is a defensive instinct which, once indulged in, is difficult to break when the skier learns the parallel. Why teach the pupil how to edge, plough and stem when you spend the rest of the time breaking all these habits?

Horst Abraham, on the other hand, says: 'The skier in the wedge position feels more secure and therefore can get more terrain experience. Most ski areas do not offer the gentle flat slopes you need for direct parallel on 3-foot skis. Skiers have to learn a braking movement — and using a 5-foot ski straight away helps you to learn to appreciate the ski as a tool. You get accidents in direct GLM, too. Not to the legs but to collar bones and hands because balance is reduced.'

Curt Chase, the director of the Aspen ski school, says: 'When the ski becomes so short that it ceases to act like a ski, when it ceases to perform its basic function as a stable base to stand in balance on, it should be obvious that we have gone too far. Certainly it can be fun to slide around on a 3-foot ski, but the skills required to stand in balance on it, the movements required to make it turn and the feelings and reflexes that are developed as a result, do not relate, and are not transferable to the sport of ski-ing as we understand and practise it today.' Chase advocates teaching a wide track parallel: 'It is independent leg action. It relates to stemming, pivoting, skidding and steering and the fundamental skills of modern ski-ing. It is not to be confused with direct parallel approaches where the feet are simply swivelled around'.

GLM Vs. ATM

Who is right? The argument is really only between GLM and ATM. Nobody any longer should allow himself to be taught the traditional long ski way; even when the teaching is traditional you can and should insist on a compact ski of about 170 cm or less (see Chapter 3). If there is no compact ski, go for a shorter version of the traditional ski. Between ATM and GLM we would not be as

dogmatic. Comparative tests by *Ski* magazine in 1970 (vol. 135, no. 4) suggested that the total time required to learn to ski at speed using basic parallel turns was about the same for both GLM and the contemporary American teaching method, but the GLM people reached higher skiing speed sooner.

The decisive change in progress came with the introduction of a side skid phase in the turn, and that proved easier to master on shorter skis. John Shedden* reports other tests that suggest that shorter skis enable beginners to learn the basic movements more easily. Shedden, however, supports the British Association of Ski Instructors in recommending one length of ski for learning (170 cm), largely because it seems so many ski resorts will not want to go in for the capital costs of providing each learner with two or three pairs of GLM skis.

Our own experience supports the idea that GLM learners progress quickly and fewer give up. We took a mixed party to Les Arcs in France where Robert Blanc has pioneered an original system similar to the direct GLM schools mentioned above. Our group included beginners and poor skiers taught by traditional methods, who gave every appearance of being no-hopers. All improved fast and the beginners reached a level in one week that would have taken two to six weeks of traditional ski-ing. One of our beginners was a photographer who got up, and more or less down the mountain, to take some of the pictures for this book, after only a couple of days of lessons. The drop-out rate in the class was also far lower than in traditional classes. And the learners had a lot of fun. Another influence on us was Fred Reilly, our general adviser, who has a lifetime of traditional teaching behind him; he watched with scepticism, if not scorn, but became convinced that GLM has a lot to be said for it.

So far so good for GLM. But we have reservations.

First, we are sceptical of *some* GLM claims. Only a natural and gifted athletic GLM beginner, for instance, can expect to be able to ski parallel within two weeks. None of the beginners in our trial group did — and one did wrench a knee.

Secondly, we believe the stem christie — a narrow wedge turn in which the skis are closed in the fall line — is relatively easy to learn (easier than good parallel) and often comes in useful on the mountain. Defensive? Yes, but there are times and places for defen-

sive ski-ing. Sometimes our nerve for parallel fails on a tough slope or in poor visibility or bad snow. The stem christie is another weapon in our armoury. It opens up more terrain. 'I can go anywhere with my stem christie' is the solacing remark of many an experienced but non-expert skier. We are certainly glad we learned one.

A third reason for regretting the reluctance of GLM schools to teach the stem is that in a simple plough turn you can very easily get the feel of carving a turn (Chapter 19) and an understanding of what the ski will do for you. Fourthly, and finally, there is something in the worry that GLM tends to produce excess upper body motion.

Summing up

There is thus something to be said for both systems. There is, in our judgement, not enough in either at the moment to make the choice for the absolute beginner anything other than marginal between a good GLM and a good ATM school. (In Europe, as we have said, we think GLM has the advantage over traditional schools.)

There are three kinds of people we think would benefit most from GLM:
- Any skier who has tried traditional or ATM and finds it unappealing or who has even given up.
- Any intermediate skier who is stuck in his progress.
- Any advanced skier with a twitch of a stem still in his parallel. A day or two on 3-foot skis, then 4-foot, helped us greatly.

There is also a compromise approach we recommend: to begin GLM but learn the stem after graduating to 160 cm skis and a fair parallel.

The decision for each skier between GLM and ATM must, in the end, be based on the best permutation of resort convenience, reputation of school, and a judgement of his own personality and athletic ability. It will help the judgement, as well as being instructive in itself, if we describe in detail what happens in France's Les Arcs — for Les Arcs, as we say, you can near enough substitute the direct parallel GLM schools in the U.S.

---

* *Ski Teaching*, by John Shedden, published by John Jones, Cardiff Ltd., U.K., 1974.

Direct parallel

The whole system places great emphasis on spontaneity. Teachers are encouraged to develop their own methods within the framework of the equipment and philosophy of ski évolutif. So no two teachers at Les Arcs taught in precisely the same way, though the difference lay not in what they taught but in the order, emphasis, and manner of their approach.

At Les Arcs those of us in the ski évolutif school who had skied before were amazed that we did not have the sensation of the skis running away from us. Short skis go so much slower. Secondly, we were astonished at how little force was needed to turn.

We now found it was we who turned the skis; the skis did not turn us. Because our skis did not have the necessary edge to 'bite' the snow, there was no possibility of their developing a mind of their own. They simply went in the direction we pointed them. (Although for the first few minutes some of the party did find it a little difficult pointing them.)

The psychological impact of all this on confidence is enormous. Probably the single most important difference between short ski teaching and the traditional method is that from the outset the pupil has the initiative. Our attitudes were offensive, not the defensive ones to which those of us who had skied before were used. As Robert Blanc told us: 'It's an aggressive way of ski-ing.'

We did not feel inhibited by the equipment. We always felt one jump ahead of whatever we were doing. Whatever we were asked to do seemed well within our abilities. There was no hesitation, no fear factor. The first lessons, at least, progressed at a cracking pace. There was little explanation and a lot of action (an unforeseen bonus which minimizes difficulties where instruction is in another language) and we clocked up a lot more mileage than we would have done in a traditional school, where there is a lot of hanging about.

Much of what we were taught is a duplication of material already contained in the chapters on traditional ski-ing. There is no difference, for instance, between herring boning up a slope on short skis or on long ones (except that it is harder on the long ones, and is therefore usually taught at a later stage). So in what follows we will skip the explanation where there is too much duplication.

How the skis 'evolve' at Les Arcs, left to right: 1-metre, 135 cm and 160 cm 'evolutif' (GLM) skis. Plus 'full length' 185 cm and 2-metre ones (note that the bindings are further back on the mini-skis, which means they have proportionately less 'tail' than standard ones.)

stationary (star) turn

traverse

traverse with uphill checks

stop

herringbone

twisting down the fall line

stationary exercises

sidestep

The short ski pupil packs a lot into the first lesson. At about the point when the traditional pupil is going down a slope in a controlled snowplough (after 20 minutes), he is doing a schuss with parallel turns (i.e. twisting down the fall line, bottom right of diagram)

Getting the feel of skis

The one-metre skis were so much easier to get the hang of than full length ones. Even those of us who had never worn skis before had little difficulty standing. But we did not have much time to think about the difficulties. First we side-stepped up a slope without poles (these came later). Some fell—because they did not keep their skis at right angles to

the fall line. Then we climbed up with a Charlie Chaplin herringbone (pp 94), weight on the instep.

Exercises

When we reached the top of the slope we started to do exercises on a flat piece of ground.

These exercises were to be constantly repeated whenever we had a moment or two to spare; whenever we experienced new snow conditions; and especially when we graduated onto a new length of skis. Each time we changed onto new skis we would repeat this entire first lesson. This, at least is the theory. On a subsequent visit to Les Arcs we noticed that this was not always done. We think it should be.

1. Jumping

First jump up and down. Arms out in a 'wings' position.

Keep the skis together if you can.

Try not to open them. Try to jump just by lifting your legs, rather than by leaping into the air with your entire body. Imagine there is a ceiling just above your head.
Make sure that both skis leave the ground at the same moment, not one before the other. And make sure they return to the ground at the same time too—again, not one before the other.
In this exercise jump up and down on the same spot. After about ten seconds of this try a variation.

2 Jumping and turning

Instead of landing on the same spot twist your skis while you are in the air. Twist one way the first jump, the other way the next. Land first to the left, then to the right. And so on. Try not to move your shoulders, and always face in the same direction.

Try as much as you can to use your legs rather than the top half of your body. Your outstretched arms should not flap up and down as you jump, nor flail around wildly as you turn.

3. Just turning

As soon as you have got the hang of that try the same twisting motion, but *without* the jump. No beginner would be able to do this on full length skis whilst stationary. There is too much resistance from the snow. This is one of the very real advantages of short skis: the beginner can practise the movements without having to cope with the problem of downhill motion at the same time.
This exercise makes an hour-glass pattern on the snow, and is rather like dancing the Twist.
Having worked at stationary balance you next tackle moving balance.

4. Moving across the slope (traverse)

'Now,' our instructor told us, 'hold your arms out. Put your uphill ski slightly forward. And follow me.' Whereupon he set off in a gentle traverse across the slope. No more instruction was given. (Those of us who had skied before noticed that there was no talk of edging or weighting.) But no more seemed necessary. We followed. It was only after our progress had been brought to a gentle halt by an upward slope of the mountain that we realized that we had received no instructions on how to stop! It seems incredible to those of us who had skied before that there had been no squeals of protest from the complete beginners—in traditional classes the first question is always 'how do we *stop*?' They had seemed quite happy. We travelled so slowly on the small skis that those who fell found getting up easy. This is another bonus with short skis.

5. Turning through 360 degrees

We did exercises 1, 2, and 3 again, then tried No. 5—turning on the slope. You are standing sideways across the fall line. You wish to turn so that you are facing in another direction. For the beginner on short skis standing on a gentle slope this is miraculously simple.

Imagine your skis are the hands of a clock. The fall line runs from 12 to six. Your skis point to three o'clock. To turn uphill round to, say, nine, you must first move the uphill ski. So make sure that your downhill one is firmly set on its uphill edge to prevent you slipping sideways downhill.

Now lift the tip of your uphill ski and move it round to about one o'clock. This opens your skis into the 'V' configuration of the herringbone: tips apart, tails almost touching. As you place the uphill ski back on the ground you immediately adopt the herringbone stance: weight on each instep to set the skis on their inside edges, knees bent and ankles pressing forward hard against the boot. This stance will stop you sliding backwards. Just as it did when you herringboned up the slope.

You now move the downhill ski round a bit, to about two o'clock. And so you shuffle your way around, moving first one ski and then the other until you are facing the way you want. But remember, at all times:

- Maintain the edging
- Bend the knees.

Traverse with checks and stop

a skier moves across a slope in a traverse

his impetus is controlled by uphill checks

the shoulders do not turn, only the skis

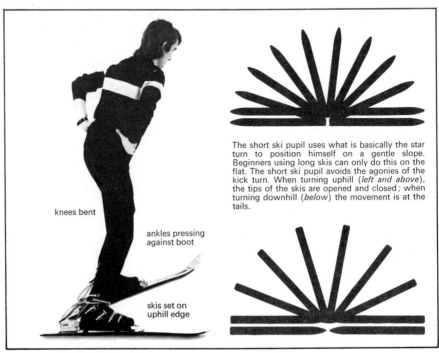

knees bent

ankles pressing against boot

skis set on uphill edge

The short ski pupil uses what is basically the star turn to position himself on a gentle slope. Beginners using long skis can only do this on the flat. The short ski pupil avoids the agonies of the kick turn. When turning uphill (*left and above*), the tips of the skis are opened and closed; when turning downhill (*below*) the movement is at the tails.

as soon as the uphill twist of the skis is relaxed the skis return of their own accord to the traverse position

keep the knees supple and relaxed

do not edge the skis

a stop is merely an exaggerated check; in this case a gliding uphill turn which is the easiest way for a first day skier to stop

Turning *downhill* from the fall line, from three to, say, six o'clock, involves a variant of this technique. The uphill ski is still moved first, but this time it is to form a 'V' the apex of which is at the *tips* of the skis, with the tips practically touching. The tails are apart. Once again edge the inside of the skis. Bend your knees. Now they will probably be tight together.

Step on round as before, widening and narrowing the 'V'. The tips stay together. You end up facing downhill. This useful exercise is much less complicated than it sounds, especially on short skis. (You will notice—cf. p. 88—that it is basically the star turn.) It enables you to position yourself just as you want on the slope, facing in whichever direction you wish.

6. Moving across the slope—checks
All that took longer for you to read about than it did for us to practise it. We found the instructor would show us the rudiments of an exercise or a movement, but would not give us time to perfect it. This annoyed some of us. Others reacted as they were meant to do—it awakened their aggression towards the snow. They were attacking. They were not on the defensive. 'Well, I didn't get that last one right,' one of us commented, 'but I'm damn well going to do *this* one.'

Now do a traverse again, but this time with little twists, the same twist as in the exercises with the skis on the ground. Twist in the direction that brings the tips uphill. *Do not move the shoulders. Turn the foot not the whole body,* and do not edge. Your knees should be relaxed. These little uphill twists will slow you down. At the end of each twist allow the skis to return to the traverse position. Pick up speed, and then twist again. It is a good feeling. You will be able to control your speed, and it will already be obvious how to stop.

7. Stopping
Whether you are going across the slope or straight down it, what is needed is a determined twist of the skis to bring their tips uphill. But this time hold the turn. You glide round (do not bother to face downhill any more). And stop. On steep slopes you will find you slide backwards after a stop. So what do you do? Remember the herring-bone, and also the exercise for turning through 360 degrees. Open your skis into a small 'V', tips facing uphill and apart, knees bent and close together edging the inside of the skis. This will stop you sliding down the hill. Now you can reposition yourself for wherever you want to go next.

The first time the short ski pupil does a schuss, the speed of descent is controlled with a series of twists and jumps (left). Soon it can be done by just twisting (above). The next step will be to make the turns more rapid and less pronounced.

8. Fall line with twist and jump

Next go straight down the fall line. Once again what seemed incredible to those of us who had been through the traditional teaching process was that there were no protests from the beginners.

Now, while moving, try one of the exercises you will have done standing still—the jump and twist. The skis only *just leave the ground*. Jump and twist to the left, then to the right. Keep your shoulders still, so that you are always facing downhill. Your legs should move from side to side, but the rest of your body should remain still. These jump-twists slow you down.

Where we went wrong

Our group fell about all over the place doing this exercise. This was our most common mistake: we leaned too far back, the skis shot away from under us, and we sat down with a bump. Even on short skis you do not always have the courage you need, yet you must commit yourself to the plunge.

We tried to correct this. On a gentle slope body weight should be directly over the feet, and the steeper the slope the further forward your weight should be. But just standing upright is ungainly and does not give you any flexibility to manoeuvre. Anyway, it is physically impossible on all but the gentlest of slopes.

Getting the bottom down is the secret. Down but not out. Keep the trunk as erect as possible. Do not lean forward if you can help it. This way the body is supple. It is poised for movement. The weight is directly over the feet, and there is no force pushing the skis away from under you, neither backwards nor forwards.

Once we had corrected that fault we discovered there were other things we were doing wrong. It was the same mistake we had made in the stationary jump and twist exercise, a tendency to lift the skis from the ground one by one. Of course it all happened so quickly that we were not aware of it. We just fell over because we were trying to go in a different direction to the ski that was still on the ground. Or, for the same reason, we went all over the place. Or, worst of all, did not turn at all.

Skis together?

Those with an enquiring mind will have noticed that we had received no instructions for the straight part of our downhill run. We

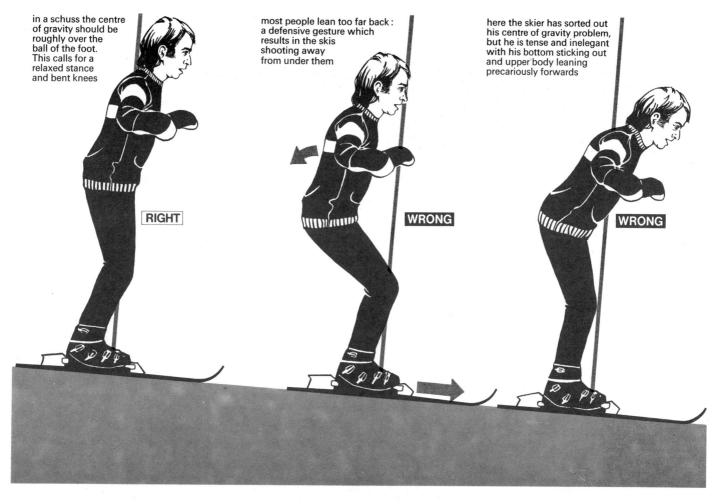

in a schuss the centre of gravity should be roughly over the ball of the foot. This calls for a relaxed stance and bent knees

RIGHT

most people lean too far back: a defensive gesture which results in the skis shooting away from under them

WRONG

here the skier has sorted out his centre of gravity problem, but he is tense and inelegant with his bottom sticking out and upper body leaning precariously forwards

WRONG

were just told to go. Needless to say, our skis should have been parallel. They were *always* parallel in motion by the ski évolutif method. But should they be tight together?

Or far apart?

To tell the truth, none of us had given any thought to the matter. Either way would have been difficult. We had done what seemed natural. And those of us with wide hips tended to have our skis further apart than those of us of smaller build. About four inches (10 cm) was the average.

When we asked the ski évolutif instructor about this, he simply said: 'If it feels right, it *is* right.' It was a phrase we were to hear often at Les Arcs. The French make no fetish of the 'feet tight together' way of ski-ing for beginners. *Their* obsession is with acting naturally. They are apt to dismiss anything

else as a 'tyranny'. Naturally those of us who had skied before, and who had gone through agonies trying to keep our skis together, were rather relieved about this.

9. Downhill with twist only

This time we came downhill with a twist but not a jump. The skis stayed on the ground all the time. Again we checked our impetus by twisting left and right. The common fault here is *not moving the skis together*. They must both twist at the same moment, and they *must remain parallel*. Some of us had them *too* far apart. We could not always get enough leverage this way, and anyway, it looked ungainly. Some of us had a tendency to gaze fixedly at our ski tips; we should have been looking at the terrain ahead. Who looks at the pedals when driving a car?

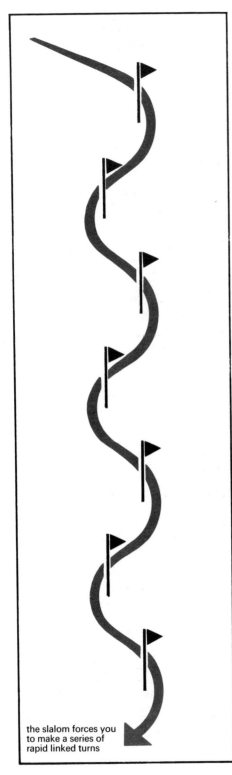

the slalom forces you to make a series of rapid linked turns

10. The slalom

The instructor bundled up our poles. We thought we were going to use them at last, but instead he stuck them in a row down the fall line, one every three yards or so, like a slalom run. It *was* a slalom run.

So far we had been twisting down the fall line as we chose. As soon as we recovered from one twist we would think about the next.

The poles were to force us to turn, not when we wanted to, but when we *had* to. For the skier does not always have the luxury of being able to turn at leisure.

The slalom poles would also help us build up a *rhythm*, we were told, one of the most important things in ski-ing.

Down through the poles we went, our arms out like wings still weaving into the rhythm of continuous turns. We used the same twisting motion as before, but we kept facing down the fall line, our arms at right angles to it, and turned only the lower part of our bodies. We were told to keep our feet on the ground and only give a little hop if we had to. Of course, we did not always manage to turn in time, and often we missed one gap, but this was all very enjoyable work.

Setting the poles as 'gates' down the slope is not the only way of teaching rhythm. One French teacher played a harmonica; another got the class to sing. The idea was to have a Viennese Waltz, or something else slow and rhythmic, and on every 'boomp' (as opposed to 'ta-ra') the entire class would twist to change direction. Ski-ing to the music, getting the rhythm—it is vital. You can, of course, always sing to *yourself*.

11. Getting the feel of the poles

Now it was at last time to use the poles. (On p. 77 we tell you how to choose them, and on p. 83 how to hold them.) But this first exercise was just to give us the feel of handling the poles. By now we were finding our 'snow feet': learning the feel of the snow and how to react to it. We were beginning to notice that some places were easier to turn on than others. In this exercise we were not using the poles to help us turn, but accustoming ourselves to yet another sensation. And, our instructor explained, we were using the poles as a timing device. This is one of their most important functions.

It is exercise 9 again, a schuss with twists. The difference here is that you don't just twist, you plant the pole at the same time.

(You will find a detailed description of how to plant your poles on p. 178.) Briefly, keep the forearm parallel to the snow, the other arm tucked close to the body. Plant the pole by bringing down your entire body, bending at the knees. As your body comes down so does the arm, and the pole. Use the right pole for turning to the right, the left to turn left. So, starting with a schuss, this is how you get the feel of the poles:

- When you are ready for your first twist, plant the pole lightly in the snow with a downward movement of the whole body from the knees. Put no weight on the pole.

The pole is removed from the snow by an upward movement of the body. The next move is to go down to plant the other pole, the aim being a series of linked turns

the turn is completed; note that the shoulders have hardly turned at all

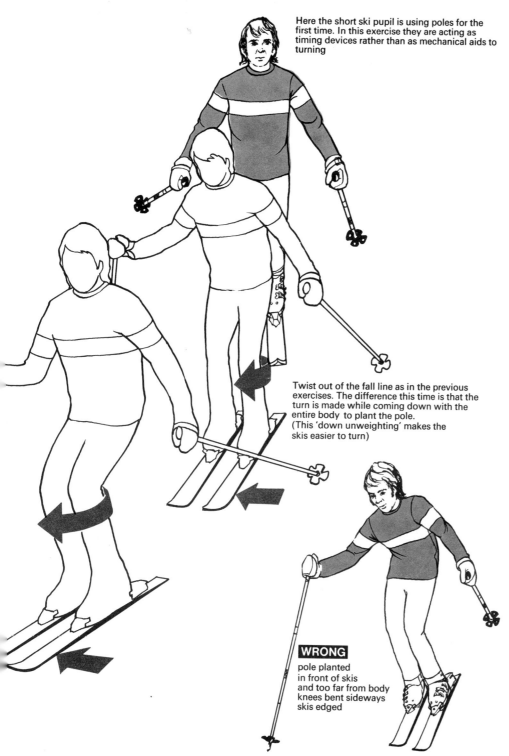

Here the short ski pupil is using poles for the first time. In this exercise they are acting as timing devices rather than as mechanical aids to turning

Twist out of the fall line as in the previous exercises. The difference this time is that the turn is made while coming down with the entire body to plant the pole. (This 'down unweighting' makes the skis easier to turn)

WRONG
pole planted
in front of skis
and too far from body
knees bent sideways
skis edged

As soon as you start to move down, twist as before. Twist to the side on which you are planting the pole. As always, the shoulders should not move, but remain at right angles to the fall line.

- The pole remains in the snow only for a moment. As soon as your twist is completed come *up* with your entire body. This removes the pole from the snow. It is the reverse of the planting movement.
- Now plant the other pole (from now on it is always the downhill one).
- Twist again, but in the other direction.
- And up.

Repeat: down, turn, plant, up; down, turn, plant, up.

Our mistakes: At first we found the poles confusing. We had managed to make a schuss with continuous twisting checks without poles. Yet all we were being asked to do now was to poke the snow with the pole by going down at each twist. We had a coordination problem. We would go down when we should be going up, or plant the left pole when we wanted to go right. We lost our rhythm, and it took a while for some of us to get it back.

We were also guilty of mistakes of technique, and these often made us fall. The chief trouble was diagnosed as 'pole-leaning'. We were either leaning on our poles too hard or planting them too far away from our skis, or both. This made us keel over sideways, and edged our skis. This kind of continuous 'wedel' turn with smooth snow and a modest slope requires flat skis. Edging can make you fall.

To cure ourselves of the pole-leaning habit we went down the slope like this, schussing with continuous twisting turns, with the poles as an aid to balance only.

Others amongst us were guilty of rigid knees. This exercise is rhythmic and—when it works—very satisfying. It calls for a lot of work at the knees, a constant down, up, down motion. Even when the body is poised to plant the pole the knees should be slightly bent. And, when the pole is planted, your bottom should be well down.

Here is a tip which helped us. You should always be able to feel the pressure of the boot against the front of your ankle. Press it hard as you go down. Beware of the tendency to bend your legs to the side. This edges the skis.

12. Anticipation

There is a minimum of explanation and theory in ski évolutif teaching. The emphasis is all on action. In that last exercise—although nobody had told us so—we had been turning by 'down-unweighting'. This means that we had taken the weight off the skis, and made them easier to turn, by going down with the body (to plant the pole). Now we tried a different way of turning. Again we were given no theory or terminology, but what we were about to do was to turn with 'anticipation' and 'up-unweighting'. (A ski can be unweighted by a sharp upwards movement of the body as well as a sharp downwards one. See p. 168 for more on this.) Once again we would go down the slope in a series of continuous linked turns, but this time we would plant the poles more firmly in the snow, and leave them there longer.

This is the sequence for turning with anticipation:

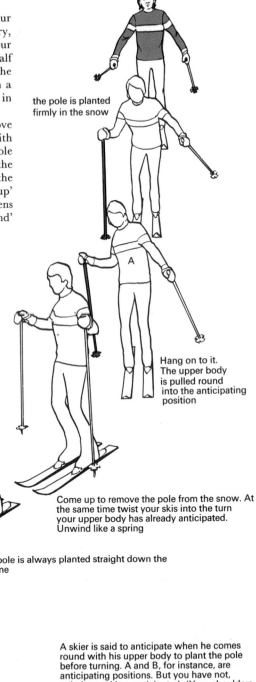

the pole is planted firmly in the snow

- Start with a schuss.
- Plant the pole vertically and *firmly*.
- Hang on to it. What happens? Your hand is suddenly virtually stationary, but the rest of you is travelling on. Your arm pulls your shoulder and the top half of your body round. If you are using the right pole you twist from the hips in a clockwise direction. All this happens in a fraction of a second.
- Now, two movements at once. Remove the pole from the piste, as before, with an upwards movement of the whole body (you are up-unweighting). At the same time, twist the bottom half of the body round to the right to 'catch up' with the top of your body. This happens almost automatically; you will 'unwind' like a spring.

Hang on to it. The upper body is pulled round into the anticipating position

Come up to remove the pole from the snow. At the same time twist your skis into the turn your upper body has already anticipated. Unwind like a spring

The pole is always planted straight down the fall line

the pole is removed with an upward body movement as you turn

A skier is said to anticipate when he comes round with his upper body to plant the pole before turning. A and B, for instance, are anticipating positions. But you have not, strictly speaking, anticipated. (Your shoulders have been brought round by your impetus *after* the pole has been planted.) This exercise gets you used to the *feel* of anticipation

Anticipation in practice: in this sequence (*bottom to top*) the more advanced short ski pupil learns to anticipate by turning his upper body to plant the pole straight down the fall line. This becomes his basic turn (and he soon discovers that the easiest place to do it is on a mogul)

The point of this exercise is to enable you to turn at the moment of up-unweighting. It was this that gave us co-ordination problems again. Instead of twisting our skis and bringing up our body all in one movement, we had a tendency to do first one and then the other. Some of us were unweighting too fiercely—leaping into the air—whilst the majority were unweighting gingerly and therefore insufficiently. In either case a fall was usually the result. It was at this point that we were introduced to another aspect of the ski évolutif philosophy, the 'minimum force' concept. We should unweight, our instructor told us, as much as we needed in order to turn, no more. In practice this might mean an imperceptible lift of the skis from the ground—certainly no more.

The placing of the pole in this turn is crucial. You should plant it straight down the fall line. But not, whatever the length of your skis, in front of them. This will give you a pole-planting zone which curves from the tips of your skis around to a point on an imaginary line drawn at right angles to your bindings. Thus a skier on a shallow traverse should place the pole almost at his side. A skier who is going practically down the fall line should plant the pole near his ski tips.

The maximum radius of this arc is determined by how far away from your body you can plant the pole whilst keeping your forearm horizontal. Just how far away you will want to plant the pole depends on the steepness of the slope. This is because the steeper it is the more likely you are to be edging your skis in a traverse. Leaning well down hill to plant the pole has the effect of flattening the skis and making them easier to turn. Thus the steeper the slope the further away you should plant the pole.

And that was the end of our first ski évolutif lesson. With the cryptic comment that turning with anticipation was 'easier on the bumps' our instructor dismissed the class. We had packed a lot into those first two hours, and returned cock-a-hoop to the hotel where our more 'expert' colleagues greeted our claim to have wedelled in our very first lesson with howls of derision.

If you learn the short ski way we hope this will give you some idea of what to expect, and what you can practise in your own time.

MORE EXERCISES

As we have said, no two ski évolutif instructors teach in quite the same way. A number of them only introduce the poles once their pupils are on 135 cm skis. Others place greater emphasis on unweighting and edging. (For instance, we had been specifically told not to edge our skis. When we asked our instructor about this he said he wanted to discourage edging as a *conscious* movement unless we were in difficulties. The same applied to weighting the downhill ski in a traverse.) It is excellent to have this varied approach and a variety of exercises. What works for one might not work for another. No two champions ski in quite the same way; there is no reason why two beginners should ski in the same way. For this reason, it is impossible to describe the entire ski évolutif process exactly as you are likely to be taught it. We shall, however, be taking a brief look at how the ski évolutif pupil can expect to progress, and what additional techniques he will be taught.

First, however, we would like to describe a few exercises which we have seen. Our particular instructor did not teach them, but we feel they will be useful in coping with any early difficulties. Do not worry if you cannot do one perfectly. Move on and try the next. This is one of the proclaimed virtues of ski évolutif: there is no single exercise at which you must succeed before moving on, no 'plateau'.

Ski-ing on one ski at a time is not as difficult as it looks, and helps combat rigid knees

The Jump and duck exercise

13. One ski only

Our chief difficulty was that we were still ski-ing rigidly. We were not relaxed. We felt it was all very well for the instructor to yell 'relax' at us, but this was more easily said than done. Yet clearly a relaxed movement was one of the vital clues to good ski-ing. So:
Ski down a slope. Lift one ski off the ground. Replace it. Lift the other ski. Go down the slope first on one ski, then the other. This teaches weight transference from ski to ski, and helps your balance.

Do the same again, only do a twist to change direction each time you are on one ski. Lift, turn, replace. Lift other ski, turn, replace. *Always* turn so that the ski you are turning on is to the outside of the turn. When you are on the left ski turn to the right. And vice versa.

14. Jumping on the move

This involves going down the slope in a series of jumps. The movement should be in the legs only—for instance, keep your head still. Lift both skis at once. Be careful not to lean too far back, as you will sit down with a bump when you land; or too far forward, when you are likely to take a header. This exercise helps your stability and your nerve.

15. Jump and duck

This helps discipline the jumps. Take four ski poles. Place one flat on the ground at right angles across your projected path of descent. About five yards (or metres) further down the slope stick two more in the ground on either side of your projected path. Place the last stick across the top of them, like a goal.

Now ski down the slope. Jump the first pole by lifting the legs only—*not* the trunk of the body. Then go *down* under the goalposts formed by the other poles. Now move the first pole closer to the others. Try again. See how close you can put the first pole to the rest and still get under them.

Your poles will make perfect 'goalposts' for practice runs

16. Weight transfer fore and aft

This exercise teaches you to transfer your weight from the tip to the tail of your skis. Neither this nor the exercise that follows should be attempted until you are on 135 cm or longer skis. Your instructor will tell you when you are ready for this length of ski. Standing still jump to lift the *tails* of the skis —but only the tails. Next, jump lifting only the tips. This is harder.

Now stand on the skis. Lean well forward without bending any body joints. Now lean well back.

17. Weight transfer on the move

Now, still using the longer skis, put the theory of Exercise 16 into practice. This will give you the feel of transferring weight either to the front or to the back of your skis when you are on the move.

Ski down a slope. Bring your weight forward as in the stationary exercises, but without keeping your body rigid. Ski in the normal knees-bent position, but feel the front of your ankles pressing on the boot. Now—with your weight on your toes—turn. Turn several times, both to left and right.

Having the weight on the toes is useful for steeper terrain.

Find a gentler piece of slope for the same exercise, but this time get your weight well back. You need a gentler slope or you will fall. Ski down it with your weight on your heels, your toes pressing on the 'roof' of your boot. Turn to the left and right as before. You will find turning on your heels is best when you graduate to deep snow, or when turning as you go up a bump.

18. The turn test

We detected a certain difference of opinion about the twist turns taught in ski évolutif. Some instructors seemed to expect pupils to waggle their feet only. Others expected a twist from the hips.

Clif Taylor, whom we mentioned as the pioneer of GLM in the United States, teaches exercises which distinguish three distinct twist turns—feet only, legs and feet only, and the hip turn.

Feet turn test. Stand with knees tight together. Bend down and place your hands on your knees. Twist the feet from the ankle. Your hands will tell you if your knees are moving. They should not.

Leg twist test. Stand with your hands on your

turning with weight on the tails of the skis: this exercise introduces a technique which is useful in deep snow

hips, arms akimbo. Twist with your legs and feet. These will be bigger twists. Your hands will tell you whether your hips are moving. They should not.

Hip twist. Hold your arms horizontal and twist hips, legs and skis. This time your *arms* should not move—you only move from the hips downwards. With this exercise you will be able to move the skis through a still bigger arc.

In the Taylor system, the pupil would then try the following turns on the move.

- Arms out in the wings position.
- First the short, sharp foot-turn.
- Then the more powerful leg turn.
- Finally, the hip-turn. This has enough power to turn the skier through as much as 90°. It is therefore obviously the most useful turn when on steep terrain or sharp braking is required.

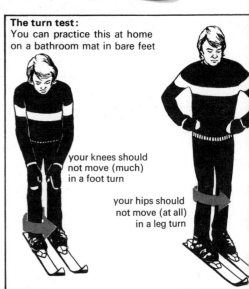

The turn test:
You can practice this at home on a bathroom mat in bare feet

your knees should not move (much) in a foot turn

your hips should not move (at all) in a leg turn

We found this was the clue to the dilemma about how much of the lower half of the body you should move when turning. The answer was minimum force. You should put no more power than is necessary into the turn.

The principle factors which would govern the necessary power are the nature of the snow, the steepness of the slope and, to an extent, your speed. The softer the snow the steeper the slope, and the greater your need for braking action the more power you need to put into the turn. And the necessary gradations of power are **1.** foot movement only; **2.** leg movement; **3.** hip movement; **4.** hip movement with progressively greater up-unweighting and anticipation; and finally **5.** some use of the pole to assist un-weighting. Long skis need more turning power, too. This is precisely why we had been using short skis, but we discovered that our technique and strength increased as our ski lengths did.

19. The cha-cha

The pupil is then encouraged to link these turns together in what Taylor calls the 'Cha-Cha'. Two slow hip turns. Three fast foot turns. Cha-Cha-chachacha.

In the Taylor system this is the most important exercise of all. It gives the skier both rhythm and control. He can suit his turn to the terrain. No slope is of constant steepness. If the slope gets steeper or the snow softer then the skier steps up the fierceness of the turn. He abandons the foot turn in favour of the hip turn.

and your arms should not move in a hip turn

the cha-cha: two slow hip turns then three fast foot ones

SHORT SKI VERSUS TRADITIONAL TEACHING

The two most obvious differences between ski évolutif teaching and traditional methods are that the skis are different and that with the short ski method the parallel turn is taught from the outset (with the stem as a later refinement). There are also some more subtle differences of ski-ing technique. Edging, for instance, is discouraged as a conscious movement. As a result the ski évolutif pupil is taught to traverse a slope not in a straight line with sharply edged skis but in a diagonal forwards side-slip (see p. 162). Or, even better, to descend with smoother, continuously linked turns. If he asks why, he is given two reasons. **1.** The traditional traverse is a remarkably fast manoeuvre. This is precisely where most beginners come unstuck: they pick up so much speed in their traverse that they can't turn properly at the end of it. **2.** The most common mistake in executing a parallel at the end of a traverse is failing to relax the edges. If they haven't been set in the first place then a major impediment to turning has been removed.

The second major difference in technique, in the French teaching at least, is the clue to our instructor's parting comment that it was 'easier on the bumps'. Ski slopes are full of bumps—or moguls, as the bigger ones are called (see p. 219 for how to cope with moguls). For the traditional beginner these are merely one more ski-ing hazard when ploughing and stemming. But our instructor was right: they *are* easier to turn on, when you know how. This in fact becomes the standard turn of the ski évolutif pupil once he has graduated to 135 cm skis. Instead of avoiding bumps, he heads straight for them, and turns on them (see p. 220).

This accords well with the ski évolutif philosophy: it is logical, and it is aggressive. However, it also provides the one major flaw in the argument that ski évolutif has no plateaux. Turning on the bumps is something that has to be mastered before you can progress. It is also a relatively complex manoeuvre, and so needs more explanation by your teacher than most. It was the one time during our ski évolutif experience that we had a language difficulty.

THE SHORT SKI TIMETABLE

How long will it take me to learn to ski? That is what everyone wants to know. With ski évolutif it is possible to give at least a

moderately concise answer. After our first two hours on short skis we had a sense of achievement nobody could possibly have had after two hours learning tennis, swimming, or riding. We were already playing the game. But, of course, we were not on 'real' skis. Even at the end of a week we were still on short skis, and still falling constantly. Even to the most casual observer we were still manifest beginners. But we *were* getting down mountains—and that is what ski-ing is all about.

Because of the relative absence of *plateaux* in the early stages of ski évolutif, it is possible to project the average pupil's first week on skis with some confidence. Our definition of this 'average pupil' would be a male under 40 or a woman under 30 (men progress more quickly) and moderately fit (capable of running up two flights of stairs without puffing).

This average beginner then could expect to have a first week something like this:

DAY ONE.   Morning on one-metre skis. Not so much ski-ing as learning to handle the equipment. Afternoon: use of poles. Working on the simpler exercises. Building up confidence.

DAY TWO.   First use of ski lift. Working on anticipation and pole usage to prepare for the 135 cm skis (which the stronger pupils may already be using). Small bumps: how to absorb them, how to turn on them. Linking turns.

DAY THREE.   On to the 135 cm skis. Doing it all again, especially turns with anticipation. Getting used to the longer skis. The afternoon will probably be spent 'going for a ride', abandoning the beginners' slope and taking a long run down the mountain with minimal instruction, just correction of errors. You are building up mileage. 'You judge an airline pilot by the hours he has flown.'

DAY FOUR.   (For the moderately active pupil this could be day three.) The longer skis enable steeper slopes to be tackled. This is done. Your work on side-slipping, bigger bumps, and continuous rapid turning, controlling the sharpness of the turn.

DAY FIVE.   Is spent in much the same way, and going faster. You get used to the things that can be done on the longer skis. Trying still steeper slopes and a few fast downhill runs to get used to speed.

DAY SIX.   On to 160 cm skis. (Although this could be day seven or eight or even a fortnight for weaker pupils.) Getting used to the longer skis, building up the extra power to turn them. Repeating everything that has been done before.

DAY SEVEN ONWARDS.

The 160 cm ski: It is now a matter of doing everything better, faster, and in more difficult conditions. These skis are to all intents and purposes full length in what they enable you to do. You can use them in powder snow and on all but the steepest slopes. You are, needless to say, ski-ing parallel. It could be said that, at this point, short ski teaching joins forces with traditional methods. You are working on your parallel turns. Perfecting, refining and varying them, just like any other pupil. Your skis are still shorter, though, than those of pupils taught by the traditional method.

When do you move onto full-length (180 cm–210 cm) skis. The simple answer is when you want to. Which might be never, especially if you are a woman. You will only need skis that are longer than 160 cm if you want to go faster, or if you want to ski off-piste a lot, or if you find yourself eyeing steep, bumpy and icy slopes and then discover that your 160 cm skis don't give you the necessary grip and control on them. When you are this good or ambitious you will begin to value the ability of longer skis to hold you steady at speed or on difficult terrain, as well as the support they give you on deep powder snow. More important: you will also have the ability to use them. But there is no reason why just a small jump up to, say, 180 cm for men or 170 cm for women should not give you all the things you need. It all depends on your ability, weight, strength and daring.

The short-ski pupil on full length skis

Advocates of ski évolutif contend that even on full length skis their pupils have several advantages over those who have learned on full length skis.

The first advantage is psychological. The short-ski graduate will be positive and aggressive in his ski-ing. He will have a certain *panache*. The traditional pupil, on the other hand, will be more defensive.

The second advantage is that he will be used to making short sharp turns. He will have better control than the skier who has lumbered through the plough and the stem to the parallel, who will often have picked up too much speed on the turn.

We felt these two arguments had some validity, but these differences would be more apparent in a comparison between the beginners on short skis and the traditional beginners stemming and ploughing. To do good parallels on long skis everyone has to conquer defensive instincts.

We agreed that the biggest advantage the short-ski graduate enjoys is when it comes to ski-ing in powder snow, where the technique is to keep one's weight further back and not to edge or open the skis (pp. 226). The short

skier's whole training has taught him to keep his weight evenly distributed on both skis, not to edge them. The traditional skier tends to perform parallels pivoting at the tips of his skis. He has, moreover, an instinctive urge to open his skis when he is in trouble. Anyone finding themselves on powder snow for the first time is convinced that he is in trouble; opening the skis ensures that his expectations are fulfilled. The short-ski graduate is also never guilty of 'parallel' turns that are in fact merely surreptitious stems.

Changing to longer skis

The one real doubt in our minds about short ski teaching had been just how easily pupils would manage the transition to longer skis. Clearly in theory the method was virtually impeccable. But what about the practice?

The first difference we noticed about longer skis was that they were faster. When we changed from 1 m to 135 cm skis, for instance, we set off down the slope a good 50 per cent faster (or so it seemed) than we were used to travelling.

It was then that we noticed the second difference. They were harder to turn. Moments of despondency and despair! All the zip and zoom we had seemed to have had on our 1 m skis had vanished. We had leaden feet—and, what was more, we tangled them up. The critics were right. We had not been ski-ing at all. We had been skating. How could we *ever* cope with even longer full length skis?

We soon discovered what the trouble was. We were trying to do on the 135 cm skis exactly what we had been doing on the 1 m skis. What we should have been doing was starting from scratch. This was what we then did. We went through the first lesson again—the side-stepping, the exercises, the descent with checks. By the end of the morning we

were as happy and as competent on the 135 cm skis as we had been on the shorter skis the day before.

The transfer to 160 cm skis was far easier, perhaps because the proportional increase in length was less, perhaps because we had learned our lesson from our first experience with the 135 cm ones.

Children on short skis

Children have always skied on shorter skis than adults.

But, although skis of less than one metre are now being produced for children, few teachers are yet convinced that they need them. Having absorbed this surprising piece of information, we therefore expected that the children at Les Arcs would start on 1 m skis, but would end their progress with, say, 135 cm ones.

This they did. But, to the consternation of those of us in the ski évolutif school, we noticed that their teaching was otherwise purely traditional. Plough and stem before parallel. We had heard so much about ski évolutif being logical and natural, yet here were eight-year-olds on skis that were relatively long for their size doing natural plough turns and plough stops.

We never succeeded in worming an entirely satisfactory explanation for this from the ski évolutif proponents, who scowl at ploughs and stems. Why were they teaching children this, or at least tolerating it?

Their argument went like this. One metre skis are almost full-length skis for a small child. They are much bigger, in proportion to his size, than a one-metre ski is for us. The child is therefore being taught on more or less traditional equipment. Traditional methods are therefore called for.

At this point the one flaw we had already detected in the argument was conceded. The plough and the stem *are* natural defensive reactions. Put a child on skis and he will plough instinctively. *But*, the argument continued, children are also natural and gifted learners. They pick up a new skill quicker than adults, and discard obsolete ones with equal facility. They therefore have none of the difficulty the adult experiences in progressing from the stem to the parallel turn. For them it comes naturally.

The short ski method for us was therefore an antidote to the crustiness of old age. Consolingly, it could help us to learn to ski as easily as a child.

6

Lessons for advanced skiers

19 CARVING THE TURN. 20 THE JET TURN: Anticipation. The sit-back style. 21 TIGHT TURNS: Short radius parallel turn with check. Classical and braking wedel turns. 22 HOW TO MASTER THE MOGUL: The Avalement turn. 23 OFF- PISTE SKI-ING: how to ski parallel in deep powder.

19 CARVING THE TURN

There are thousands of people who have been ski-ing for years who have never heard of the difference between turning by making the skis skid and turning by making the skis carve an arc in the snow. There is no mystique about carving turns. It is simply a way of getting your skis to work more efficiently for you. Unfortunately skiers are hardly anywhere told what the skis will do for them; one often feels the teachers themselves have never analysed or understood what kind of tool the ski is. Instruction books have not dealt with carving, and few ever use the word skidding; yet the difference between the turn which is skidded and the turn which is carved is fundamental. The carved turn is:

1. faster
2. smoother
3. more sensuous

It is all these things because the skier 'rides' round the corner on the smooth edge of his skis. They have to be bent into reverse camber to do that, but once you are 'riding' on your edges you are locked into an arc and will track along it like a tram on a curving monorail. The ski is thus doing the work, while the skier enjoys the ride. Once the weighted ski is in that position, it does not matter whether it is a man or a bag of potatoes on the ski: it will still follow the same curve. Of course the skier has to maintain balance and keep his nerve. The carved turn goes so much faster that when we first practised it even the most dare-devil of us had his breath taken away. The skidded turn is slower, and follows a less precise arc because it is the *skier* pushing the skis outwards who is dictating the arc of the turn, rather than the ski.

We had come across the carved turn in our research into the design of the modern ski (Chapter 9, section 3). Then we read a book which is already beginning to have a profound influence on ski teaching, and we talked to its author in the United States. He is Warren Witherell, Director of Burke Mountain Academy, Vermont, and his book —which we mentioned earlier—is called *How the Racers Ski*. Witherell was a world water ski champion before he took up snow ski-ing, and he now trains ski racers for the American national team. His basic message is that racers win races because they carve turns, but he also believes that holiday skiers can and must learn to carve turns. So what is this carving and skidding distinction?

Use the skis to create turning forces

Skiers say they turn by using a 'parallel', a 'stem christie', and so on. In fact, they mostly have not a clue what the ski is really doing in the snow. They simply use names to describe turns without realizing that turns can be executed in two very different ways.

Skidded turns are what most of us do. The skid is, of course, controlled and the side slip is the controlled skid. Yet you rarely hear the term skid when you are told to do the movements that will encourage the tails of the skis to make a skid. You will go on skidding, as we did, but the more you ski the more you will want to enjoy the thrill of carving some or all of your turns or some part of the turns.

Carved turns are different. The skis are not pushed round the corner. There is no heel thrust. The edges are not used for braking. There is no side slip in the true carved turn. The skier puts one of his skis on its edge and transfers his weight to that ski. This makes it bend into 'reverse camber' (which we described in Chapter 9, section 3). If the skier maintains that position—and it requires

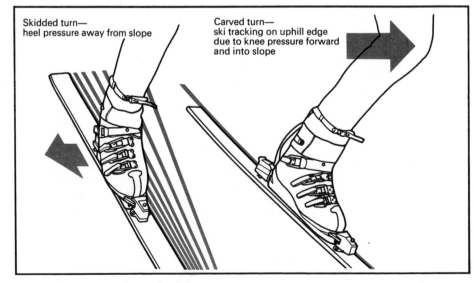

Skidded turn—
heel pressure away from slope

Carved turn—
ski tracking on uphill edge
due to knee pressure forward
and into slope

balance—the weighted ski itself will describe an arc in the snow and carry the skier with it. *In the skidded turn* the skier is pushing outwards so that the edge bites into the snow and slows him down in a regulated sideslip. *In the carved turn* the skier pushes forward and into the slope with his knees, and the edged ski runs along in a groove in the snow. The edges 'carve' a smooth arc in the snow, hence the term 'carving'.

These photographs illustrate the difference. The carved turn (below) has left a very narrow track in the snow. The skidded turn (on the right) has left a wider track.

The wide track of the skidded turn

The narrow track of the carved turn

The skier who skids when turning is always pushing across the snow and fighting to control his skis. The skier who carves a turn is using the qualities of the ski and does not need to fight the slope. Skiers do learn to control their skids, but there is no need to struggle at all when the ski is locked on an edge in a carved turn. The sidecut and reverse camber of the edged, weighted ski dictate the arc of the turn, and the skier just enjoys the ride.

Beginners, whose first prayer is to control speed, will not be very excited at the prospect of learning a faster turning action. This is why we have included this chapter in the advanced section. Yet Witherell believes that beginners, too, should be taught about carving before they build up muscular habits related to skidding.

We have all learned to skid our turns, so it is hard for us to say how a beginner would react to learning a faster kind of turn. The braver would no doubt do it. It would be a pity if the rest were put off because they could not control their speed.

Speed *can* be controlled—by doing more turns across the slope. Of two skiers of equal ability coming down the same slope the man doing carved turns will have to turn more often. This is another reason why we all have to learn to skid, despite the superiority of the carved turn. For the beginner, certainly, every turn is an agony of anxiety, and he will want to keep the number of turns he does to a minimum. That said, most people who have done the stem christie turn can control their speed, and should have the confidence to attempt carving more of their turns. This is the stage that the better of us writing this book have reached. Sometimes when we do not get it quite right we begin a turn with a skid, but then we continue with a carving action as the ski is locked on its edge, and thrust forward with a movement of the knees. It is a marvellous experience.

Even the best racers may skid a bit at first, until they get the ski tracking on its edge in the new direction. And many racers lose their balance as they ride on their edges, and can fall over.

All this talk about racers, we realize, is likely to put you off. 'What, me? Do that?' is the reaction of the first year skiers when asked to race between slalom poles. You will be astonished to find you can do it. In the challenge you will start stepping from ski to ski like a racer. You will ski aggressively, and forget about conscious movement of this and that shoulder.

There are certainly some holiday skiers who will never want to attempt carved turns, and who are happy enough pottering and skidding down the slopes. So be it. There are many ways to enjoy ski-ing.

However, the average holiday skier who can put his or her skis on edge to an angle of 30 degrees should try carving. That is ample to make the edges carve on slopes of modest steepness. You do not need to be able to balance over skis edged at an angle of 60 degrees like a racer. But you are following the same principle.

Here are some exercises which will help to get the idea of carving. We have tried them all, and when we get them right there is nothing in ski-ing quite so exhilarating—but we confess that we find it easier to write about carved turns than to do them!

Long radius carved turn

Position yourself on your friendly slope in a 5 o'clock traverse—almost straight downhill. Put your skis about 1–2 ft apart, but parallel. Roll the intended outside ski of the turn on to its edge—say about 30–40 degrees. The other can stay flat and with only a little weight on it. Give the *edged* ski most of your weight by just standing on it. This will seem very awkward at first. We kept wanting to stand on the flat ski—naturally, since it is easier. When you have got the weight right, let yourself go.

Your weight should produce reverse camber and your ski should describe an arc in the snow, helped by the impetus of your downward slide. The faster you go the easier it is to 'carve'; but extra speed needs extra nerves. It will be a long arc, and it will take perhaps ten yards before the arc begins. You will be gathering speed. This is necessary, so try not to panic. That is the importance of trying carving first on a wide slope of moderate incline, where you will have room to move and where you will not be moving so quickly. Whatever you do, avoid sideways skidding. If you find you are frightened you will push with your heels and slow yourself with a skid. We know: we did. But that is completely against the point of the exercise. So find a slope you can 'dominate' and say 'Here goes; what does it matter if I don't stop?'

Once you have done a few single turns either side, try changing the angle at which you have edged the ski and see what happens. Given enough pressure the more you edge the more you will tighten the radius of the turn. Then experiment with different leverages. Begin with forward leverage—pushing your feet forward. Then, when the turn has begun, move to neutral leverage, with pressure over the centre of the ski. Keep trying different angles and pressures and get the idea of the edged, weighted ski gradually and smoothly doing the carving of the turn for you. Do not rush and push. Relax. You will probably find at first that you cannot

Above: practising carved turns in wide-stance parallel; more than half the weight should be on the edged ski which will carve the turn.
Below: edge-changing in the carved snowplough turn (see facing page)

hold yourself on the edge of the ski and then you will skid in the snow. Keep trying to ski on the railway line of the ski so that you get the feeling that your arc is the arc of reverse camber in the ski.

Linking the turns

Intermediates (and brave beginners) should try to link these turns.

After you have turned one way with one ski edged, flatten it and edge the other ski. Then stand on the newly edged ski and, gradually, you turn. Keep the skis apart but parallel. Let the newly unweighted ski lie flat and light and follow the weighted ski.

You may find the linking a bit difficult at first. What you are aiming for is smooth transition with no skidding in between. You should try to initiate the change by gradually rolling the ankle and knee (and then, depending on the steepness of the slope, letting the hip angulate).

Carving snowploughs

If you find it hard to change edges with skis parallel but apart, you can—surprisingly—get some feel of carving by doing linked snowplough turns. If that seems humiliating, reflect that Witherell uses the snowplough

Henri Duvillard, French downhill and slalom champion : note the erect upper body

with racers. 'I had a national team skier who was jamming his skis in the turns,' he told us. 'We did a morning of snowploughs getting him to let the ski lead the turn.'

Witherell takes his students on miles of gentle runs doing nothing but snowplough turns, learning to make turns of a smooth arc by constant pressure and edge on the ski. Slower speeds are best for getting the feel of the snow. Most of us doing snowploughs will push with our heels and do it with a skid. Some initial skidding or steering may be necessary in a slow turn, but try to get the ski carving *forward* and on its edge as soon as possible. Concentrate on experimenting with knee, ankle and foot pressures, and forget about the upper body. Do not lean forward. Your hips should always be over your knees. Look back at the snow from time to time and identify skidded and carved tracks.

Edge changing

Since the hard part in carved turns is to change from riding on one edge to riding on the other, here is a short exercise which helps.

Start in the fall line in the wedge position— tails apart as in the snowplough but tips further apart than normal—say 1–2 feet. Make sure the slope is fairly easy and wide. will be worrying about moving too quickly.

1. Start with both skis flat, and with your weight on both skis.

2. Edge one ski by pressing your knee inwards.

3. Put your weight on that ski.

4. As soon as the ski begins to carve, transfer your weight to the other ski and set that edge with a push inwards with the knee. The ski previously edged is flattened.

5. Do this quickly. Do not wait for the turn to build up as you have been doing in earlier exercises. As soon as you feel the carving action begin, jump to the other ski.

6. Keep facing downhill and forget about your upper body and pole. Witherell does a similar exercise. He hops from edged ski to edged ski, saying perhaps a hundred times 'Left edge, right edge'.

This is an excellent way to learn how to make quick changes of edges and weights.

Watch the racers

Until we learned about carving—and we are still skidding a lot!—ski racing was all right as a spectacle but seemed as relevant to holiday ski-ing as motor cycle racing is to pottering about on a scooter. Now we find there is so much more to watch, especially in slalom. We try and check who is skidding most. Are there great plumes of snow at each turn (skidding) or very little (carving)? What is the effect on the time?

We watch how the racers step from ski to ski (at 70 mph!). We try to spot the moment when they push off the uphill edge of downhill ski and step on to the uphill edge of the uphill ski. We note how few bother to keep the skis close together. We watch the leverage created by knees thrusting forward. We note the angulation of ankle, knee and hip and how quiet their upper bodies are. We try to see reverse camber in the weighted ski. And occasionally we reflect, with an approving nod, that we did something like so-and-so on that lovely last afternoon down the blue run.

20   THE JET TURN

We thought the jet turn was going to be far-out and flashy, something strictly for experts and 'hot-doggers'. (The word comes from America, and describes dare-devil experts who go in for especially skilful moves and dangerous antics.) In fact it is only a modern variation of the parallel christie. Basically, it is a parallel turn which relies on a sudden check (edge-set) and 'anticipation' (downhill-turning) of the upper body to bring about the critical split-second of unweighting. Nevertheless, it's a good turn. Once you can do good basic parallels there is no reason why you should not be able to take the jet in your stride.

The jet turn; a stylish modern variation of the basic parallel technique in which the skier assumes an apparent sitting-back position in mid-turn

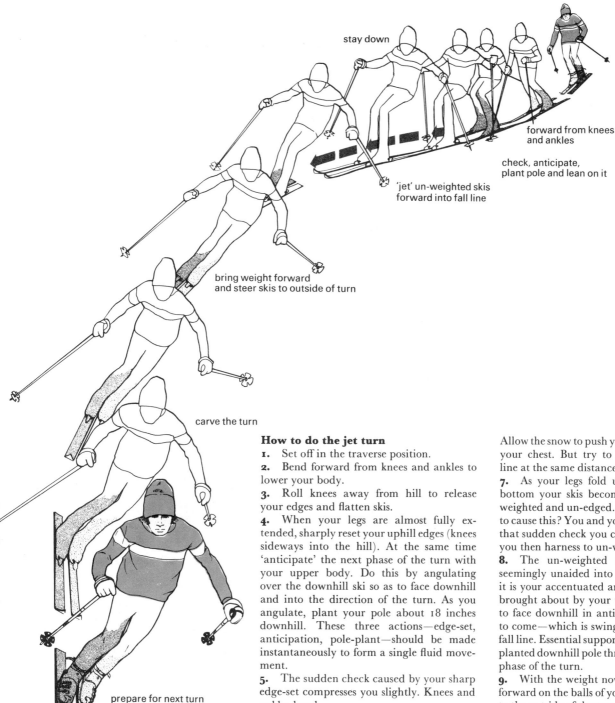

stay down

forward from knees
and ankles

check, anticipate,
plant pole and lean on it

'jet' un-weighted skis
forward into fall line

bring weight forward
and steer skis to outside of turn

carve the turn

prepare for next turn

How to do the jet turn

1. Set off in the traverse position.

2. Bend forward from knees and ankles to lower your body.

3. Roll knees away from hill to release your edges and flatten skis.

4. When your legs are almost fully extended, sharply reset your uphill edges (knees sideways into the hill). At the same time 'anticipate' the next phase of the turn with your upper body. Do this by angulating over the downhill ski so as to face downhill and into the direction of the turn. As you angulate, plant your pole about 18 inches downhill. These three actions—edge-set, anticipation, pole-plant—should be made instantaneously to form a single fluid movement.

5. The sudden check caused by your sharp edge-set compresses you slightly. Knees and ankles bend.

6. Then, like a coiled spring, the build-up of force bounces you into an 'up-forward' motion. But instead of allowing the force to raise your whole body, you 'ride' it, just as you would 'ride' a bump. Relax your legs.

Allow the snow to push your knees up towards your chest. But try to keep your shoulder line at the same distance from the snow.

7. As your legs fold up underneath your bottom your skis become momentarily un-weighted and un-edged. What has happened to cause this? You and your edges. By making that sudden check you created a force which you then harness to un-weight your skis.

8. The un-weighted skis begin to turn seemingly unaided into the fall line. In fact it is your accentuated angulation position— brought about by your upper body twisting to face downhill in anticipation of the turn to come—which is swinging the skis into the fall line. Essential support is provided by your planted downhill pole throughout this critical phase of the turn.

9. With the weight now off your heels and forward on the balls of your feet, steer the skis to the outside of the turn.

10. As you move out of the fall line into the final phase of the turn make your uphill edges bite more sharply.

11. The final phase of the jet turn is the same as the basic parallel christie.

Anticipation: how the upper body leads the legs into the turn

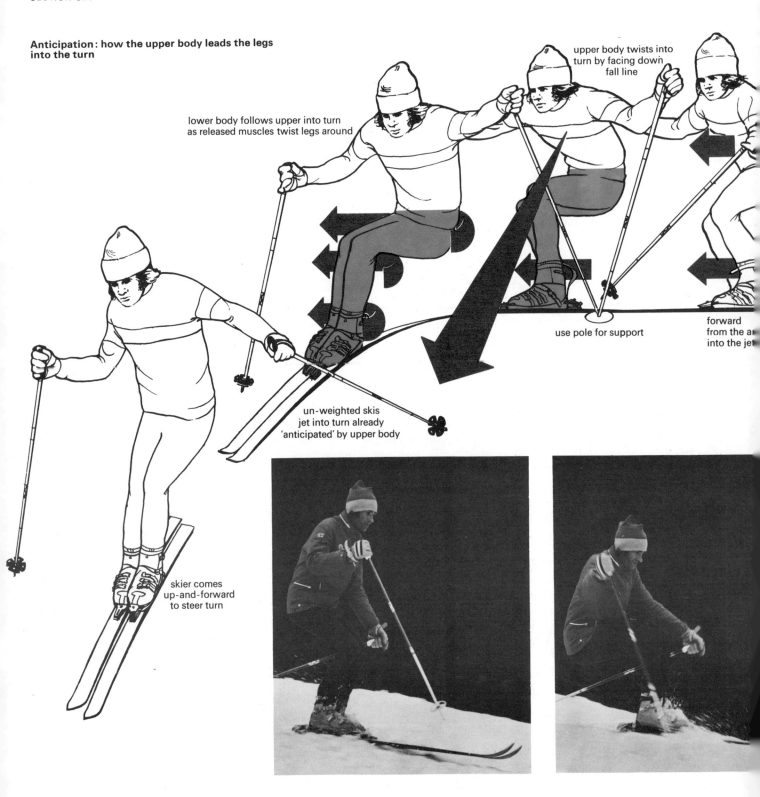

upper body twists into turn by facing down fall line

lower body follows upper into turn as released muscles twist legs around

use pole for support

forward from the a into the je

un-weighted skis jet into turn already 'anticipated' by upper body

skier comes up-and-forward to steer turn

Anticipation—how it works

Anticipation is what the American skier calls 'split-rotation'. The body is split in two halves—upper and lower. In a turn such as the jet turn, which relies on anticipation, the upper half of the body twists into the turn first and draws the lower half of the body around after it. This is what happens.

1. The upper body twists to face downhill —in anticipation of the turn the skier is about to perform. He supports himself by planting the pole downhill.

2. This twisted, accentuated angulation position stretches muscles in the hips and small of the back.

3. When the skier bounces out of his check position, those stretched muscles are released and immediately contract, pulling his legs back into the axis of his body.

4. This automatically turns the un-weighted skis into the turn already anticipated by the upper body.

Sitting back is 'in'

Like every cult from pop music to fashion, ski-ing is, we repeat, subject to sudden fads and fancies. This applies not only to ski clothes and equipment but even to technique itself. Currently 'sitting back' is all the rage. The craze was detonated by the skill of the French superstar ski racers Jean-Claude Killy and Patrick Russel in the late 1960s, who perfected a style of turning on their tails to make their skis accelerate faster through the slalom gates. Sitting back was only a phase of their technique, which required just as much if not more time balancing in a neutral or forward stance. But the sitting back movement created more dramatic action pictures, and the ski-ing press was not slow to pick this up. The result was inevitable. Suddenly, sitting back was 'in'. The jet turn, the avale-ment and its extreme form, the kangaroo, became terms of common currency on the ski slopes. Boots grew higher and stiffer to give the sit-back skier something to lean on. Thigh muscles bulged to bursting point with the strain and the agony of jacking-up eager but sagging stylists in an attempted armchair stance.

There is no doubt that sitting back is due for a long run. It's fast and it's fun. But it should be kept in perspective, used in moderation and never exaggerated.

Sitting back is a reaction movement adopted in the beginning or mid-phase of a turn where the feet are launched forward towards the fall line, as in the jet turn, or when 'swallow-ing' the bump, as in 'avalement'. The sitting movement lasts for just a fraction of a sec-ond, when it is no longer possible to remain balanced directly over the feet. To conclude the turn, the skier must always catch up with his feet again. In other words, for every 'sit-back' movement there is a 'come-forward' position, which is just as important.

Even as used by the racers, sitting back is only an additional aid to turning, and not a whole new replacement for basic technique, which still demands a consistently well-balanced position over the skis. Furthermore, we are not racers. The average holiday skier has neither the muscle needed to stave off collapse on to the tails of his skis nor the skill to recover from near-spill situations when sitting back. So use the technique by all means whenever the modern avalement-based turns demand. But don't let it colour your whole approach to ski-ing. Otherwise, instead of sitting back, you could end up as a backward skier.

Below (left to right): in this sequence you can see how the skis 'jet' forward into the turn from beneath the skier's compressed body. For a brief moment he is in an extreme sitting-back movement over his un-weighted skis. But he quickly returns with an 'up-forward' motion to bring his weight forward and steer the final phase of the turn

21 TIGHT TURNS

The short-radius parallel turn with check

At this stage in your ski-ing career there are plenty of situations when a tight, short-radius turn is wanted in a hurry. This is the time to introduce the parallel christie preceded by a short uphill check. It's the ideal turn for steep slopes and tight corners. It's stylish. It's aggressive. It's sharp, twisty and fun to do. Here's how it goes.

1. Begin to traverse a slope of average steepness.

2. Exaggerate your traverse position a little. Increase the angulation of your upper body over the downhill ski. Prepare to plant your downhill pole.

3. Roll your knees down the slope to flatten your skis. As your ankles relax and your skis flatten, begin to side-slip. Thrust the sliding tails away down the slope with your heels.

4. Instead of letting your deliberately induced mini-side-slip develop, cut it short. After a yard or two smartly reset your uphill edges. Make them bite hard and fast. Really stab on the brakes. The effect will be to create a platform in the snow, something on which the skis can grip. It is also a launching pad from which you can safely spring into the turn without slipping.

5. As you check you will feel your momentum compressing you into a semi-crouch. Your knees will flex. Bend forward from the ankles as your legs start to concertina.

6. At the moment of maximum compression plant your downhill pole. Immediately you will 'rebound' lightly with an 'up-forward' motion. Your upper body will remain square to the fall line. The two movements combine. Your un-weighted skis will swing underneath you towards the fall line.

7. Land on flattened skis and apply turning pressure with your knees. Your lead ski will change as the turn progresses (your inside ski now leads). Your upper body is angulated so that the shoulders remain facing downhill. Again assume a traverse position. You are now ready to make a turn in the opposite direction. As you have finished your turn in a 'down' position, you use this to trigger the 'up' movement for the next turn.

Say to yourself: 'end of last turn is beginning of next'.

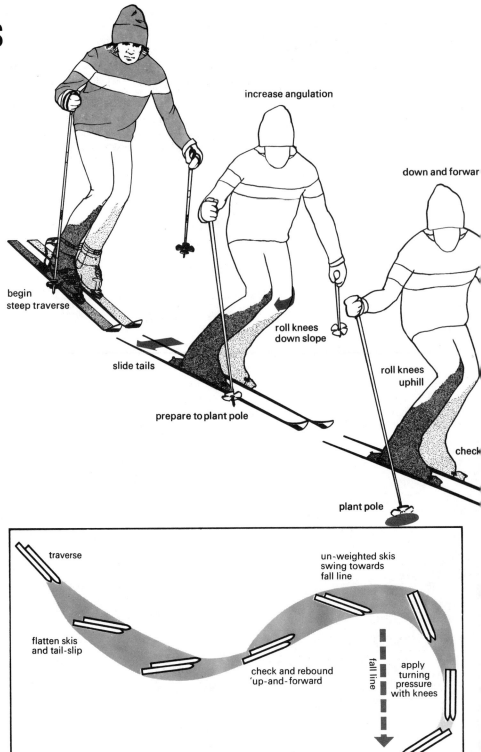

increase angulation

down and forwar

begin
steep traverse

roll knees
down slope

slide tails

roll knees
uphill

prepare to plant pole

check

plant pole

traverse

un-weighted skis
swing towards
fall line

flatten skis
and tail-slip

check and rebound
'up-and-forward'

fall line

apply
turning
pressure
with knees

up and forward

body square to fall line

In the main illustration (left) the short-radius turn has been expanded in order to show more clearly what happens in every phase of the turn. The illustration above gives a more accurate impression of the tightness of the turn

un-weighted skis swing to fall line

complete turn with angulation and knee steering

land on flattened skis

Sharp, twisty and fun to do; the short-radius turn

Wedel turns

In German, 'wedeln' means 'to wag', as a dog wags its tail. The French call it 'godille', meaning 'to scull'. The two words give an accurate picture of what the movement is like. It is the art of the linked short-radius parallel turn down the fall line. In each turn the tails swing out the same distance either side of the fall line. The traverse is abolished. One turn flows directly into the next, leaving a serpent track behind. The skier 'wags' his skis like a dog. Perhaps a more accurate image is the regular movement of a windscreen wiper.

Few of us honestly thought we would ever progress so far when we first joined a ski school. Now here we were (those of us who made it) among the ski school élite. We shall not deny that we felt highly pleased with ourselves the day we entered the wedel class.

There are several variations of wedel, but the average wedel-class pupil need only concentrate on two.

The joy of wedel in powder snow. The serpent trails show how one turn flows directly into the next as the skiers 'wag' their skis from side to side

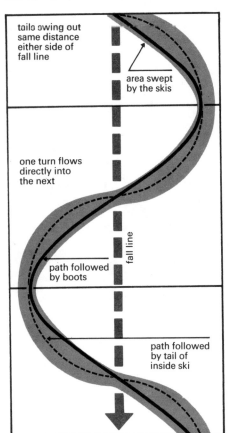

tails swing out same distance either side of fall line

area swept by the skis

one turn flows directly into the next

fall line

path followed by boots

path followed by tail of inside ski

Classic *wedel* on a gentle slope. In the *wedel* the upper body goes downhill all the time. Note the hips and the pole planting.

Braking wedel

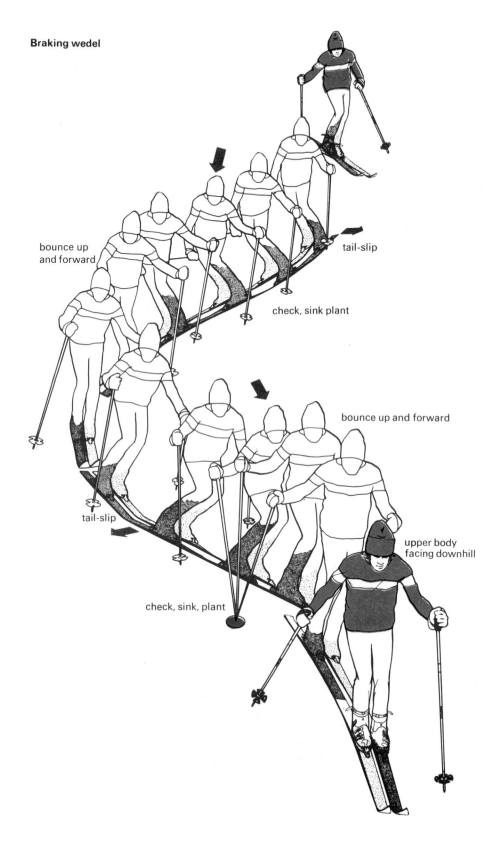

bounce up
and forward

tail-slip

check, sink plant

bounce up and forward

tail-slip

upper body
facing downhill

check, sink, plant

The braking wedel

This is nothing but a series of the short-radius parallel turns with check we have just learned. It is a useful method of slowing your speed on steep or intermediate slopes, or on a narrow piste, for instance, when a schuss would prove impractical or unwise.

1. The skier comes straight down the fall line. Skis together and flat on the snow. Body facing squarely downhill.

2. He sinks forward and plants his pole.

3. Leaning on his pole he rebounds with an 'up-forward' motion to un-weight his skis.

4. As his skis un-weight he swings them out of the fall line.

5. He lands on flattened skis. They tail-slip downhill. He angulates over the downhill ski so that his upper body remains facing downhill.

6. Before the tails have slid too far out of the fall line he checks them sharply, energetically setting the uphill edges of his skis with a quick 'down' motion. Simultaneously, as he sinks and checks, he plants the other pole.

7. At once, like a compressed spring that has been freed, he rebounds off his edges into an 'up-forward' motion. The forward part of the movement keeps his ski tips on the snow. The 'up' part un-weights the tails. The pole gives added support and triggers the rebound. The un-weighted tails swing back through the fall line again.

8. He lands on flattened skis. They tail-slip downhill. His upper body remains facing downhill.

9. He checks, sinks, plants his pole, ready to rebound into the next turn.

215

The classical wedel

Unlike the braking wedel there is no practical purpose for learning the classical wedel. It is really nothing more than an exercise in hedonism, a stylish piece of frivolous nonsense to impress your friends and maybe improve your sense of co-ordination. Nevertheless, mastery of this technique gave us more fun than anything we had learned so far.

For the classical wedel you need a smooth, not-too-steep slope.

The skier still relies on planting the pole to trigger each turn, but the rebounding action is far more relaxed and subdued.

The tails move only a short distance out of the fall line.

The skis are flatter on the snow.

The turns are quicker.

The shoulders stay at right angles to the fall line. In other words, the skier's upper body faces directly downhill all the time.

The upper body remains 'quiet'. The shoulders stay at the same height above the snow. All the movement comes from the hips downwards as the legs swing from side to side like a pendulum.

Because the shoulders stay the same height above the snow the skier's legs are at their maximum point of compression when they are directly under the body with the skis in the fall line.

And they are most fully extended when at the end of their sideways thrusts away to either side of the fall line.

Try to think of the leg movement like this:

1. Skis are in fall line. Legs are compressed directly under skier.

2. Skis are thrust to one side and legs extended, pushing heels down slope.

3. Pole is planted. Edges set. Skis are *pulled* back under skier's bottom into the fall line—then in same uninterrupted movement *pushed* away down the slope on the other side.

Ski tips to remember

Concentrate on acquiring a good rhythm above all else. This is the secret of wedeln. Rhythm, rhythm, rhythm.

Keep your weight forward on the balls of the feet. We often found ourselves starting well but losing control after the first few turns. Usually this was due to the fear factor forcing us back on our heels.

Keep your upper body 'quiet'—and facing down the fall line.

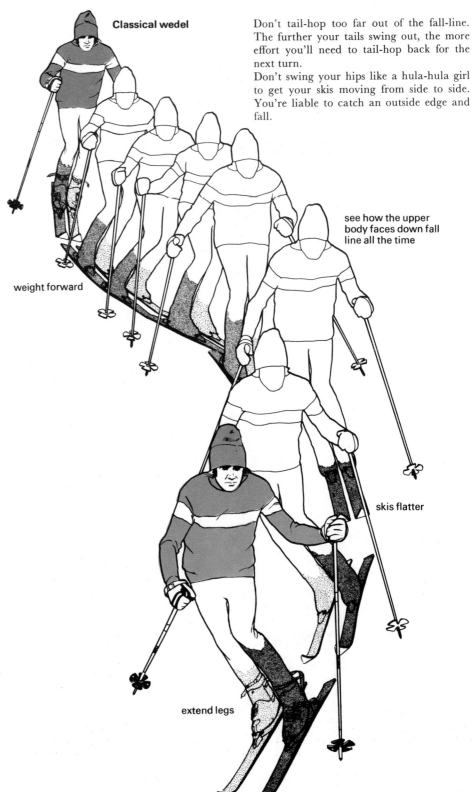

Classical wedel

weight forward

Don't tail-hop too far out of the fall-line. The further your tails swing out, the more effort you'll need to tail-hop back for the next turn.

Don't swing your hips like a hula-hula girl to get your skis moving from side to side. You're liable to catch an outside edge and fall.

see how the upper body faces down fall line all the time

skis flatter

extend legs

How to prepare yourself for wedel

Find a smooth and gentle slope and practise the following two exercises.

1. *Pole-planting and tail-hopping down the fall line*

We've already explained this one in Chapter 17 (the parallel christie). It is the same exercise that introduced us to the long radius parallel turn.

Simply:

(**a**) Ski down the fall line.

(**b**) Sink forward and plant the pole.

(**c**) Hop with an 'up-forward' motion to un-weight the tails.

(**d**) Sink forward and plant the other pole. And so on.

2. *Pole-planting and tail-hopping out of the fall line*

The same again. Only this time when you tail-hop keep your skis flat but shift your tails slightly out of the fall line, first to one side then the other. And so on.

If you can do this you are almost wedeln.

In both exercises it is important to concentrate on keeping a steady rhythm. Remember that your pole-plant is your trigger and your support.

Rhythm, rhythm, rhythm. It really helps if you can say aloud to yourself—rhythmically—what you are supposed to be doing. 'Pole plant. Edge set. Thrust.'

In wedel it is important to keep the skis together. The skier in front has a good position but his companion's skis have begun to open. Leaning back defensively or too much upper body movement can cause this

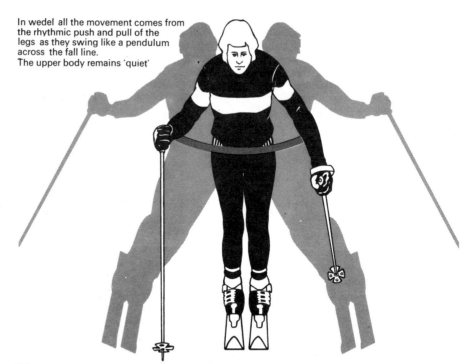

In wedel all the movement comes from the rhythmic push and pull of the legs as they swing like a pendulum across the fall line.
The upper body remains 'quiet'

Where we went wrong

- We started well but lost control after the first few turns. Usually this was because the fear factor had forced us back defensively on our heels. Keep your weight well forward on the ball of the foot.
- Sometimes we found ourselves swinging the tails with more and more effort at each tail-hop until we lost control altogether. The mistake was to swing them too far out of the fall line so that they did need this extra effort. Again, it was defensive—the more out of the fall line the slower we went.
- We found ourselves losing control and rhythm because the upper body kept swinging about. We lost our position, which was pointing our navel down the valley, all the time. Again, the mistake was almost always swinging too far out of the fall line.
- We caught an outside edge and fell. Cause: we had been swinging our hips like a hula-hula girl to get the skis moving from side to side.

COUNTER-ROTATION

Counter-rotation is an old-fashioned term used to describe the movement of the upper body when it turns in the opposite direction to the lower body. Right into the 1960s it was still being taught as an aid for easier turning, but modern theory now frowns on excessive upper body movement.

In ski-ing it is the lower body that does all the hard work. The legs provide the power. Hips, knees and ankles are working to provide steerage and control.

The upper body (or rather, the arms) has only one main purpose—to provide balance. Here's a quick demonstration to prove the point.

Stand on a rug or towel on the bathroom floor. (Any smooth or slippery surface will do.)

Now, with knees bent, legs and feet together, twist your feet vigorously from side to side. You'll notice that as your arms go one way your feet twist in the opposite direction.

In other words, you are counter-rotating. It is an automatic, subconscious reaction to help you maintain your balance. It's exactly the same on the slopes. When your skis turn one way your upper body should be counter-rotating in the opposite direction.

If ever you are in doubt as to which way you should counter-rotate, remember: your upper body should always be turned so as to be facing downhill.

22 HOW TO MASTER THE MOGUL

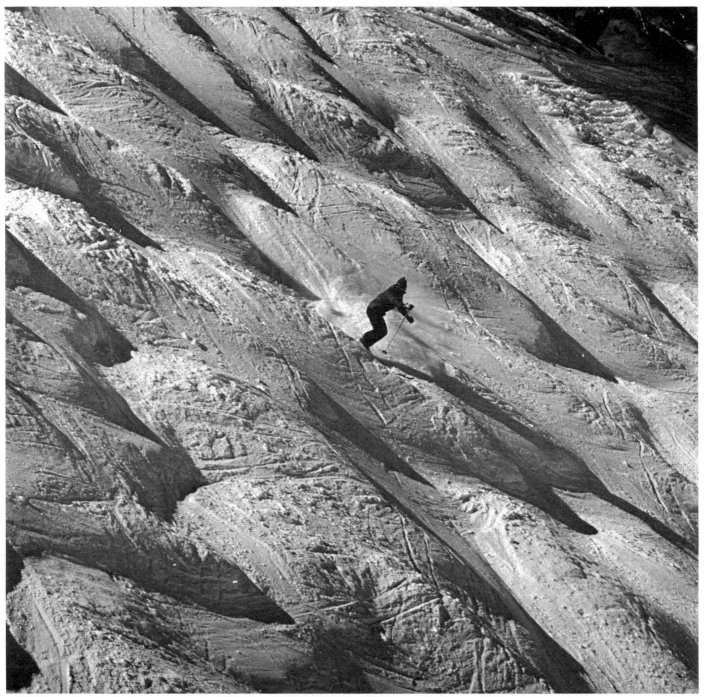

A lone skier navigates his way through the moguls on Look Ma at Vail. To ride these daunting bumps demands a whole new way of turning—and the new compact skis are creating tougher moguls.

Every winter the ski fields are afflicted by a strange malady. The steeper slopes come out in bumps. As the season progresses the bumps get bigger. The smooth snowfields have become a sea of billowing hummocks, and it is these hummocks which are known as moguls. The cause of this curious affliction is you—the skier.

Moguls are formed by the constant passage of skiers carving tight turns in each other's tracks on steep slopes. They grow larger very quickly, because it is easier to turn on a slight bump. The more skiers who turn around a slight bump, the more it becomes a big bump, and the deeper the trough beneath it.

Moguls don't turn up in ones and twos. Entering a mogul field is a bit like trying to find your way through a maze—or a mine-field. Even the name, 'mogul', smacks of something powerful and sinister. Certainly our first meeting with the moguls was a very apprehensive affair. Our initial reaction was to crawl across the slope in a shallow traverse looking for a likely spot to turn. Usually there wasn't an easy spot, and we finished up on the opposite side of the piste with an undignified kick turn to get us out of trouble. In short, we hated moguls. Now we love them. Why? The answer is the 'avalement' turn. This is the technique the French have devised for mastering the mogul, and means, literally, 'swallow'. We have no doubt ourselves that it is the most stylish method. With avalement the mogul ceases to be an obstacle. It becomes a positive aid to easier turning.

Moguls—the good, the bad, and the ugly

Moguls come in a variety of shapes and sizes. Long, ugly whale-backed moguls. Deceptively gentle half-moon moguls with scary, near-sheer ice walls hidden on their lower sides. But the skier who knows his moguls is constantly looking for a shapely, well-rounded mogul, preferably one with just the hint of a flat, turn-table surface on top. This is the kind of mogul on which it is easiest to turn.

Why moguls make turning easier

The first time we entered a mogul field our reaction was to try and sneak along in the troughs instead of riding the bumps. Somehow it felt safer than being perched on those hostile hillocks. But this never proved easy. We had not the skill to turn fast enough. Nor was there always room enough to turn without tips or tails catching between the bumps. We fell a lot.

The essence of mogul ski-ing is that you turn on top of the bump. Just think about it for a minute. If you sat your empty skis on top of a mogul you could turn them with a flick of your little finger. The reason is that the skis are only in contact with the snow over a small area in the middle, the fulcrum. So they turn much more easily than when they are on the flat. It is exactly the same when you are standing on your skis. Pivoting on a bump is astonishingly easier than trying to turn on a flat surface. Try it.

Pivoting on a bump is a good stationary exercise for avalement. Pick out a friendly mogul, one with a smooth convex slope on the downhill side and a tolerably flat surface on top. Stand on top of this mogul and across the fall line with skis parallel: they can be apart if you like—say up to six inches. Tips and probably tails will be poised in mid-air, with snow contact only at the centre of the skis. But note:

- The uphill ski, which is normally ahead, is in line with the downhill ski.
- The weight, which is usually predominantly on the downhill ski, is more evenly on both sides (unless the slope is steep and you are sliding).

Drop into a semi-crouch by bending the knees well forward. This lowers your centre of gravity and gives you better balance for the exercise. This is to twist your feet and knees first one way and then the other. Your skis will swing round and back like propeller blades through an arc of about 45 degrees.

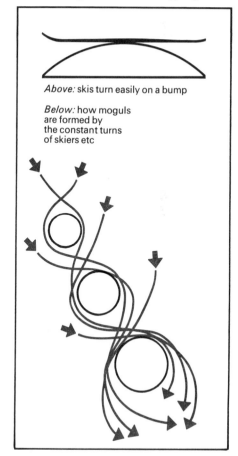

Above: skis turn easily on a bump

Below: how moguls are formed by the constant turns of skiers etc

Anticipating the turn

When you've got the feeling of this pivoting movement you are ready for the next exercise. For this one you'll need a bigger mogul. Stand on top of it, across the fall line as before, with ski tips and tails clear of the snow. Double up into a good semi-crouch, bending at ankles, knees, and waist.

The upper body should be slightly forward and turned away from the direction of the skis to face downhill. Both skis should be slightly set on their uphill edges. Now plant your downhill pole directly below and to the side of your feet. Plant it a good two feet away from you downhill—further still on a very steep slope. Some of your weight will

inevitably be transferred to the pole. You are now in what is known as the 'anticipation' position. In other words, your skis and knees are still driving forward in the traverse position. *But the upper half of your body has already begun to twist and lean downhill in anticipation of the new turn.*

That is easy enough. The difficult bit is to complete the exercise by doing the following three movements simultaneously. Supporting yourself firmly on your planted pole:

1. Bring your evenly distributed weight forward onto the balls of your feet, so that both your ski tips slide down the mogul at the same time.

2. Release your edges by the downhill roll

of the knees, so that the skis are flat and therefore able to turn more easily. (If you do everything else right you'll find this happens almost naturally.)

3. Steer the skis into the turn, using the knees-and-feet pivoting movement learned in the first exercise.

If performed correctly, this will bring you down and around the face of the mogul in a curving side-slip.

Your skis turn almost as if pulled around of their own accord. What has happened?

By anticipating the turn with your upper body and planting your pole well down the hill, the rest of your body is drawn into the turn a split second later.

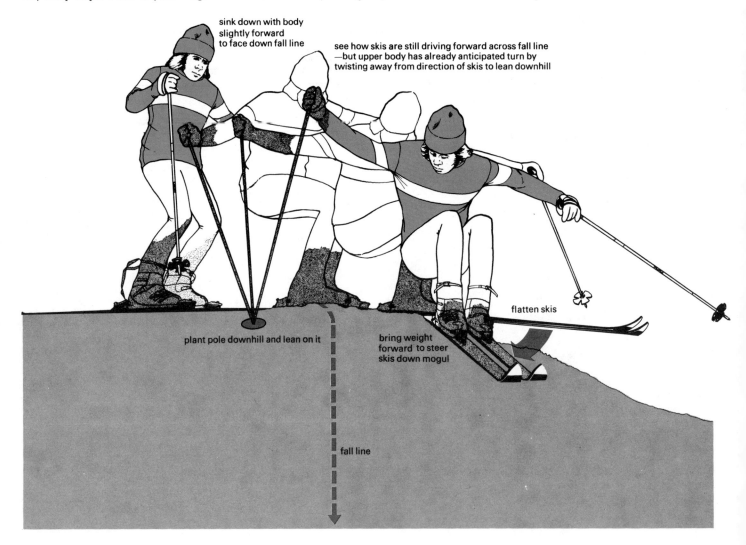

sink down with body
slightly forward
to face down fall line

see how skis are still driving forward across fall line
—but upper body has already anticipated turn by
twisting away from direction of skis to lean downhill

flatten skis

plant pole downhill and lean on it

bring weight
forward to steer
skis down mogul

fall line

How leaning too far back can cause un-weighted ski tips to cross

Double fault! The pole should be planted farther down the mogul and the skier is too upright

Where we went wrong

This part of the exercise gave us a lot of trouble.

1. We knew clearly what we were trying to do but our ski tips kept crossing as we turned on the mogul and again we fell. What went wrong? We were leaning back. Instead of coming forward onto the balls of the feet we still had our weight back on the tails. This left the tips free to wave about and get us into trouble. This was our commonest fault. We were not quite ready or bold enough to dive down the mogul. The fear factor at work again! And, as it usually does, it produces errors more surely than boldness. We had to keep picturing the un-manned skis pointing in the air and realizing that we had to force them down into the hollow with our toes.

2. Sometimes we got the first bit right but fell just as we had completed the exercise. Our skis went ahead of us—again because we were sitting back.

3. Sometimes we began in the anticipation position on top of a mogul but had difficulty making the skis turn. Why? We had not planted the pole far enough downhill, and were too upright.

4. Reduce un-weighting actions to the minimum. Learners put too much effort into whipping the skis round quickly. Make the shape of the snow work to your advantage and reduce your own effort.

When trying the same exercise on the move, it is important not to let the bump launch you into mid-air! For perfect control it is essential that the skis remain in constant contact with the snow. We had already learned to do this when running over bumps and dips (Chapter 5); but a little revision is always useful.

As you pass over the bump you concertina into a sitting position. Let the bump do the work for you. Allow it to push your feet up towards your bottom. Then, as you drop into the dip you extend your legs as if reaching with your feet for the bottom of the trough. In this way the bump is 'erased', or swallowed, without disturbing the upper body.

When turning on a bump at speed, then, you must remember to *stay down low* on top of the bump. And extend your legs into the dip as you come off the bump. You come off in a controlled side-slip. Set your edges. You are looking ahead and ready to begin your next turn. Think of it this way: you are flattening out the bumps by folding and stretching your legs.

Right (from top to bottom): fold up in a sitting position on top of the mogul—then extend the legs down into the dip as you slide down the crest and be ready for the next one

221

Planting the pole

Let us refine a bit. First, timing on the move. Let the pole trigger the turn. Plant your downhill pole as your tips reach the top of a bump. Then you can dive into the turn at the very moment when your tips have come forward off the snow and your feet are on the crest of the mogul. Don't be afraid to lean on the pole. It helps to flatten your skis, and that makes the skis turn more easily.

Second, position: Planting the pole correctly is half the secret of avalement. Also, the more anticipation you have in the movement the greater your turning power. If your skis are right across the fall line (as they might be on a steep hill), the further they have to turn and the more turning power you need. So you must anticipate that much more. This means turning your upper body downhill that much sooner, while your skis are still across the fall line. The movement of the pole sets your upper body in the right position, and helps you get the timing right.

Below is a drawing of the pole position for a sharp turn. Note how far back it is from the tips, and how it has brought your shoulders back so that you are facing down the valley while your skis are still pointing across. Conversely, if your skis are nearly pointing down the fall line as you approach the mogul, you do not need such a big turn or such anticipation. Here the pole need not be as far back.

The shoulders

It is easy to get confused about your shoulders. We did at first. We hope this helps.

Some of us had been told that we should punch with our uphill hand at the moment of turning, so that our shoulders (and skis) came round. It seemed to work for the punchers, and if they found it helpful it seems pedantic not to mention it. One instructor made vivid and effective use of the idea of a punch:

'The mogul punches me in the stomach. I double up. I spike the mogul. I swivel and I punch back. That mogul does not bother me any more.'

Some of us who had been taught in Austrian schools did tend to leave our shoulders behind: we had been drilled into having our uphill shoulder way in front and tended on the mogul turns to be like a man who walks round a corner with his feet first. The idea of the punch is a reminder that we are all going round the turn—and it is a good aggressive image. But this is what sometimes happened—we have punched the mogul all right but so hard that our downhill shoulder has come round and we are facing uphill again. We are not ready for the next bump. Our conclusion is that if the idea of the punch helps, use it. You do what you need to do. But 'minimum force' is a good doctrine in ski-ing. A short jab, not an uppercut—and do without it when you can, as there is always a danger of overturning.

run to crest of mogul

sink forward and down from ankles, knees and waist to 'swallow the bump'

anticipate turn with upper body and plant pole well down mogul as ski tips reach top

Avalement — the French technique for mogul skiing

leaning on poles helps to flatten skis which shoot ahead

bring weight forward and dive into dip

knee-and-foot steering swivels skier down and around mogul

look ahead for next mogul

How do I slow down?

The French are aggressive skiers. They like speed. So they try to ski as 'flat' as possible. They don't have to stray too far from the fall line. For the ordinary holiday skier this is probably asking too much—particularly in mogul country. His biggest problem is usually: 'How do I slow down?'

In a mogul field the best snow lies on top of the moguls. The lower run-off slopes are usually harder. This makes braking twice as tricky. If you want to brake you must do it on the run-up to the crest of the bump. Just add a quick uphill check (p. 212) before turning on the crest.

Down the giant staircase

Moguls should lose their terror in a week of hard practice. Your avalement turns will probably be a bit like our attempts at French; people will understand what you are doing, but will realize you've obviously not done it from birth. But we found we went looking for moguls. Some of the steeper ones proved a bit tricky, and sometimes we were not ready for the sharpness of the drop on the other side. But we could ski over moguls without a fall, and with controlled speed. Once you can link a few turns together the moguls become less of a maze, more like a giant staircase. They seem to acquire a regular, logical pattern.

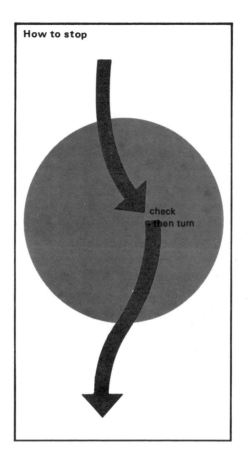

How to stop

check
— then turn

A flight of steps on which you turn on the treads and slide down the risers.

We found, though, that it helped to keep talking to ourselves as we went down the staircase:

  Sit on the mogul
  Spike the mogul deep down
  Anticipate
  Spin on the mogul
  Dive into the dip

What can you do if you come across moguls before your nerves are ready for the avalement movement? We hope this mood won't last long. It shouldn't do, so long as you graduate from practice movements to friendly moguls. If you really find it difficult—and some people do—we suggest that the best way to avoid bumps is to keep to the outside edges of the run or the longest way round a bend. Most of the traffic will be keeping to the centre, and so most of the bumps will be there. In addition, the snow at the edges is not so hard, so there is a chance of more loose snow to make turning easier. If the run is hemmed in by steep walls of hard snow, then lose height to see which side of the run has the least bumpy terrain. Do it by side-slipping down the crest of the bumps: don't try that in the hollows, or the tips and tails of your skis will catch on the side of the mogul.

Below: the idea of 'punching' the mogul with the outside arm of the turn can be helpful so long as you do not overdo it
Right: what happens if you punch too hard with the outside arm when spinning on the mogul; over-punching has led to overturning and leaning into the slope

23 OFF-PISTE SKI-ING

Holiday skiers are spoilt. The snowy slopes they ski on are tended as lovingly as a champion golf course. At every resort teams of men set out with their giant snow-cat machines to pack and roll the snow until it is as firm and smooth as icing on a Christmas cake. It is upon this easy and artificial surface—the piste—that the skier acquires his ski-school skills.

Unfortunately, even the prepared piste is at the mercy of the weather. The fresh-packed powder that flatters the style of the most ordinary skier soon becomes hard or even icy. Some days we blundered about it a new fall of wet, heavy snow before the snow-cats had time to beat it down. Later in the season we encountered spring snow like coarse granulated sugar (good) and slow, slushy end-of-season snow (bad).

Always on either side of us stretched great wastes of unbeaten snow, acres virtually unmarked except for the occasional trail of some solitary explorer. This is what the true art of ski-ing is all about—the ability to travel anywhere on skis. Yet we tended to regard unpacked snow rather as a novice swimmer looks upon the deep end of the swimming bath. Frankly, we were out of our depth. Off-piste we just floundered.

By learning to adapt our technique we found we could cope reasonably well with different snow conditions, both on and off the piste. Knowing exactly what to do boosted our confidence, and we began to plunge off-piste more often. The reward was a taste of the most joyous sensation ski-ing can offer—the exhilaration of parallel ski-ing in fresh knee-deep powder.

Left: In the shadow of the Matterhorn. The joy of ski-ing off-piste on the vast open snowfields above Zermatt, Switzerland

Right: Blazing fresh trails through knee-deep powder, the stuff that skiers dreams are made of. But first you must learn to adapt your technique for off-piste conditions

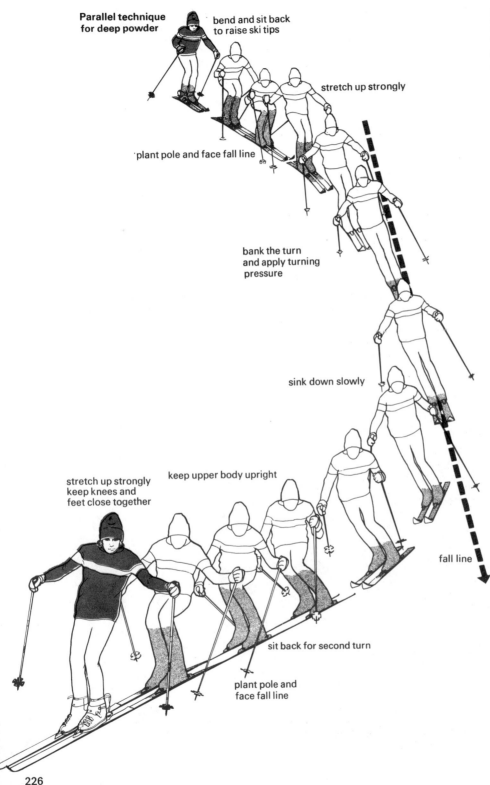

Parallel technique for deep powder

bend and sit back to raise ski tips

stretch up strongly

plant pole and face fall line

bank the turn and apply turning pressure

sink down slowly

keep upper body upright

stretch up strongly keep knees and feet close together

fall line

sit back for second turn

plant pole and face fall line

Coping with light powder

If you wake up one morning to find the piste covered in a foot of dry, light powder snow, stop worrying and head for the slopes as fast as you can. These are the conditions skiers pray for. There is virtually nothing new you need to know. You can use your existing technique quite happily. Once you overcome the psychological barrier of not being able to see your skis you will find light powder easy to ski in. Control is easier. You can keep your skis flatter, use your edges less. The snow slides as smooth as silk underfoot. But sometimes you'll need to use a slightly more exaggerated 'down-up' motion to make your skis turn.

Coping with deep powder

When ski-ing on a hard-beaten piste your skis run *on* the snow. When ski-ing in deep powder they float *in* the snow. That is why deep powder—a foot or more, on or off the piste—demands a special technique of its own.

We found the easiest way to tackle deep powder was to make a steady string of medium-radius parallel turns. But first we had to adapt our hard-piste technique.

How to do it

Instead of keeping most of your weight on the downhill ski *weight both skis equally* most of the time. This is one of the most important points to remember when ski-ing in deep powder. Too few instructors ever bother to tell you this before taking you out in powder snow.

You also have to bring your ski-tips to the surface of the snow before you can begin to turn. This you achieve by bending your knees and sitting back slightly with your upper body upright. As your weight sinks back onto your heels your ski-tips will break the surface in front of you.

Plant your downhill pole to 'trigger' the turn, stop your 'down' motion, and rebound with a strong, high-standing 'up' motion towards the fall line. When you rebound into this strong 'up' motion, launch your body, not forwards towards your ski-tips, but at an angle between the tips and the spot where you have planted your pole. This produces a banking effect. The greatly exaggerated motion is needed because the skis are harder to turn in the deep snow.

Your un-weighted skis will now be on the surface and will begin to turn. Banking the turn will make it easier for you to thrust your skis towards the fall line.

Weight your skis again by coming down from your 'up' position softly and steadily. Resume your slight sitting back position, but keep your hands well down in front for good balance—like a gorilla. Note how little your upper body should be angulating. This is because much less edging is needed in powder snow.

Ski tip to remember

When ski-ing in powder snow try to hold your knees and feet close together. This togetherness is essential in powder, because there is a constant tendency for deep snow, if allowed by a wide stance, to pull the skis apart and hook the tip of the uphill ski to the inside of the turn.

WRONG! Keep those feet and knees together

Powder turn using avalement

This is beyond any doubt the most stylish of deep-snow turns. But this is strictly for good parallel skiers and it is really only effective at higher speeds. To perfect the avalement turn in deep powder calls for high-back boots, thigh muscles like iron bands, split-second co-ordination and long hours of practice. To be honest, none of us had the muscle or the know-how to surmount this pinnacle of snowmanship. Besides, we were happy enough to concentrate on our ordinary parallel powder turns. Nevertheless, for those with the skills and strength we lack, this is a beautiful turn.

The skier begins from a fairly high upright position. Skis and knees are close together.

Now he must bring his ski tips to the surface to begin his turn. To do this he pulls his knees up towards his chest with his thigh muscles and stomach muscles.

This leaves the skier in a sitting back position. (Hence the need for high-back boots and strong thigh muscles. Without them the skier would collapse on his tails.) His upper body is already anticipating the turn by facing downhill. At the same time he pushes his feet forward with a sliding motion in front of him. In this position he has planted his pole well downhill for extra support during the turn.

As he leans into the turn his skis start to curve out into the fall line.

Having anticipated the turn by twisting his upper body downhill, the skis now follow round into the turn as if of their own accord.

As the turn is completed the skier comes up to his original high-standing position. The end of this turn becomes the beginning of the next one.

Above: sit back slightly with upper body upright to bring the ski tips to the surface

Below: banking the turn

How we stopped worrying and learned to love powder ski-ing

It took us a while to lose all our inhibitions about ski-ing in the powder. Much or our trouble was psychological. We could not *see* what was going on down there under a foot and a half of snow. Therefore we imagined our skis crossing and doing all kinds of terrible things. The following two-stage exercise managed to dispel most of our fears.

Stage 1: into the powder

Our instructor chose a medium slope of pisted snow and told us to ski straight down the fall line within a few yards of the edge of the piste.

Still on the piste, we began a long-radius parallel turn. We used the exaggerated deep-snow 'up' movement to un-weight our skis. As we sank back we let our turn take us off the piste and into the deep snow. We advanced our inside ski more to increase our wheelbase for better balance. (There is a slight but sudden shock of slowing-down as you enter the deep snow.)

Once into the snow we drove the skis strongly into the turn by pressing the knees well forward over our boots—so much so that we could feel the boot pressure—and then sideways into the slope. At the same time our body was back in a slightly defensive position. Our arms were forward and our hands held fairly low to compensate for our modest sitting back position.

We repeated this same turn several times, to the left and the right, before moving on to the second stage.

Stage 2: out of the powder

The same exercise as before, but this time we began in a straight schuss through the powder. We began our turn in the powder and let it take us out onto the piste again. As we left the deep snow and rejoined the piste we felt our skis suddenly accelerate. We were prepared for this and counteracted the potentially unbalancing moment by coming forward from our slight sitting back position.

Advice on ice

One of the first phobias we picked up on the slopes was a hearty dislike of ice. On icy days we blossomed with bruises. Nor did we much care for the hard-beaten, well-worn piste that Americans call 'boiler-plate'. But ice and

What one admires in this girl is her angulation—note the hip into the hillside.

boiler-plate are so frequently encountered that they are virtually unavoidable. Sooner or later every skier must get to grips with white ice on the piste. This, as we discovered the hard way, is impossible unless your skis have sharply-honed edges that will bite on the boniest patch of ice.

Even with razor-sharp edges on your skis an icy piste will quickly set you slithering unless you apply the correct technique.

In a straight schuss downhill swallow your pride, open your skis and settle for a wide stance. Weight both skis equally. To stop them wandering, apply equal pressure lightly to both inside edges.

A fairly wide stance—say 12 inches—is also useful for traversing an icy slope. A pronounced angulation of the upper body is important, but at the same time let your weight rest on the uphill edges of *both* skis.

(Normally it is the downhill ski that takes most of the weight.)

When turning on ice keep your movements light and gentle—especially those 'up' and 'down' un-weighting motions. Bend your knees well forward and exaggerate your angulation. This will enable you to place almost all your weight on the inside edge of the turning (outside) ski. Failure to angulate (lean out boldly over the downhill ski with the upper body) was our most common cause of falling on icy slopes.

In wet heavy snow

The Americans call this kind of snow 'mashed potatoes'. It's hard to turn in, and there is no doubt that it boosts the accident rate. Use the same technique that you would use for powder ski-ing. *But use it with ten times more caution.*

In breakable crust

'Breakable crust' is the most treacherous of all snow conditions. As the name suggests, it is a layer of frozen snow which is not strong enough to support the skier's weight. His skis sink down into the soft snow where they can be trapped underneath the crust. It is possible to ski in breakable crust conditions using acrobatic jump turns. We did not try this. We do not recommend that you should attempt it, either. Our advice is that, when breakable crust is about, stay out of it and go home.

Enjoying the view

One day, when we were struggling more than usual, a particularly good instructor remarked: 'You really ought to appreciate the mountains a little more. Here you are, in a wonderful setting, and all you are doing is getting steamed up about ski-ing. Why don't you just stop a minute and look around?'
It seemed a pretty shattering comment after the hammering he had been giving us all morning. Yet, in its way, it was the best single piece of advice we were ever given.
So we did stop, and we did look at the view. We looked down at the resort, a swirl of ant-people below us; we looked up to where we had come from, to the peaks of the mountains—slabs of snow and rock silhouetted against the bright blue afternoon sky. And, all around us, was the snow, and a still silence, broken only by the occasional hiss of skis or the cry of a bird. This, we realized, was what all the struggling, cursing and falling had been for. Our skill on skis had opened a new world for us: that of winter in the mountains.
We skied much better after that. Enjoying the view can do wonders for your ski-ing.

Ski tip to remember

When ski-ing in deep powder do stay close to the fall line. The nearer you are to the fall line the easier it is to weight both skis evenly. Also you will be able to keep your skis flatter so that they 'cut' sideways through the snow. Shallow traverses mean more edging which builds up snow resistance.

Above left: Into the powder; sink back then drive the knees forward and sideways into the slope
Left: Out of the powder; come forward to counteract the sudden acceleration as the skis meet the piste

7 Lessons for us all

**24 GETTING OUT OF BAD HABITS: Common faults analyzed.
25 SKI CRAFT: How to read the piste. Trails, gullies, ruts and ice.
26 GETTING FIT. 27 SKIER'S HIGHWAY CODE.   INDEX.**

24   GETTING OUT OF BAD HABITS

In each teaching chapter we have identified the commonest faults of people learning the movement. Later when you can do the movement tolerably well you will begin to develop your own style and strengths. Some apparently difficult things you will do easily, to your gratification. Others, perhaps less obviously hard, will puzzle you. There is something wrong . . . What follows is an analysis of the commonest worries voiced to us by competent holiday skiers, with advice on correction.

1. *'No matter how I try to ski parallel, my lower ski always sneaks out into a small stem.'*
Analysis: This happens to many skiers just as they go into the action of starting the turn. The lower ski is pushed out as the arm is brought forward to plant the pole. Often it is because the skier wants to brake more with the lower ski, which anyway bears most of the weight. Often the pole-planting arm is swung too far forward at the same time, displacing the hips. The result is not a parallel turn in the true sense, but a kind of step across from one ski to the other. It is not entirely bad technique, but when linked turns have to be made very quickly close together the movement becomes magnified.
Remedy: Both legs have got to work together. A small edge set, with both skis, helps. It creates a platform from which to unweight the skis or initiate them into a new turning direction. It also cuts speed, persuading the skier not to panic with excess braking of the lower ski. Get the feeling of using both skis to make the edge-set. Reflect, as you practise, that it is to your advantage to have two lengths of edge to make a snappy bite into the snow. Any movement after this will have to involve both feet staying together, as the turn is already under way. We confess it is not quite as easy as it sounds to get both feet working together. It requires a lot of practice exercises. One of the best is to try doing a series of skid-bite-hops in a long traverse line. Try to develop a rhythmic pattern of movements of both legs.

Other clues if the skis split: the binding may be placed in the wrong position on the ski. Poor fitting boots may not give immediate response to edge bite action. Or it could just be fear creating a defensive attitude.

1. One of the most difficult habits to eradicate: the lower ski breaking away in a small stem at the start of a parallel turn

2. Bad pole-handling technique; swinging the pole too far forward is the commonest fault

2. *'They say use your pole for turning, but I find that it is always getting in the way and doesn't seem to be of any help.'*

Analysis: We have heard this dozens of times. Almost certainly because of poor instruction the skier has never got the hang of co-ordinating all the movements so necessary to parallel ski-ing.

The commonest bad habit is to swing the pole too far forward, and then allow it to drop back into the snow close to the ski tip. This makes the actual plant-and-push reaction through the arm a fraction too late to be of any real use.

It is not possible to make a smooth push off the handle of the pole, because it is too close to the ski and the arm gets in the way. The result is that the skier has to make vigorous leg actions to get both skis turning together. Much more effort is required, and the turn is jerky.

Remedy: If turns are to be triggered off smoothly and with a minimum of effort, a correctly-timed sequence of movements is essential. Plant the pole *at the moment you sink down*—not before, not after. Get the timing exact, so that the reaction that sets the skis into the turn is coupled with the use of the pole as a way of displacing the skis. Do not reach out to plant the pole ahead of you. The nearer the pole is to your body on the down-hill side the easier it is to displace the tails of the skis. Nor should you hang on to the pole after it has been planted. This pulls the shoulder back, and prevents a clean carving of the turn.

3. *'I find that quite often my skis turn too far round the slope.'*

Analysis: Heavier people tend to have this bad habit more frequently, but it is rooted in the natural defensiveness we all have. As the skier makes the swing of the turn, the skis point down the fall line. He shudders and acts quickly for reassurance—but simply prevents the skis carving the turn correctly. He uses his bulk—hips and shoulders—to skid the heels round fast. Doing this, he moves his weight pressure to the inside of the turn by leaning towards the slope. Consequently, the skis *overturn*. The tempo of the turn is lost, and to stop the skis skidding out from under, the skier bites more on the edges.

Looking down at the skis will produce a similar effect. The body sits back over the heels and when coming out of a turn the backs of the skis will be pressed out even more. We have done this scores of times.

Remedy: Summon up nerve enough to let the skis carve the turn. Concentrate on feeling that you can alter the tips of the skis *with your knees*. Press them forward in the direction you want to go, and forget about pushing the heels to brake with the backs of the skis. Only bad car or motor cycle drivers ever brake on a curve. They control their speed before they reach any bend. So it is with ski-ing. It is difficult for heavily-built people, as they have only to move a little to shift their weight pressure along the skis. Hands and ski poles are a good guide. Keep your eyes on them—

not the ski tips. If you see them swinging forward across the body, then it is a sign something has happened to your basic natural stance over the skis.

4. *'I get round, but the turns are hard on my legs and the turn is jerky. Sometimes I stop when I don't really want to.'*

Analysis: Excessive braking is indicated. Even skiers who have had several holidays are prone to put the brakes on when the skis begin to pick up a little more speed. They develop the habit, perhaps unconsciously and often unnecessarily, of stemming or side-slipping to check the speed of the skis. Or they develop Fault No 3, and push hard with a stiff outside leg. The result is that, instead of driving the skis in the direction required they sit back and stiffen up into a defensive posture.

Remedy: Save your leg muscles. Make the skis do the work. Press them into a full frontal attack. Quick reaction and knee thrust forward are required. By reading the snow correctly, you can be ready for hazards or sharper falls and so eliminate unnecessary braking. Stay relaxed as much as possible, with the knees and ankles well flexed in the 'driving position'. Do not sit back on your heels. Breathe! Sing now and again to relax, especially as the skis pick up a bit more tempo. You will then find that long parallel turns are a delight, and that really you are not going all that fast. Like many other things, it is all in the mind.

3. Overturning caused by flinging the outside arm and shoulder in front. This in turn causes the skier to lean into the slope

4. Unnecessary stemming and side-slipping to reduce speed is hard on the legs and produces ugly, jerky turns

25 SKI CRAFT

By now your mind will probably be racing with thoughts about ankles and knees, but that is not the whole story. The complete skier will 'read' the slopes in the same way that a good motorist will be aware of everything around him. Just as a motorist acquires 'road sense', so a skier will learn 'ski craft'. You can make your ski-ing safer and more enjoyable if you try to get into the habit of using your eyes and brains to make the mountain work for you. That may sound patronizing. 'Of course I'll do that,' you say. But it is astonishing how obsessed you can become with the immediate foreground, and how little the average holiday skier plots his line down the mountain. Too few of us make the best use of the snow or read a line so that we can anticipate any necessary turning or slowing down. Yet this facet of ski-ing is seldom emphasized by ski schools. Only the gospel of technique matters, and the craft of ski-ing is often looked on as 'crafty' or cheating your way down. We do not agree. Here, in a simplified form, is a sketch of two skiers of the same ability coming down the same mountain—one a cunning woman, the other a beefy man. The girl comes down smoothly and has the exhilaration of a long run. The man keeps getting in a hopeless mess—not because his leg movements are inferior but because he does not use his eyes. Our illustration is not intended as a gesture to women's lib; girls just seem more able to use guile. If girls are the 'goodies' in this example, we certainly have felt like the 'baddies' on many outings.

This is a run we have imagined but it has many elements of chance and challenge that you will meet in the average resort. Next time you come off a run, count how many times you made the mistakes of the snarled-up skier and how often you kept moving like the crafty skier in our illustration. Without worrying about the second hand on your watch, time yourself over two descents of the same run at the beginning and end of the week, making a determined effort in the second run to use your ski craft. If you follow the lessons of this example you will be astonished at the improvement in time and in enjoyment.

Snarled-up skier
1 Starts too fast for his ability, has to stop at edge of piste and kick-turn round

2 Tries three stem christies but second one takes him too high up side of valley wall, forcing him to attempt tougher turn. Catches edge, falls

3 Blunders into a tightly-massed mogul field. Flounders through with frequent stops

4 Fails to look ahead, becomes tangled up with ski school class waiting its turn

5 Meets woodland path, easy he thinks, but fails to notice ice. Skis go from underneath him

6 Prudent at last, does not like look of steeper slope. Runs across top of valley instead. But finds himself at the end, poised on brink of even steeper valley. Shock un-nerves him. Stops, performs awkward star turn in difficult spot

7 Runs into wet snow, realises he is in trouble and stops by sitting down

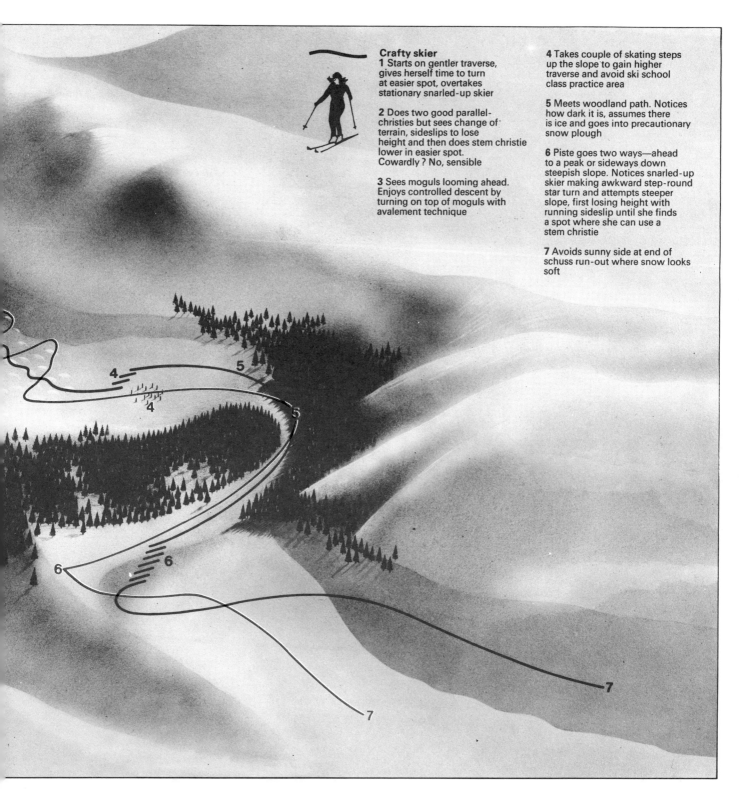

Crafty skier

1 Starts on gentler traverse, gives herself time to turn at easier spot, overtakes stationary snarled-up skier

2 Does two good parallel-christies but sees change of terrain, sideslips to lose height and then does stem christie lower in easier spot. Cowardly ? No, sensible

3 Sees moguls looming ahead. Enjoys controlled descent by turning on top of moguls with avalement technique

4 Takes couple of skating steps up the slope to gain higher traverse and avoid ski school class practice area

5 Meets woodland path. Notices how dark it is, assumes there is ice and goes into precautionary snow plough

6 Piste goes two ways—ahead to a peak or sideways down steepish slope. Notices snarled-up skier making awkward step-round star turn and attempts steeper slope, first losing height with running sideslip until she finds a spot where she can use a stem christie

7 Avoids sunny side at end of schuss run-out where snow looks soft

What to look for on the way down

There are several things to look for when you set off for a run.

- The shape of the snow terrain.
- The state of the snow.
- Hazards on and off the piste.

You can learn a lot by spending a few moments watching other skiers go before you. Watch the line they take and the difficulties they encounter. Identify the places where a muffed turn will force you to stop and kick-turn out of trouble. Identify where you might schuss, side-slip, and so on. Learn how to make deliberate use of the terrain to give you the best line through hollows and flat spots and moguls. It is no use plunging down into a likely-looking stretch of snow if it is going to be tough to ski. You should find it easy to recognize loose fluffy snow on a piste: it lies two or three inches deep and will be a delight to ski. It is also not too difficult to recognize patches of ice, shiny grey-blue that are

definitely unpleasant. When you hit a wood trail, realize that the parts that have been in the shade are likely to be icy. And when you see a turn ahead in the sun, be ready for soft snow, even slush: this will stop your skis but throw you forward.

Rocks, tree stumps and holes in the snow are some of the more common hazards. Sometimes they can be seen from some way above; sometimes they are hidden. So never ski blindly. This is where watching others helps. Once you have done a run successfully, or are past the intermediate stage, decide that next time you will do it differently. If you make each run as varied as possible within the safety margins, you will get the best out of ski-ing. One of the skiers we met was good enough to wedel down most slopes, but he complained that he got bored with ski-ing down some of the easier runs. His fault was that he never changed his tempo of turning, but skied only in a set rhythm. He was

admittedly fluent, but after a while his rhythm became monotonous to the point of boredom, relieved only by having to avoid other skiers and marker poles. People of this standard should pick out a terrain that will develop a variety of turning techniques—short linked turns on steeper ground, long sweeping turns on smoother slopes, and so on.

Ski tips to remember

Ski craft evolves slowly, with experience and practice. But you can learn a lot from a good instructor. Here are some of the hints we wished we had been taught earlier.

How to survive on narrow trails and woodpaths

Open slopes above the treeline usually allow you plenty of room to manoeuvre and time to decide when to turn. Sometimes, however, especially below the treeline in older resorts, turning room is restricted to a few feet either side. If you are a wedel expert, woodpaths will cause you little trouble. For the rest of us they can be more formidable than a mogul field. On one side the path usually falls away steeply into the trees. On the other there is a high wall of ice hemmed in by rocks and roots. The middle of the path has been beaten down to a hard and often rutted surface by the passage of many skiers in a confined space. If you schuss down it you may go too fast and catch an edge in the ruts. If you try to snowplough, the surface may be too icy for your skis to grip effectively.

What do you do? First, keep your ski tips clear of that dangerous wall. Running into it is much more risky than falling over the edge of the path. So ski in a running side-slip on the downhill side of the path. There is usually a bank of loose snow here, piled up by the ploughing and scraping of other skiers struggling to stay in the centre of the trail. Keeping to this bank may mean moving along with your ski tips jutting over the edge. This will frighten you at first, but it is nothing to the shock and even injuries you can suffer by colliding with the ice wall.

If you lose your nerve and have to snowplough you can increase your braking power by sitting on your poles. Purists may sneer and your poles may suffer, but it is effective. Hold your poles between your legs with the points trailing behind you between your stemming skis. The further down you sit the slower you will go.

If you have to sideslip down a narrow path keep tips away from the ice wall (*left*)

How to get up in deep snow

Getting to your feet after a fall in deep powder can be difficult, because there is no firm snow against which you can push. If you try to push yourself up with your poles the baskets sink down through the snow, unable to support your weight. If this happens to you, take both poles in one hand, hold them by the middle in the form of a cross laid on the snow and push off from that.

If you come out of your bindings in deep snow beat out a base of firmly trodden snow before trying to put your skis back on.

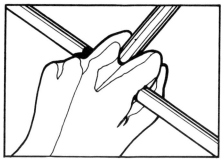

To get up in deep snow hold crossed poles in one hand and push

Shooting a 'gunbarrel'. Good skiers ride and turn on the bumps. Others stick to the edge and use a diagonal side-slip

How to cope with glass ice

This is when you'll be grateful for sharp edges and all the hard work you put in to learn how to make them bite. For without a good hard edge-set your skis will be constantly trying to skid away downhill underneath you. That slithery, out-of-control feeling is likely to make you tense and nervous. What you must do, though, is stay as relaxed as you can. Stiff legs spell downfall! What else? Increase your angulation and put much more weight on the downhill ski. By giving your downhill ski more weight this will really help those edges to grip. If you still find yourself slipping crab-wise down the slope try a few quick 'down' movements to produce a series of short edge-checks. Use the braking wedel (Chapter 21) for turning down an icy slope, again with lots of edge-set.

If you run across a sheet of pure glass ice there is not much you can do except remain as relaxed as possible and keep your knees and ankles flexed to help you to bear down on the front of your skis to stop the tails breaking away downhill.

We never enjoyed ski-ing on ice. If we saw it gleaming in front of us we took avoiding action whenever we could, trying to pick out the less shiny, more grainy spots which would give our skis more chance to grip.

How to shoot a 'gunbarrel'

Sometimes the shape of the mountainside funnels a ski run into a steep bottleneck gulley or 'U'-shaped ravine. These 'gunbarrel' pistes can be fun for competent skiers, but tricky for others. The bed of the barrel often ripples with choppy moguls. The steep descent coupled with the high-curving sides tends to whip you through the barrel like a bullet. If you can ride and turn on the bumps (Chapter 22), you can stay in the middle. If you want to take it slowly it is better to stick to one side of the gunbarrel and run down it in a diagonal sideslip.

How to get out of a rut

On narrow trails and ski-tow tracks the snow often becomes deeply scored by rutted tracks or tramlines. If you feel unsafe with your skis trapped in the ruts, step out of trouble, one ski at a time in quick succession.

Say aloud to yourself
● Look ahead.
● Smoothly does it.

26 GETTING FIT

You do not need to be Superman (or Super woman!) to ski. You do need to be reasonably fit. It is probably the most demanding sport, mentally or physically, most of us ever take up. This is one of the reasons for its appeal: the absorption is total. Of course, you can moderate the effort you make. You can miss a run or a class or go slower or sit in the sun all afternoon discussing turns at the mountain restaurant. But you will enjoy even a modest ski holiday more if you take the trouble to do some pre-ski training. That sounds boring, but there are ways to make it more palatable, and the benefit is out of all proportion to the pre-ski effort. Some of us did go ski-ing for the first time without any training. We enjoyed ourselves all the same, but now we know that we need not have had the irritating aches and pains; that we did endanger ourselves by ski-ing closer to our physical limits than was wise; and that we would have been better skiers at the end of the first holiday if we had prepared for it. Think of it this way: dry slope training and a get-fit programme take half-hours at home but they add hours of ski-ing to the ski-ing holiday.

You may tell yourself that you are fit enough already. Self-deception. Ski-ing will detect and worry muscles you did not know you had. Children under fifteen, incidentally, need no special pre-ski training. They should be fit and agile enough already. The programme we follow is in two parts—something to make you looser and something to develop muscles you will use on the mountain. We owe a good deal of what follows to Freddy Reilly, who has spent years preparing Londoners at the Crystal Palace dry slope for ski-ing holidays. Freddy in turn wishes to acknowledge his debt to his friend Georges Coulon, who has trained the French National Ski team. For additional advice we thank A. E. Lett, the London physiotherapist who straightened out any of our ski strains. There are, of course, a number of general exercise pamphlets or books you can buy—for instance, the 5BX plan of the Royal Canadian Air Force or the *Sunday Times* wall chart commando exercises. Neither is specifically for skiers, nor are they restricted to battle-hardened veterans.

• *Timing:* begin five weeks or so before you go. The man who starts pre-ski exercises the week before he goes merely arrives at the resort with muscle aches already developed.

• *Content:* nor is it any use just concentrating on the muscle exercises. You need flexibility as well as strength and endurance. If you simply build up your leg muscles, you invite being muscle-bound—and the rest of the body will not be ready for the surprise twists and turns it will have to do. Look at the champion skier. He is not obviously muscular. He is lithe. You *must* therefore include stretching and relaxing exercises in your routine, or you may do yourself more harm than good. Some of these may not seem very dramatic, but they are essential.

EXERCISES

The first four are for limbering up. They are necessary if you are to reap the full benefit of the other exercises. Make yourself a schedule of, say, a minute a day for each exercise, and keep a daily record of how many times you have managed to do each one. Try gradually to increase the number. Or, in an exercise like No. 6 hold the position longer. With the later exercises, for muscles, you will find a little rivalry goes a long way. Casual challenges at the office work wonders for your dedication to exercise No. 12, and you can get the family to try exercise No. 11.

1. Reaching: stand upright, knees together, feet together. Raise both hands in the air. Reach as high as you can, but keep your heels and toes flat on the ground. Hold that position and count up to ten. Then bring your hands *slowly* down. Repeat three or four times.

2. Swinging: in the same position, stretch your arms sideways, palms upwards, arms horizontal. 'Flex' them a few times. Swing your arms back as *far as possible*. Hold them there a second or two. Relax. Push them back again a few times.

3. Knees bend: extend your arms, palms upwards as in Exercise 2, keeping them as far back as you can. Keep your feet flat on the floor and bend your knees. Keep your knees together and your upper body upright. Start by doing this five times, and try to go down a little further and a few more times each day.

1

2

3

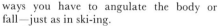

4

5

6

7

4.   Knees bend 2: this time go down on your toes throughout the knees bend. Go down as far as you can. This is much easier; but it helps you graduate to the next exercise.

5.   Jumping: feet and knees together, feet flat on the ground, arms at your side. Bend the knees keeping your heels on the ground —but this time *jump* up and land on your toes. Repeat as often as you can and then add a varient for agility. As you jump up, jump back also. Or sideways. This exercise gets your leg muscles ready for unweighting. Jumping back helps conquer the fear factor. Most people are frightened to jump where they cannot see. Check: are you really jumping well back? When you jump side-ways you have to angulate the body or fall—just as in ski-ing.

6.   Leg lifting: lie flat on your back, legs together. Bring your feet as close to your bottom as possible by raising your knees. Then straighten your legs by lifting your feet off the ground. Keep your legs as straight as possible and raise them until they are in the vertical position. Try to stay in this position, *forcing your toes down* towards your body.

At first we could only hold this position for a few seconds. But our aim was 30 seconds, or even a minute. This is good for the stomach muscles. As one Olympic skier told us, 'most people don't realise that we ski from the stomach.'

7.   Leg Lift 2: this time, as soon as your legs are vertically out above you, open them to make a 'V' position of about 60 degrees. Still try to force your toes down. Hold this position for as long as you can. This works on the calf muscles as well.

237

8. Legs sideways: arms at your side, stand on one leg and raise the other sideways in the air. The aim is to raise it to the horizontal position, or as near as possible. Hold the position. Try to point your toes inwards. Then outwards. We are still working on the same muscles, but this also helps our balance and motor co-ordination. Repeat with other leg.

9. Trunk swinging: stretch out your arms, (either above your head or in line with your shoulders; both exercise important muscles).

Then swing them as far to the left as you can a few times, and then to the right. Do it rhythmically. This loosens you up and prepares you for counter-rotation.

10. Ankle flexing: lie face down on the bed with your toes just over the end of the bed. Bend the ankles inwards so that the toes dig into the end of the bed. Hold it a second. Do 10 the first day, 15 the second and so on to a maximum of 50. This exercise completely got rid of an ache that used to make late afternoon ski-ing rather trying.

8

9

Life-style exercises

We can always pick out the skiers at *The Sunday Times* because come late autumn they start acting strangely. They are to be seen cycling to work, running up the stairs instead of using the lifts, or sitting on their chairs with their legs in the air. They are, of course, preparing for the ski-ing season. We always feel it is a pity that these good intentions don't survive the spring. Living more energetically is one of the easiest and more satisfying ways of keeping fit.

So in the month or two before you go ski-ing: walk or cycle where you would catch a bus; run where you would walk (even better, run in the park, weaving among trees like a slalom star); go swimming or play squash.

Use the stairs. Go one at a time and, with the full foot on the stair, raise yourself by straightening the knee at each step. (Going up on tiptoe tends to produce muscle-bound calves.) There is one man over 60 who trains by climbing the Monument in the City of London—345 steps—every lunchtime.

Try to develop rhythmic breathing, breathing in through the nose as the body stretches, and out through the mouth with a contraction of the stomach muscles as the body relaxes.

Endurance

These life-style exercises will help build up your endurance. If you don't take up cycling, rowing, jogging, walking or running —or even if you do—there is skipping. This has the advantage that it can be done indoors. It also assists your agility, balance, rhythm and muscular co-ordination, and 10 minutes' skipping can give as much exercise as 30 minutes' running.

There is no need to buy a special skipping rope with handles. A length of washing line or window sash cord is ideal. The right length is this: When you stand on the middle of the rope both ends should reach your armpits.

Most people have a tendency to 'step' over the rope when they start skipping, lifting first one (usually the left) then the other foot from the ground. Instead, try to jump with both feet at once. After a while you should get the hang of it again. Start at about 60 jumps a minute. We usually found a minute or two plenty at first, but within a few days of starting your training you should hope to get up to five minutes, or even ten.

The best plan is to decide on how long you are going to skip, and then do it every day. But try to speed up the number of skips per minute rather than increase the time you spend skipping. This will prepare you for the short, sharp energy burns of ski-ing.

There are also exercises you can do whenever you have a moment to spare involving objects from daily life: the groceries, an office chair, or bottles.

11. Lifting the groceries: begin with a weight of four pounds in a shopping basket (two bags of sugar) and place it conveniently near a table. Sit on the table with the edge of the table under your knee. Put your foot in the handle of the basket and slowly lift the basket until your knee has locked. It is pointless to go higher. Hold it for five seconds. Let the basket down, pause, and do it again nine more times. After a week, increase the weight to ten pounds and then build up to 20 lifts. Later you can go to 15 pounds and 20 lifts or so of five seconds duration. You can feel your thigh muscles losing their flabbiness. This exercise is a great insurance against wrenching the knee—one of the commonest ski injuries.

11

12. Look! No Chair: sit unsupported against a wall, feet flat on the ground, hands on hips, thighs horizontal to the floor, back straight. Thirty seconds is enough for the first week of this, then you can build up to a minute or more. Killy uses this exercise. It is another for the quadracep muscles.

13. Bottle party challenge: place a wine or milk bottle by your right heel. Now swing round to your left and, without putting your arm between your legs, grab the bottle with your *right* hand. Do the same on the left hand

side. You can make it a bit more difficult each time. It makes the top of the body work as it does in ski-ing.

14. Leg raising: an exercise that can be done at work. Sit in a chair and grab the underside of it with both hands. Raise your legs till they are horizontal and hold them there as long as you can.

15. The Twist: stand with legs and feet firmly together, and do a knees bend. An angle of 110 degrees at the knee is about right. More will do, but not less. Then jump

13

12

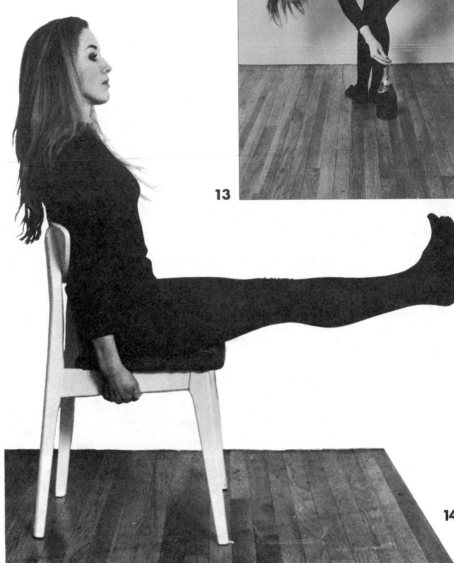

14

240

nine inches or a foot to the left. As you jump, twist your entire body clockwise through an angle of about 90 degrees. Land on your toes, and then sink back into your crouch position. Reverse the process and jump back to the right, rotating your body anti-clockwise. You should land on the same spot and face in the same direction as when you started.

Once again try to do this a little faster for a little longer every day. Speed is just as important as endurance in this exercise.

As a real test of agility, you can make this exercise more of a challenge by forcing yourself to jump high as you twist. Do this by placing some books to the left. To jump to the left you must jump *over* them. To jump back

do the same. Start off with two or three phone books, then build them up each day. Between 12 and 16 inches is the final height for which you should aim.

It is rather like dancing the Twist while hopping at the same time, and is a fair simulation of ski-ing. Now you know why you have been doing all the other exercises.

15

16

16. **Back exercises:** always end even an abbreviated session with this exercise. It will reinforce the axis for all the swinging mobility exercises. Lie face down on bed or floor, arms folded back. Gently pull up your upper body. Hold the arched position for 5 seconds, relax for a few seconds and repeat. Do four each day in the first week, then increase to six (in second week) and eventually 12. You will feel stretched and straighter.

27 SKIER'S HIGHWAY CODE

A ski-ing holiday is fun, but it also has risks. The happiest results will come if everyone observes the codes of ski-ing so that there is neither accident nor unpleasantness. The worst skier can follow the rules, and he will appreciate it if he does. Nobody can think of himself as a 'good skier' if he cuts the corners. There are some technically competent people who are oafs, spoiling other people's fun. The vast majority of skiers should gang up on these cowboys. Don't be inhibited by the fact that it is your first week on skis. Observe these rules—and expect others to observe them, however experienced they may appear.

On the lifts

- Don't queue-jump (or, if you are American, 'don't jump the line').
- Remember you are wearing skis. You don't have to be very close to someone to step on theirs.
- Don't tow hog. If there is a long queue (or line) at the tows, then, providing it is a tow built for two, share your tow with someone else.
- Keep in the ruts—unless there is a bare, bumpy or icy patch. Weaving from side to side on the tows (a) increases the chance of a collision with a skier; (b) increases the likelihood of your falling, and the suddenly released tow hitting someone; and (c) strains the equipment.
- If you fall, try to get out of the way of those coming up behind you as quickly as possible.

As you leave the lift

- If you are sharing a tow, establish in advance which of you will get off first.
- Once off the tow, get well out of the way of the people behind you before stopping to admire the view or adjust your equipment. Otherwise you could cause a nasty pile up at the top of the lift—or be hit by a bar as it is released by the skier coming up behind you.

When ski-ing

- Remember you have no rear view mirror. Don't do anything unpredictable without glancing behind you first.
- Remember other skiers are also without mirrors. If you are about to overtake another skier assume that he has not seen you.

Overtaking

The skier's highway code has no hard and fast rules, and nowhere is this more apparent than in overtaking. If there is a golden rule it is that *in all cases the responsibility is that of the overtaker*. It is up to him to get past safely, not for the slower skier to give way. Use your common sense and stick to these general principles, unless there is a good reason for doing otherwise.

- When you find yourself bearing down on a skier slower than yourself, turn where he turns. If both your turns are not synchronized in this way, you run the risk of colliding when traversing in different directions.

- The cry of 'Achtung' (German), 'Track' (American), 'Piste' (French) or 'Attenzione' or 'Pista' (Italian) serve the same purpose as the motorists horn. In fact, though, you are far more likely to hear simply an agonized yell from behind. When we found ourselves panicking, we just yelled the first thing that came into our heads. It seemed to work. When you are about to overtake another skier a suitable shout warns him not to make a sudden turn across your path, but like the motor horn this has its aggressive and futile uses also. It is pointless, selfish and possibly even dangerous to yell 'Achtung' at a skier who has no option but to turn at that moment—particularly if it is a beginner who is running out of piste on a traverse. Nor can any use be served by shouting at a skier who cannot possibly get out of your way. Should you find yourself the victim of such a piste hog, don't allow him to fluster you.
- All other things being equal, overtake on the left. An example of all other things being equal would be when you and the slower skier are both schussing down a wide piste.
- When overtaking a skier who is traversing, always do so on his uphill side, ie *behind him* (although you may encounter

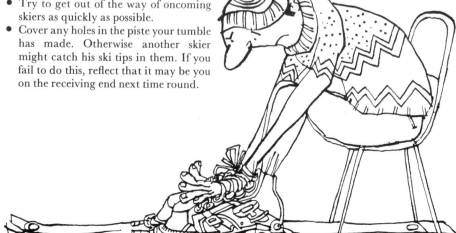

Some vital rules

- Always wear and fasten the retaining straps on your skis.
- Always keep to the edge of a piste if you are walking. (And you should be walking *on skis* if you are on a piste.)
- Always observe mandatory signs—especially ones indicating a piste is closed.
- Always take a map with you, one which marks as clearly as possible where the pistes are, and how difficult they are. Keep a mental note of landmarks and piste-marker numbers as you pass them, so that, in the event of the sudden loss of visibility, you will have some idea of where you are, and so can use the map to get home.
- Always ski within your abilities. Don't hurtle out of control down the piste assuming that you will be able to slow down and stop on a relatively flat section ahead. Your assumption might well be right, but what if you have to stop *before* then? What if another skier falls right in front of you?
- In the same way, always be prepared for the unexpected and the idiot. You should never ski round a blind corner or over the top of a blind drop too fast to stop safely. There may be a fallen skier lying on the piste, or someone admiring the view where they should not be.

situations, especially on a narrow piste, where common sense dictates otherwise). The sooner you overtake after he has made a turn the less likely he is to turn around and come back at you. As he turns, you go straight on.

- Never cross in front of any skier too closely. The criterion of 'close' is: 'If I fall can he avoid me?' This involves knowing the skier's abilities. If in doubt assume them to be minimal.
- When overtaking on a narrow path the overtaker must pass on the most dangerous side—ie if there is a drop then it is the overtaker who must ski close to it. If there are trees on one side then he must go close to the trees.

Stopping

If you wish to stop, for any reason, there are still times when it is safer to continue. In particular:

- Do not stop at a bottleneck, or on a narrow stretch of piste.
- Do not stop just below the brow of a hill, or just around a corner, where oncoming skiers will be unable to see you. Move to the edge of the piste or off it altogether.

In other words, it is the motoring analogy once again. Don't park where you can't be seen until the last minute, or where you are in the way.

- Resist the temptation of showing off by screeching to a stop in a spray of snow just in front of other skiers, especially at lifts. You may not be as good as you think you are, and could hurt both them and yourself. Always stop *below* a stationary skier, or *well above* a lift queue/line.
- Whenever you move off, *look both ways first*. Make sure there is no skier bearing down on you from above, or one who has fallen below you.

If you fall

- Try to get out of the way of oncoming skiers as quickly as possible.
- Cover any holes in the piste your tumble has made. Otherwise another skier might catch his ski tips in them. If you fail to do this, reflect that it may be you on the receiving end next time round.

- Have a warm-up first thing in the morning. Your muscles will be stiff, and you won't be capable of doing what you did the afternoon before. If you go straight down a run which was testing you to your limit, you are likely to hurt yourself. Either start off on a run that is well within your capabilities, or side-step or herringbone up a short slope as fast as you can and ski down several times. This will get you breathing deeply and loosen your muscles.
- Always glance uphill to see if anyone is coming where your piste joins another.

Equally, there are some things you should never do:

- Never throw a ski on the ground. It could just sail off downhill.
- Never ski through a ski class. Remember what it was like when *you* were having lessons and someone bombed through the file that was following teacher. Give ski classes a wide berth and be particularly understanding of the pupil who is out in front trying a turn. He or she has enough problems without you.
- Never walk on a piste without skis. You will make holes in it.
- Never ski far off-piste on your own, unless you are an experienced off-piste skier, know the terrain intimately, and are prepared to pay a high price for solitude. If you want to ski off-piste, it should be with someone experienced.

- Never go out inadequately clothed in doubtful weather. Assume it will get worse rather than better.
- Never ski alone in bad visibility.
- Never have 'one last run' if you have to ask yourself first whether you have enough energy. If you ask the question then the answer is probably no. Many a good day is spoiled by a miserable 'last run'. Statistics also show that this is precisely the time when people have accidents.
- Never attempt 'going up a standard' when ski-ing on your own. Your first crack at a piste of a harder category than you have attempted before should always be in the company of a more capable skier. At the very least, there should be plenty of other skiers on the piste.
- Never ski across the path of a ski tow, or even near it if there is any alternative.

In the event of an accident

- Don't move an injured skier.
- Ideally one person should stay to comfort the victim (and to warn on-coming skiers of the hazard). Another should go for help. If you are alone with the victim, then just go for help. But remember that help is useless if it can't be got to the injured skier. Make sure you know where you are. If necessary, leave a garment or a pole in a prominent position to help navigation on the return journey. Wrap the injured skier in any clothing you can spare. You'll be warm on the move.
- One of the first things you should do at any resort is to prepare for such an eventuality by establishing what the procedure is in an accident: who is responsible for the toboggan (a sledge-cum-stretcher) and where the SOS points are. Nearly all ski lifts have phones.

Mountain safety

If you follow the skier's highway code you should never find yourself lost, or alone and in difficulties.

None of us have ever got lost. We may have been lucky rather than prudent, but we can still see how it *could* easily happen—even if one observes the ski-ing code. For instance, if you lingered too long in a bar at the top of a lift, you could come out to find it was snowing, visibility was almost nil, and everybody else had gone. Well, not *everybody* could have gone. There would still be the bar staff and the lift operator. If you find yourself in this predicament, *wait and go down with them*.

Being caught in a 'white out'—a sudden blanket of cloud and snow—is precisely like being plunged into the dark. Only everything is white, instead of black. (Your yellow lenses—cf p. 59—are the remedy.) The first time this happened to us we were safely in a ski class, but it was a sufficiently unnerving experience for us to resolve never to risk it alone in unfamiliar territory.

If for any reason you still manage to find yourself alone on a piste in bad visibility *stick to the piste*. Unless it is snowing heavily, you should be able to 'feel' your way down. A change of surface will warn you if you are straying off the piste. If you can see them, follow the markers. If you lose the piste *go back* until you find it. *Never* set off through unknown country straight down hill. *Never* take your skis off if you can help it. If you are with others in this predicament, follow the same rules, and stick together. Should you become hopelessly lost, *stop*. Find a sheltered spot, wait there and shout for help. Six calls or whistles a minute followed by a minute's silence is the international mountain distress signal. The answer is three signals a minute, followed by silence. Sound carries well in the mountains so this is not as futile an exercise as it may seem.

Avalanches

These may seem a somewhat hypothetical hazard, rather in the abominable snowman league. True, we have never seen one ourselves, but we have arrived on the scene just after a fall. So they do exist, and are something about which you need to know. They can begin on almost any treeless slope; it doesn't need to be at the top of a mountain, or even particularly steep. A heavy snowfall, high winds or a sudden rise in temperature can create avalanche conditions. In these circumstances it is unwise to ski off-piste without seeking expert advice. In a well-organized resort it is highly unlikely that you will ever be endangered by an avalanche when ski-ing on the pistes. Avalanche danger is the usual reason for closing them—and a very good reason for never ignoring a 'piste closed' sign.

If you do see an avalanche coming, try to escape it. Avalanches other than powder snow ones (which come down the mountain in a billow of snow and a rush of wind) take the line of least resistance. If you can ski to any piece of ground considerably higher than all around it, do so. Otherwise do a fast schuss away from the path of the avalanche. If escape proves impossible, remove your skis and jettison your poles before the avalanche hits you, and 'swim' to stay on top of it when it does. If this fails, and you are submerged, then it is vital to preserve energy, body heat and air. Do not struggle. Assume the foetal position and *cover your mouth and nose* with your hands. (To stop snow being forced into them.) When the avalanche stops create a breathing space around your face and body. If you find you can move upwards through the snow then by all means try. Otherwise save your

energies for occasional cries for help. People will be looking for you. Robert Blanc of Les Arcs survived after six hours buried in snow. If you are rescuing someone overtaken by an avalanche, *speed is essential*. If you can hear or see them try to release them from the snow. Otherwise, do your best to calculate where they may be. Probe the snow gently with an upturned ski stick. Shout and listen for an answer. If there is none, make a note of the spot, leave an identifying article of clothing or equipment firmly fixed in the snow, and go for help. If there are several of you, the best skier should go for help while the rest keep up the search.

HEATH

SKIER'S VOCABULARY

You do not, ideally, want to find yourself slithering sideways down a mountain while, somewhere above you, an instructor is yelling 'lo sci a valle deve sostenere maggiormente il peso del corpo!'—not unless you have enough Italian to know that he is suggesting that the solution to your problem is to apply more weight to the downhill ski. The beginner has enough to cope with without language difficulties. Most instructors have a smattering of ski-ing English. But the man who can speak English fluently, ski well and teach well is, you will soon discover, a gem beyond compare. Until you meet him we offer this vocabulary which, although far from exhaustive, may be of help if your instructor or the ski shop has no English at all.

ENGLISH	GERMAN	FRENCH	ITALIAN
The ski shop			
The ski is	der Ski ist	le ski est	lo sci è
too long	zu lang	trop long	troppo lungo
too short	zu kurz	trop court	troppo corto
broken	gebrochen	cassé	rotto
no good	unbrauchbar	(le ski) ne me convient pas	scadento
the tip (of the ski)	die Skispitze	la spatule	la spatola (dello sci)
the heel (of the ski)	das Skiende	le talon du ski	la coda (dello sci)
the running surface (of the ski)	die Gleitfläche	la semelle	la suola
the edges	die Kanten	les carres	gli spigoli
the binding	die Bindung	la fixation	l'attacco
the retaining strap	der Sicherheitsriemen	la courroie de sûreté	la cinghia di sicurezza
the ski pole	der Skistock	le bâton de ski	il bastone da sciatore
ski wax	der Skiwachs	le fart	la sciolina
ski boot	der Skischuh	la chaussure de ski	la scarpone da sci
gloves	Handschuhe	gants	guanti
mittens	Fäustlinge	moufles	guantoni
goggles	die Schneebrillen	les lunettes de ski	gli occhiali da sole
Could you please adjust my bindings?	könnten Sir mir bitte die Bindungen anpassen?	pourriez-vous régler mes fixations?	per favore, mi potrebbe sistemare i lacci?
They are too tight	Sie sind zu fest	elles sont trop serrées	sono troppo stretti
Too loose	zu locker	trop larges	troppo lenti
Could you put them on the lightest setting?	könnten Sie sie in die leichteste Position setzen?	pourriez-vous les régler pour qu'ils se déclenchent très facilement?	potrebbe metterli in posizione piu' lenta?
I would like softer/harder skis	ich hätte gerne weichere/ härtere Skier	j'aimerais des skis plus souples/plus durs	vorrei degli sci piu' leggeri (flessibile)/pui' pesanti (rigidi)
Could you please sharpen the edges (of my skis)?	könnten Sie bitte die Kanten (meiner Skier) schärfen?	pourriez-vous aiguiser les carres de mes skis?	mi potrebbe affilare li spigoli?
The terrain			
The fall line	der Fallinie	la ligne de pente	la linea della massima pendenza
the run is	die Piste ist	la piste est	la pista è
gentle	sanft	douce	dolce

ENGLISH	GERMAN	FRENCH	ITALIAN
steep	steil	raide	ripida
easy	leicht	facile	facile
difficult	schwierig	difficile	difficile
closed	geschlossen	fermée	chiusa
on flat ground	auf ebenem Gelände	en terrain plat	in terreno piano
trees	Bäume	arbres	alberi
mogul	die Bodenwelle	la bosse	la prominenza
the dip, or hollow	die Mulde	le creux	la conca
a rock	ein Felsen	un rocher	una roccia
track (either a path, or a mark left by your skis)	eine Spur	une trace	una traccia
the descent	die Abfahrt	la descente	la discesa
cable car	die Luftseilbahn	le téléphérique	la teleferica
drag lift	der Skilift	le télé-ski	la sciovia
chair lift	der Sessellift	le télé-siège	la seggiovia
telecabine, gondola lift	die Gondelbahn	la télécabine	le telecabine
the snow is	der Schnee ist	la neige est	la neve è
soft	weich	molle	soffice
icy	vereist	glacée	ghiacciata
wet	nass	humide	umida
sticky	klebrig	collante	appiccicosa
deep	tief	profonde	alta
thin	dünn	mince	bassa
powder snow	der Pulverschnee	la neige poudreuse	neve farinosa
breakable crust	der Bruchharst	la neige croutée	la crosta gelata
avalanche danger	die Lawinengefahr	le danger d'avalanche	il pericolo di valanghe
Which is the piste to . . . ?	welches ist die Abfahrt (Piste) nach . . . ?	quelle est la piste qui va à . . . ?	qual'e la pista per . . . ?
Which is the easiest way down?	welches ist der leichteste Weg hinab?	quelle est la piste la plus facile?	qual'e la discesa piu' facile?
Is there anywhere to eat up here?	kann man hier oben etwas essen?	où peut-on manger ici?	c'e un posto per mangiare in cima?
The ski school	die Skischule	l'école de ski	la scuola di sci
the instructor	der Skilehrer	le moniteur	l'istruttore di sci
the season ticket (for lessons or lifts)	das Abonnement	l'abonnement	l'abbonamento
the beginner	der Anfänger	le débutant	il principiante
left, right	links, rechts	gauche, droite	sinistra, destra
Put more weight on the downhill ski	den untern Ski stärker belasten	chargez davantage le ski aval	lo sci a valle deve sostenere maggiormente il peso del corpo
uphill ski	den obern Ski	le ski amont	lo sci a monte
Lean downhill	vom Hang weglehnen	se pencher vers l'aval	inclinarsi verso valle
the ankle	das Fussgelenk	la cheville	la caviglia

SKIER'S VOCABULARY

ENGLISH	GERMAN	FRENCH	ITALIAN
the shoulders	die Schultern	les épaules	le spalle
the hips	die Hüfte	les hanches	le anche
the knees	das Knie	le genou	il ginocchio
Turn to the right	nach rechts abdrehen	tournez à droite	girare a destra
Get up!	stehen sie auf!	levez-vous!	levatevi!
Brake!	Bremsen!	freinez!	frenate!
Repeat these movements!	die Bewegungen wiederholen!	répétez ces mouvements!	ripetere questi movimenti!
Keep skis parallel	die Skier parallel niedersetzen	gardez les skis parallèles	tenere gli sci paralleli
skis naturally apart, not too close together	Natürliche Spurbreite. Skier nicht zu nahe beisammen	ne serrez pas trop les skis, l'écartement doit être naturel	Larghezza naturale della traccia. Gli sci non devono essere troppo vicini
Lean forwards	der Korper lehnt nach vorn	le corps se penche en avant	il corpo è inclinato in avanti
Bend the knee	das Knie beugen	pliez les genoux	piegare il ginocchio
The whole body is supple and relaxed	der ganze Körper ist locker und gelöst	le corps entier est souple et détendu	l'intero corpo resta sciolto e rilassato
slowly	langsam	lentement	lentamente
faster	schneller	plus vite	più in fretta
look ahead	vorwärts schauen	regardez devant vous	guardare in avanti
Edge the uphill edge	die Skier auf die oberen Kanten auflegen	prennez de la carre amont	poggiare gli sci sugli spigoli superiori
side-stepping	der Treppenschritt	les pas (montée) en escalier	il passo a scala laterale
the herring bone	der Grätenschritt	la montée en canard (ciseaux)	il passo a lisca di pesce
kick turn	die Spitzkehre	la conversion	la conversione
weight on uphill ski.	den obern Ski belasten	chargez le ski amont	spostare il peso del corpo sullo sci a monte
the skating turn	der Schlittschuhschritt	le pas de patineur	il passo del pattinatore
Keep the skis flat and weight them equally	die Skier flach auflegen und gleichmässig belasten	mettez les skis à plat avec poids égal sur les deux skis	mantenere li sci piani e mantenere il peso su ambedue
Put those sticks back	Stöcke rückwärts halten	tenez les bâtons en arrière	dirigere i bastoni all'indietro
the traverse	die Schrägfahrt	une traversée	una discesa diagonale (in linea obliqua)
Bring the uphill ski forwards	den obern Ski vorschieben	avancez le ski amont (ski amont en avant)	avanzare lo sci a monte
Not too much	nicht zu weit	pas trop	non troppo
up-down-up!	hoch-tief-hoch!	haut-bas-haut!	su-giù-su!
the sitting back position	die Rücklage	position de recul	sporgersi indietro
the snowplough (turn)	der Schneepflug	le chasse neige	spazzaneve
the stem turn	der Stemmbogen	le virage en stem	la voltata a semi spazzaneve
side-slipping	seitliches Abrutschen	le dérapage	scivolata di fianco
Release the edges!	Kanten lösen!	relâchez les carres!	rilassamento degli spigoli!
Planting the poles helps unweight the skis to start the turn	die Stockarbeit erleichtert die Skientlastung und die Auslösung des Schwunges	le planté du bâton aide l'allègement et le changement de direction	i bastoni servono ad alleggerire il peso sugli sci e a cambiare direzione

ENGLISH	GERMAN	FRENCH	ITALIAN
The skis should be close together	die Skier sind geschlossen	les skis sont serrés	gli sci sono uniti
Do not stick your bottom out	den Hintern nicht hinausstecken!	rentrez votre postérieur (derrière/vos fesses)	non sporgeta col sedere
Keep the upper body upright	den Oberkörper gerade halten!	tenez le buste droit	mantenete il busto in posizione eretta
Do not crouch!	nicht kriechen!	ne vous accroupissez pas	non rannicchiatevi!
Follow me in a line	folgen Sie mir hintereinander	suivez moi en file indienne	seguitemi in fila indiana
One at a time	Einer aufs Mal	un à la fois	uno alla volta

INDEX

CREDITS

Swiss National Tourist Office, 11, 14, 24, 29, 79, 80, 119, 120, 124, 125, 203, 214, 218, 224, 225
French Government Tourist Office, 25, 123, 125
Canadian Government Tourist Board, 13
Austrian National Tourist Office, 10, 25
Norwegian National Tourist Office, 29, 36, 47
United States Travel Service, 26
Brian Wharton, 62, 68, 75, 81, 98, 99, 104, 154, 179, 182, 184, 185, 197, 236, 237, 238, 239, 240, 241
Frank Herrmann, 17, 38, 78, 91, 96, 97, 100, 101, 108, 110, 113, 114, 117, 123, 126, 127, 129, 130, 132, 134, 142, 143, 152, 153, 155, 159, 161, 164, 166, 167, 168, 174, 177, 186, 187, 196, 199, 202, 205, 206, 208, 210, 211, 213, 214, 217, 219, 221, 223, 227, 229, 230, 231
Christopher Thornton, 50, 56, 74, 75, 77, 84, 85, 106, 115, 127, 130, 139, 190, 191, 192, 193, 200
George Konig, 137
Stewart Fraser, 207

Basic movements
for the
Classic Wedel

Construct your own flip-book from the photo-strips on the following pages and see the classic wedel in action.

A. Cut out the pictures along the dotted lines.
B. Staple them, numerically, on the left side (or use a bulldog clip).
C. Flip.

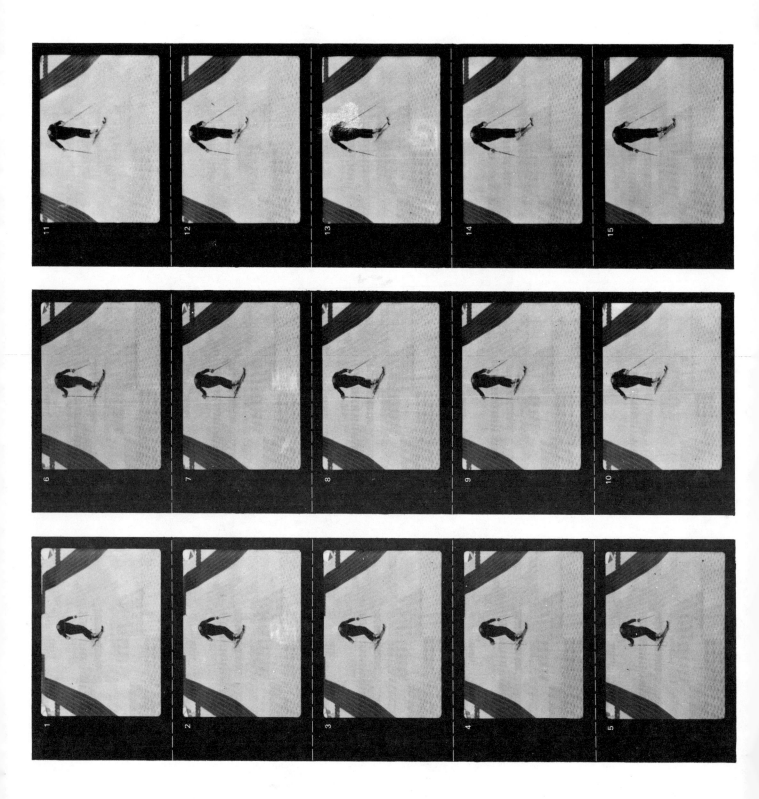

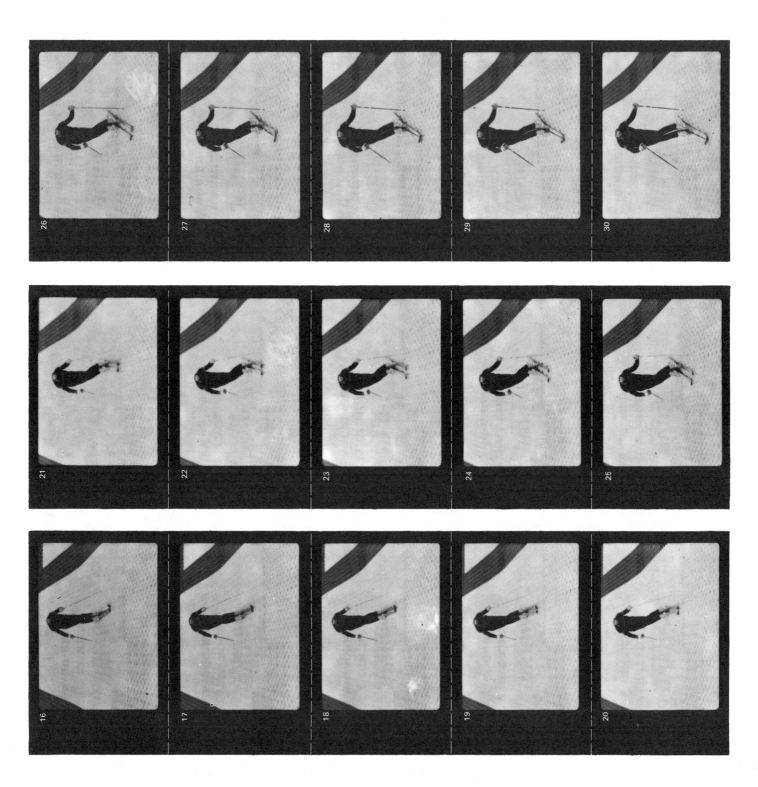